MUSLIM

In Transit

BOOK POWER PUBLISHING

MUSLIM IN TRANSIT: A LITTLE BOY GROWS UP IN PATNA, TRAVELS TO AMERICA AND DISCOVERS THE ESSENCE OF ISLAM.

Book Power Publishing, Detroit, Michigan
www.bookpowerpublishing.com

muslimintransit@gmail.com

First Edition, 2016

ISBN: 978-0-9822215-1-8

MUSLIM

In Transit

A LITTLE BOY GROWS UP IN PATNA, TRAVELS TO AMERICA
AND DISCOVERS THE ESSENCE OF ISLAM.

MOHAMMED QAMRUZZAMAN

BOOK
POWER
PUBLISHING

DETROIT, MI

With each passing second,
I condemn myself for what I was;
Each folly makes me blush, at memories I wince;
Each thought comes with a desire to change.

For Bin Yamin, Yusuf, Mariem, and You

May you find the answers you seek
and may the answers lead you to Allah

Contents

Why a Second Edition?

All praise belongs to Allah who helped me publish this memoir and has now enabled me to work on the second edition that lies open in your hands.

Allah created the earth as a beautiful dwelling and placed the humans as vicegerents on it. He intended for them to build it and live on it for a certain time. He clearly expounded that this duration was to be a test; in the hereafter, every soul is going to reap what they sow in the world. Whoever follows the true guidance shall succeed and whoever rejects it and goes astray shall fail.

ALLAH CREATED MANKIND IN THE PUREST FORM AND COMMANDED HIM TO MAINTAIN IT:

To enable man to fulfill his role as a vicegerent, Allah created him in the purest of forms – in the state of fitra, and equipped him with love, compassion, empathy, faith and virtues. Allah equipped mankind with the abilities that would enable him to be an obedient slave of Allah. In the beginning, mankind remembered this test and adhered to the path of Allah's pleasure. But Shaitan tricked him and made him forget, pulling him into his evil schemes. Gradually, the test was forgotten; tawheed was replaced with polytheism, love with malice, and virtue with vice and materialism.

Allah, being All Loving, kept sending His prophets and messengers to remind the people of their true purpose on earth, and to redirect them to their pure state of fitra. The last of these messengers was Prophet Muhammad (pbuh).

HATE AND GREED LEAD US AWAY FROM FITRAH

Here one may question why Allah kept sending prophets one after the other to remind and redirect us to our pure state of fitrah? To understand the importance of this question we must understand the importance of our state of fitrah. Allah created us in this state because the purpose of our creation cannot be fulfilled unless we stay in this state, or are working hard to maintain this state - to purify our hearts and souls from all vices, especially hate and greed.

A person full of hate and greed is like a heavily intoxicated person who loses the ability to determine what is good and what is bad for him. In the Quran, Allah has called such people dumb, deaf and blind and we continue to prove ourselves to be so with our contradicting actions and empty words.

Mohammad (pbuh) came to deliver the Message of Allah, the Quran, and to establish the Kingdom of Allah so that mankind can live on this earth in peace and harmony, social justice, equality and compassion towards each other. Allah wanted us to live in peace and harmony, but because of our desire to control we always struggled for power and wealth, degraded our pure form, corrupted our moral character and filled our hearts with hate and greed. Once we are full of hate and greed, we turn into a different kind of human being, different from the one that Allah had created.

MANKIND ALWAYS HAD A PROBLEM SUBMITTING TO ALLAH, NOT IN ACCEPTING HIM AS THE CREATOR:

When Mohammad (pbuh) started preaching, the Quraish were already convinced that Allah is the creator and owner of the whole universe. The acceptance of Allah was not a problem for the Quraish. The problem lied in submitting their entire being to Allah, and to His demand that human beings must behave to each another with justice, equity and compassion.

If we look at the history of civilization, we find that mankind seldom had a problem accepting Allah's super power and authority. Their only problem was to give up control; absolute control, and surrender themselves to Allah.

THE DESIRE TO CONTROL MAKES
MANKIND DISOBEY ALLAH:

Mankind is struggling for control since day one. Allah wants mankind to submit and trust, but mankind refuses to obey and give up control. Allah has told mankind that their worldly sustenance is predetermined and guaranteed, that they would not get any less or more. Nonetheless, they would have to strive for it. However, to win a place in heaven they have to make sacrifices to please Allah, otherwise their destiny is Hell.

Mankind's desire to control is so intense that they never give up any opportunity. They don't necessarily have to be kings to exercise control, they do it on any level, even controlling their younger siblings.

MANKIND WAS CREATED PURE
IN ORDER TO DRAW CLOSER TO ALLAH:

A person with a pure heart understands the wisdom of Allah. He understands that even though Allah promised us sustenance and always fulfills His promise, He gives more to the people who are sincere, loving, caring and compassionate. Those who take all the commandments seriously and understand that Allah is always Just and He would be Just on the Day of Judgment. He believes that the winner in both the worlds would be the one who works hard, sincerely obeys and pleases Allah and doesn't fall into the Devil's deception. He knows that physical and mental comforts are illusions. The only reality is making every effort to obey and please Allah; honor, respect and take care of parents; and believe that everything he has – health, intelligence, family, employment, house, respect, power and honor, all belong to Allah. So sacrificing any or all of them is just returning them to the real owner.

Because of his connection with Allah and his spirituality, the person with a pure heart has mental, physical and moral strength. He is always eager to hear words of wisdom and to learn how he can get more and more close to Allah.

WHEN MANKIND LOSES HIS PURITY
HE LOWERS HIS STATUS:

Those of us who have lost the purity of our hearts appear to be human but have no connection, confidence and trust in Allah. Consequently, we believe that our success depends on our own abilities and thus we have to lie, cheat, manipulate, break promises and do whatever we have to do to get what we want and need. Our mental, physical and moral conditions become weak because we have lost the spiritual connection with Allah, the source of ultimate strength and success. Unfortunately, we don't even realize this loss, especially those of us who perform all five religious rituals or even one, such as prayers.

ALLAH GIVES WHATEVER WE DESIRE.
WHETHER WE DESIRE THIS WORLD OR
HEREAFTER DEPENDS ON THE PURITY OF OUR
SOULS:

We assume that every achievement of ours is a reward from Allah and that He is pleased with us. Unfortunately, we don't understand that materialistic gains are not a sign of Allah's pleasure. They are simply part of the promised worldly sustenance, and are even given to the atheists. On the contrary, the actions and consequences that stay with us after we pass away are the real rewards and signs of Allah's pleasure; like helping people, making others happy purely to please Allah (not for self-glory) and controlling the desires of our *Nafs*. Our success depends on firm determination to stay away from all sinful acts. Nonetheless, we will not receive Allah's mercy on the Day of Judgment, based on the outcome of our endeavors. Rather, it will depend on how hard and sincerely we have tried.

The people who have lost the purity of their souls stay in the box. They believe they know all there is to know and are not interested in learning how to get close to Allah. They are more interested in talking than listening. Because they are so disconnected with Allah and have no spiritual strength, they are cowardly, self-centered and do not possess the ability to make good judgments.

They believe what they are doing is right and Allah is pleased with them. They don't understand that Allah is not pleased because we are praying, reciting Quran, or even attending Islamic lectures and seminars. Allah is pleased when we also bow down to Him in gratitude and serve His creation to make their lives pleasant by sacrificing our time, money and comfort.

LITMUS TEST:

There is a simple litmus test to know whether one has a pure heart; a person with a pure heart makes every effort to stay away from sinful acts and if a sin is committed by him, no matter how small, then he gets upset, cries and begs Allah for forgiveness. He makes every effort not to repeat the same sin. When doing good deeds, he does not raise his head with a proud and arrogant feeling, instead he thanks Allah with humbleness.

THE DEVIL – HE MAKES EVERY EFFORT TO MISLEAD US:

Recall the conversation that took place between Allah and the Devil when the Devil asked Allah to give him respite until the day of Resurrection. He wanted to prove that mankind does not deserve the honor that Allah gave them. The Devil promised to mislead mankind, and he is doing his utmost to fulfill this mission.

Those who believe Heaven is guaranteed should not brush off the Devil's threat. He is out there to prove that mankind is not worthy enough. Why do we take the Devil's threat so lightly, especially since it is mentioned in the Quran, and the Devil has sworn that he would disqualify us from reaching Heaven? We should examine Devil's strategy carefully and avoid falling into his trap.

If we ponder and use all the senses and faculties Allah has blessed us with then it would be clear like day light that even though the Devil was full of knowledge, his hate towards Adam and greed to have his position as vicegerent got the best of him. **It was hate and greed that made him disobey Allah even though he knew the consequences. Thus, it is more likely that he would use our same weaknesses to try and intoxicate us with the desires of the world, name, fame and self-glory. Once we fall prey to him, we start treading the path to destruction. We do not remain the same human beings Allah had created. We become dumb, blind and deaf; we do not read or listen to any good teaching or advice.**

THE PLIGHT OF THE UMMAH

Allah sent Mohammad (pbuh) with the most important task- to purify mankind. (Quran 2:151).

Today, fourteen centuries have passed since the death of Muhammad (pbuh). His followers have grown into the second largest nation, amounting to 1.8 billion people. Nonetheless, this nation that was once a mighty reflection of power, success and glory does not hold any significant position in the world. Collectively, they weigh no more than the froth and foam of a cappuccino.

Upon observing the plight of Muslims around the world, my heart ached – it made me think, "Why is this happening? Where did we Muslims go wrong? We had been promised victory and glory, but then where has it gone?"

The more I pondered and delved into Islamic literature the more I was able to comprehend our errors. I realized that Muslims, including myself, have wandered away from the *deen*. We are clinging on to the mere shadow and crust of Islam which includes certain customs, traditions and rituals. Whereas, the soul of Islam; the spirit of submission, sacrifice, trusting and obeying Allah, is absent. We pay heed to the purity of our body and wealth but we do not care about the seat of our actions; the purity of our heart and soul.

MUSLIMS ARE FOLLOWING IN THE FOOTSTEPS OF THE CHRISTIANS AND THE JEWS:

Prophet Muhammad's (pbuh) prediction has become clear as crystal. We are following in the footsteps of the nations before us; the Christians and the Jews.

To free themselves of the worry of practicing, Christians invented the belief that no sin would harm a person as long as they believed in Esa (as). Similarly, an exaggerated concept of intercession was propagated among Muslims, so much so that the general masses of Muslims believe the same: as long as we believe in Muhammad (pbuh), he will intercede for us and no sin whatsoever will harm us.

Consequently, Muslims have fallen prey to arrogance, hatred, dishonesty and corruption. Being free from the burden of action, we indulge in misdeeds. The belief that Prophet Muhammad (pbuh) will intercede is in conflict with the Quranic teachings. Thus, we have deviated from the teachings of Quran. Instead of relying on intercession, Islam demands dignity in our character, and that character demands that we free ourselves from all sinful deeds.

Moreover, the personal interest of scholars and learned men adds to the dilemma. All have their own pet projects and organizations to develop and look after. They do not serve to rebuild the Muslim identity. They are more interested in name and fame which they receive by talking about 'selling topics' like life history of the prophets (as), their companions and Islamic historical events. Most ulema talk only about the soft aspects of Islam which are well received by the masses: they speak about reward and good deeds, often quote misinterpreted Quranic verses, and share fabricated and unauthentic ahadith which give only glad tidings and no warnings. The ulema fail to give admonitions, forbid evil and truly educate Muslims about the trials of this life. Forbidding the evil puts them against the status quo and only few are willing to do that.

Additionally, after studying and researching the current financial system, I've reached the understanding that with the arrival of paper money, luxuries and comforts of life are becoming easily accessible.

Economic powers like the World Bank and IMF have created a false illusion of wealth using virtual currency, which has given birth to a tide of materialism. Everyone, including Muslims, is engrossed in the race for money, material comforts and wealth. Hereafter is forgotten and fitrah has become corrupt along the way.

STAY IN SUCCESSFUL TRANSIT:

The solution? I believe it lies in transition – reverting back to our original state of fitrah; of love, compassion, empathy and virtue. We are, of course, weak and sinful and may never be immaculately pure or perfect. However, that does not count. Allah promises forgiveness and mercy, and loves those who seek repentance. He does not reward us based on the results of our deeds, rather He rewards our sincerity and efforts. As long as we keep struggling to stay in transit, we shall be successful, In Sha Allah.

Before I go any further, I want to remind my readers that though it is true that Allah promises forgiveness and mercy, and loves those who seek repentance, this promise is only for those who have *iman*, fear the day of judgment, and stay away from all sinful deeds. Also, **repentance is not accepted until we complete the following four (4) steps:**

1. Accepting the fact that we did wrong
2. Asking Allah for His forgiveness
3. Making an honest and sincere promise never to do the same sin again
4. If tested, never do the same sin again.

BELIEVING IN ALLAH DOES NOT GUARANTEE HEAVEN, OBEYING MAY:

Hate and greed are the Devil's attributes and they connect us with Devil. Whereas good deeds are angelic attributes and they connect us with Allah. We know very well that we can't get connected with the Devil and Allah both at the same time. Thus, if we are full of hate and greed, we can't perform good deeds that would please Allah, and if Allah is not pleased then a piece of Heaven is questionable. However, we know that Allah has promised to reward every good deed, regardless how small it is.

Unfortunately, we take this promise and believe that Allah has promised Heaven for our good deeds and forget all His other blessings and rewards such as food, health, family, children, house, etc., not to mention eyes, nose, hands, legs, etc. Do we know how many good deeds are required to qualify for all these blessings, and **do we know how many good deeds are required for Heaven?** If we honestly think about it then we'll know that we can never do enough good deeds to qualify for Heaven.

If this is the case, does it mean we can never win a piece of Heaven? No, that is not true. Heaven is guaranteed but there is a condition. **Heaven is guaranteed to those who believe in Allah (obey Him) and the Day of Judgment, do good deeds, and submit, trust and obey Allah. Thus, to win a piece of Heaven it is mandatory to get rid of hate and greed, or in other words get rid of the Devil's attributes.**

LOVING THE CREATOR AND HIS CREATIONS IS EBADAT:

Do we know that the creation of mankind is a sign of Allah's Love? He created mankind to express His love. That is why He created him in His own image and made him so beautiful with a miraculous body. It is His love that He created so many kinds of wheat, rice, grains, fruits, vegetables, animals, birds, and fish and gave mankind a tongue to taste all of them. It is His love that He created him to be His vicegerent, with whom He would share Heaven; mankind who trusts and loves Him, and is willing to sacrifice everything, even his life for Him.

It is His love for mankind that He created the whole universe for him to enjoy but never to desire to stay there. Allah sends us on earth to discipline us so that we may love each other and live in peace and harmony for a short period, before going back and merging with the origin where we came from. Since Allah created mankind in His image, mankind is born in a pure state and is expected to go back in the same pure and innocent state.

However, only those who have an inquisitive mind can value love. Their heart cries when they see others suffering from physical or emotional pain, or when they themselves suffer from sickness, divorce, loss of employment, or loss of children, etc. Their mind automatically starts wondering and questioning "Why am I suffering, did I do anything wrong?"

If the answer is yes, then am I being punished? What mistake have I made? Did I know I was making a wrong decision? If yes, then what can I do to put it right? Have I failed to make a better decision because there is something I ought to know but I don't?

God created mankind with intelligence, logic and reasoning so he would ponder thoughtfully on these questions and try to find out who he is, who is his creator, why did He create him and what does He want from him. Mankind is supposed to keep pondering on these questions until he finds the answer that satisfies him.

Unfortunately, contrary to other living animals, mankind is born helpless and he can't even walk unless someone teaches him to walk. The first teachers in his life are his parents, then siblings, relatives, neighbors, community, teachers, khateebs (Masjid Imams), and finally religious scholars. From this chain of teachers, we see that parents play a very important role to keep their children in the pure state free from hate and full of love. But today's child is tomorrow's parent. Therefore, the final responsibility lies on the shoulders of Islamic scholars (Ulema) because they are professionals, educated and trained to teach Islam, the teachings of Quran and Sunnah to the parents, and the Ummah.

More than 1400 years ago, Mohammad (pbuh) came to purify us, to build our characters, and to teach us to be obedient slaves of Allah. After him, his companions, Rightly Guided Caliphs, continued his teachings.

Love brings happiness, success, development and progress, whereas hate destroys everything. When one falls in love with himself, he becomes greedy and selfish. He can't see others happy and successful. His heart starts filling with hate and he only loves himself. He does not even love his Creator. He is never satisfied, no matter how much he has; he always wants more- more money, more power, more control and more glory, until he is destroyed.

To save the people from destruction, Mohammad (pbuh) came to teach them to love their Creator and His creations, instead of falling in love with themselves. Love and compassion give success in the world as well as Hereafter. But unfortunately, after the Rightly Guided Caliphs, greed took over the better judgment of mankind. Hazrat Husain (ra), the grandson of our Prophet (pbuh), saw that the teachings of Quran and Sunnah (getting rid of hate and greed) were in danger. So, in order to keep the Islamic teachings alive, he fought with Yazid's huge army. To save the teachings of Quran and Sunnah he not only sacrificed himself, but with the exception of one, he sacrificed the whole family.

Ebadat is loving the Creator and His Creation, and He created mankind full of love and affection. This is the love and affection that made Muslims the most successful nation in the world for more than seven centuries. They not only ruled the world but were also successful in the fields of science, arts, medicine and astrology etc. They made many important discoveries and inventions that benefit us to date.

It was Allah's Rahmah and our Prophet's (pbuh) teachings that even though our Ulema stopped teaching us to cleanse our hearts, we were still the most loving and caring people in the world and kept progressing, but eventually our enemies learned to play with our emotions and filled our hearts with Shia-Sunni hate.

After the Rightly Guided Caliphs, our hearts were already full of greed. Then, when our hearts were taken over by hate, our downfall began. Now we are at a place where everybody in the world hates us.

Even the Muslims hate other Muslims because we have forgotten Allah and believe that we are in control.

We are still surviving because God has filled our hearts with love for our children. It is this love which helps the children to grow up.

We have understood that hate and greed destroy us, whereas love, peace and harmony make us survive and progress. Now, let us see what caused us to lose our character.

CAUSES OF DEGRADATION OF MUSLIMS' CHARACTER.

Lots of talks and videos are going around talking about how much the character of Muslims has deteriorated. Even the Muslim scholars and Ulema are saying that the character of Muslims is worse than non-Muslims. Non-Muslims are more disciplined, punctual, honest, and hardworking. While Muslims' religious, moral, ethical and social performances are less than to be desired.

They are expressing how bad our characters are but no one is telling what caused it. They are also explaining us what goodness is, but nothing about the path that leads to it. I believe the main reason for the deterioration of our Iman is that we hear our religious leaders saying that Allah promises forgiveness and mercy, and loves those who seek repentance, but we seldom hear from them that **Allah's Mercy is only for those who have Iman,** and repentance is for those who follow all four steps mentioned above.

Besides, would we expect a person to be loving, caring and obedient to Allah if his heart is full of hate and greed? Of course not, not unless his heart is purified and taught to control his Devilish desires or be ready to face the consequences.

We are also made to believe that the blessings we receive from Allah are rewards of our good deeds and also because we are followers of His beloved Rasool, Mohammad (pbuh). This makes us assume that Allah is happy with us, and thus it gives us assurance that a piece of Heaven is guaranteed. **When our conscious has a guarantee for a piece** of Heaven, then naturally our unconscious mind is satisfied and we stop trying to stay away from bad deeds. This is exactly what the Devil wants and he succeeds in it.

Unfortunately, most of us also believe that Allah has promised Heaven and forgiveness for all those who perform Islamic rituals (all five or even one) and do good deeds. We also wrongfully believe that we are born with some vices such as hate, greed, ego and arrogance and thus we can't get rid of them. Therefore, we have been commanded to make a conscious effort to stay away from 'sinful' deeds, but getting rid of these 'inborn' vices is not mandatory.

Surely, the glamour and luxury of this world has made our character and obedience to God weak, but our Islamic teachers did not make any serious effort to teach us Quran and Sunnah's teachings. They focused on rituals and ignored spirituality. To justify ignoring spirituality they tried to convince us that our *Iman* is not complete unless we believe in Hadith, and then introduced fabricated and unauthentic ahadith. They did not stop there but they further misled us by translating some of the Quranic verses and their explanations using improper translations.

It appears to me that they made an organized effort to reduce the teachings of the Quran and Sunnah to something that justifies the Devilish desires of our Nafs and to turn a prosperous and advancing nation into a religiously, morally, ethically and socially weak one – a nation that would not be able to stand up on its own feet and would have to depend on the mercy and kindness of others until it vanishes. In other words, knowingly or unknowingly, they helped the enemies of Islam to subvert our faith and to make us losers.

Here, it should be noted that Islam will never vanish, but if we forget Allah then He would replace us with other people. This is a promise of Allah and this is exactly what is happening. Conversion into Islam is significantly high and Hindu Pundits, Swamis, priests, and non-Muslim scholars are promoting Islam.

In our daily lives, we find that the non-Muslims' character, such as trust in business, keeping promises, honesty, sincerity and punctuality, is better than ours. Do we ever wonder why? What do we think we have to adopt to attain good character? Do we think a man with hate and greed can have a good character? Would he be trustworthy? Yes, he may be trustworthy but only to the extent his interest is secured, otherwise -no.

Now think a little further. A man who is always keeping his interest first (his interest may be money, power, control, self-glory, ego, arrogance or merely laziness and a comfortable life) would he ever care for our interest? And if he does not care for our interest then would he teach us to qualify for a piece of Heaven? I doubt it. Thus, as long as the world is full of hate and greed, these so called scholars will make every effort to undermine the teachings that talk about purifying our hearts. This is exactly what is happening.

The scholars who translated the Quran; and the Islamic teachers who are supposed to instill the fear of the Judgment Day in our hearts, and to motivate us to submit, trust and obey Allah, they lack these virtues themselves. Therefore, how would they teach us? To teach us to be obedient slaves of Allah, the teacher has to be free of hate and greed himself, otherwise we ourselves must take Quranic commandments very seriously and make every effort to learn to be obedient slaves of Allah - if we really want to qualify for a piece of Heaven.

One may question here about what is wrong if scholars and Islamic teachers are striving for higher and higher income, why would it be considered greed? The answer to this question lies in the understanding of Islam, and the teachings of Quran and Sunnah. We all know that our sustenance is promised by Allah and we will not get any less or more than what He has already decided. If we are Muslim, believe in His promise, trust Him, and pray for Barakah (blessings of Allah) in our sustenance then shouldn't our focus be on teaching the Ummah, helping them to acquire a piece of Heaven, and being content with whatever sustenance we receive? **If our scholars and Islamic teachers have no trust in Allah, then why should we trust them for the most important thing of our life, the Hereafter?**

I understand there are many scholars and Islamic teachers who are teaching us what is good, but they do not speak about the path that leads to it. They may be very sincere people and may be working hard to lead us to the straight path, but if they are not aware of the value of the purification of the heart and if they have not tried to purify themselves, then they would not have any effectiveness in their teachings. This is exactly what we are witnessing. These sincere teachers are breaking their backs to teach us but our character keep worsening. Now we are at a point where the whole world hates us, even Muslims hate Muslims.

The character of Non-Muslims is better than ours because, I believe, we are victims of the misleading teachings of our teachers who never tried to purify their hearts, and thus they wrongfully taught us to believe that Quran commands us to do good deeds and promises forgiveness and a piece of Heaven, but Quran does not mandate us to stay away from bad deeds. This is not true, but we would never know unless we try to understand Quran ourselves. We neither read the Quran in Arabic, nor do we try to understand its wisdom. Instead, we read its translations and explanations written by Islamic scholars who themselves never tried to get rid of hate and greed; thus they nourished their desires for admiration and self-glorification by seeing a big crowd around themselves. Teaching obedience to Allah is not of their interest. Therefore, instead of talking about Allah's anger, wrath and graveyard punishment, they like to talk only about how Allah is kind and forgiving.

To make us believe that Allah is kind and forgiving, that He will forgive all our sins and grant Heaven as long as we make a conscious decision to do good deeds and stay away from bad, our scholars and teachers changed the Arabic translation of some of the Quranic verses and interpreted some of them to mislead the Ummah. Also, at every Khutbah, almost all the Imams recite, "He whom Allah Guides is rightly guided; but he whom Allah leaves to stray, for him you will find no protector to lead him to the right way." They quote numerous Hadiths with glad tidings and no warnings, such as the ones that talk about the intercession of Prophet Mohammad (pbuh); and the hadith which says that Allah loves those who repent and if there were no sinners, He would replace them with others who would sin and repent; and the one that talks about Allah forgiving the sins even if they fill the entire earth; and that Allah will reward those who build a masjid with a palace in Heaven

With all these misleading teachings using wrongly translated and interpreted Quranic verses and ahadith, no wonder our character is worse than non-Muslims.

Here, one should note that the Quran very strongly forbids us from doing sinful deeds and gives warning of a very severe punishment. But we do not read the Quran for ourselves and rely only on the khutbahs of our scholars. Thus, we believe that Allah has promised to forgive all our sins and there is no need to change our life style. In other words, we believe that we have a license from Allah to do sinful deeds. It is just like one being a favorite employee of the chief of the organization and feeling that he can do whatever he wants and can get away with it.

Hence, living in an environment with false teachings for centuries, no wonder words of wisdom don't penetrate through our deaf ears and we have become dumb, deaf and blind.

Another atrocity of our Islamic teachers is that Mohammad (pbuh) came with a message of love and peace, and Muslims, the followers of Islam, were supposed to spread love to the world. However, we are full of hate, so much hate that the whole world has started hating us. And our scholars and Imams are not teaching us to get rid of hate and to replace it with love, compassion and understanding.

The tyrant government and ruler of India are butchering Muslims alive. Millions of Muslims are becoming a victim of their atrocities, and yet the Muslim princes and rulers are supporting, honoring, conferring highest awards and making business deals with the tyrant killer. All these sinful acts are accepted because greed is accepted in our culture and a country's economic development is considered more important than the lives of the people, especially Muslims.

Muslims are the victims of hate, the same hate we never tried to get rid of . What are we waiting for? Are we waiting for the hate to destroy us?

Parents should take extra care not to teach hate, directly or indirectly, to their children. Children learn to hate when their parents are expressing their hate against anybody in their presence.

I wish our Islamic teachers would realize what they have done to our *iman* and character, and I hope that they will make efforts to correct this misunderstanding before we get to the point where our whole society collapses. I want to make it very clear that the above misleading teachings are not the teachings of Quran and Sunnah. Rather, they are the teachings and beliefs of those people who want to worship the desires of their *nafs*. This book is an effort to convince mankind and especially the ummah to come back to the true teachings of Quran and Sunnah and not to fall into devilish traps. May Allah help and guide us, Ameen.

My aim in writing this book was to help Muslims understand the soul of Islam, **to help them to understand that *Iman* entails purity of heart and soul,** and to assist them with the transition. When I first published, I had great hopes that it would guide others, like me, in coming back to deen. However, I soon realized that most people failed to grasp the depth this book had to offer.

In this new edition, I decided to add a few reflection questions at the end of each chapter so readers can use the book as a partner en route to transition. These questions serve to help us comprehend the soul of Islam, determine where we stand, and direct us how and where we can move forward. Reflection questions help us measure our performance, and measurement brings improvement. This is exactly my goal – to help us all improve as individuals and as a nation. I hope you will find this endeavor of mine to be effective. In Sha Allah

Finally, I want to close with the note that no good deed is beneficial unless we get rid of hate and greed. I believe that if our hearts are full of hate and greed then any good deed would just be to glorify ourselves and may not be acceptable to Allah.

Mohammed Qamruzzaman

REVIEW

Gripped with an utter dismay over the pathetic condition of the worldwide Muslim community (*ummah*), the author relates his own journey through life. He believes that like himself—a "Muslim in Transit," other Muslims too may be struggling with their faith, and searching for their real identity. This is the case with most Muslims who may be Muslims by chance, but not by choice.

The Quran invites man to think and reflect upon the Creator and His creation. Those who claim to be Muslims do believe in God but they do not necessarily surrender their will to the Will of God. Pronouncing the 'Testimony of Faith' (*shahadah*) and performing the ritual modes of worship are not enough if such pronouncement and devotion are not manifested through meaningful actions. Sadly, this is the case with the Muslim *ummah* as a whole; hence the mess it finds itself in.

Life releases its purpose only to the searching soul that strives to comprehend the transcendent—the sublime truth—the ultimate reality through keen observation and humble submission. The author shares his experiences of life and the situations he had to grapple with in order to understand the true perspectives of one's transitory stay on earth.

Having understood the mystery of the fleeting time, and the exigency of arriving at the 'truth' before it is too late, the author makes a clarion call to his fellow brothers and sisters in faith to wake up and take heed. He passionately wants to take them out of their apathy and complacency, and shares with them the universal truths that he pondered upon and that finally led him to the spiritual awakening, which he found to be so stimulating, enriching, fulfilling, and rewarding.

The book is well-written, thought provoking, and difficult to put down.

Dr. Munawar Haque, Imam
American Muslim Diversity Association (AMDA)

Foreword

Bismillahir Rahmanir Rahim

THE STORY OF one man's journey to ultimate truth, this book unfolds the events that shaped Mohammed Qamruzzaman's character into the remarkable Muslim he is today. From the moment I met him, I knew there was something different about him. He knew something others didn't, and that must have been why he was able to remain steadfast and live his life with such discipline and consistency. Those qualities almost guarantee success for any goal.

As the author recounts his struggles and the outcomes, he points us to some very important life lessons. Most of us are so caught up in our daily lives that we barely even allow ourselves the time to think. Some of us find time to pray and to fast, but even when those acts of worship are completed, how often do we actually stop to reflect upon the role they play in our lives?

Contemplation in itself is an act of worship. Mohammed (may Allah grant him peace) used to spend hours and days alone in the cave just thinking. It was a big part of his life leading up to prophethood. Allah has created each of us with intellect so that we may use it to prepare ourselves for the gifts that are waiting to be bestowed on us. There are signs all around that beg us to take a closer look and spend some thought so that we may realize what this life is all about.

It is not meant to be a secret. There are many books that serve as instruction manuals on how to fulfill our responsibilities as Muslims, but this book takes it a step further and focuses on motivation. There are tangible reasons why Allah has instructed us to do certain things.

Through contemplation, we are able to notice the effects and consequences of our acts of worship and our neglect thereof. When we can identify the benefit of something, we are more likely to repeat it. Contemplation leads to understanding, and that leads to taking action, which is what Islam is all about. If knowledge is put in the right perspective it becomes very encouraging, and that leads to direction and change.

Muslim in Transit speaks to readers through the author's experiences. It is written as a story in which each chapter is complemented by a section about Islam. This book is distinguished from others with a similar message by the ease of reading and the connections of the concepts with real life experiences.

Biographies have a tendency to offer universal elements with which readers can identify on a personal level. The author's humble effort to present his moral story is no small task and should not be considered insignificant. Human beings are inclined to imitate one another and often fixate on role models. As we relate the stories of our brothers and sisters in Islam, we are encouraging one another toward the right path. This is especially true when we support our claims of guidance with the words of Allah (*subhana wa ta'ala*) and examples from the life of the Prophet (may Allah grant him peace), as the author of this book does. He writes to us about *tawheed*, the oneness of Allah, from the vantage point of having learned from the events of his personal history.

There are those of us who are blessed to understand that there is no god but Allah from our environments and our upbringings, and then there are those of us who are really blessed to know it without a shadow of a doubt because we have been exposed to circumstances that teach us what the world is like in its absence. After expounding that Allah is One, Qamruzzaman leads us to demonstrate our sincerity through the five pillars of Islam. We can say, "*La ilaha illah Allah*," but we must show that it is alive within us through practice. He then touches upon the importance of purification of the heart, as it is the heart that generates sincerity and faith, and it is the purity of the heart by which we will be judged when we face Allah on the Last Day. When the heart is in a state of purity, it is ready to be occupied by a feeling of closeness to Allah, and it is then that one can get to know the Creator. This is only one of the many jewels of wisdom that are revealed in the context of one man's story as he emerges from difficulty clinging to life's lessons and implementing them in his life. His honesty and his willingness to share are evidence of his desire to help others to see that troubles are sometimes blessings in disguise.

Hafiz Nafees Ahmed Islahi
Masters of Phil. (Biography of the Prophet); BA (Shariah Law)
Islamic University of Madinah, KSA
Imam of Tawheed Center of Novi, Michigan USA

ACKNOWLEDGEMENTS

Before I launch into my story, I would like to thank all my family and friends for the good times and not-so-good times, for supporting me and opposing me, for sticking with me and for detaching themselves when it was required.

All the people in my life played a part to get me where I am today, and for that I will be forever grateful. Here are some special mentions: Thank you, Kauser Asia Jehan, for loaning me material on Islam and giving me a head start. Thank you, Nadeem Ul Haque, for introducing me to Dr. Israr Ahmad, and thank you, Hafiz Tauseef Siddiqi, for providing me with books written by Imam Al-Ghazali. Thank you, Mohammed Al Doweesh and Mazhar Ali Khan, for lending me your ears, your patience and your valuable advice. I want to give a special mention to my late friend, Anwarul Islam. I wish he could have stayed a little longer by my side. Thank you, Shahnaz Ansari, for your unflinching support. I am truly blessed to have a sister like you.

Lastly, I want to thank my publisher, Zarinah El-Amin Naeem, and my editor, Rabia Imran. Zarinah for her timely and continuous confidence in my efforts, insightful criticism and helpful suggestions, and Rabia for her research, writing assistance and uncanny intuitiveness.

There are many others who have directly or indirectly contributed to my lifelong learning and guided me forward on my spiritual journey. I thank these people from the bottom of my heart and pray for their well-being in both worlds. Ameen.

Mohammed Qamruzzaman

INTRODUCTION

A truth as big and significant as *Tawheed*; the oneness of God, cannot be suppressed. When man recognizes Allah, his tongue automatically invites people to the right path. He wages jihad, the ultimate spiritual struggle, against his own soul, enjoins righteousness and forbids evil. It is the same with any other discovery. Whenever a universal truth is uncovered, man is impatient to announce it to the world and debunk all fallacies surrounding it.

I am not the first man coming out with a beacon to light this world. I am neither a scholar of Islam, nor a historian. If you must know, I am a nobody, who goes by the name of Mohammed Qamruzzaman. There is a small chance that you know me well, if at all but there is a bigger chance that your life and mine are travelling on the same route. You, like me, could be a Muslim in transit.

Logically, a similar route means similar problems. I could be wrong though, and you could be far, far ahead of me, jumping over bigger hurdles. But then again, you might be struggling with faith too. You might be oblivious to your real identity and gnashing your teeth every time you hear the word Islam, because that is how it is these days. We are allowing non-believers to redefine our faith for us, and, under-standably, they are tearing Nit apart.

My writing began during the time I was fighting to stay afloat, while life kept pushing me under. A drowning man will clutch at a straw. I caught hold of a single dried up stalk of my faith–the same faith that had morphed into a western monstrosity. And so began my quest.

Since the beginning of time, man has been searching for the

sublime truth. Some have been after the secret of creation while others have sought the source. Intellectual men like Moses, Jesus, Mohammed (peace be upon them), Buddha, Lao Tzu, Socrates and so many more were thirsty for answers that would give their lives meaning and purpose. These men sought a super being and found the One. The lucky ones recognized Him as Allah and others as a bigger and stronger force than anything else.

Some of these great men wanted to achieve peace, justice and freedom. They were occupied with the state of their fellow men. To achieve clarity of vision they isolated themselves from the pleasures of the world. Their tireless vigils ultimately uncovered their true spirit, which became a medium between them and their Creator. The message received was soon passed on to other men but despite its clarity many refused to accept it. The freedom that man had enjoyed in his ignorance was too precious a commodity to part with. This was where conflict arose and men divided themselves into believers and non-believers.

While intrinsic curiosity led many men to God, love for the world held many back. And instead of submitting before the Creator out of fear, awe, and gratitude, man submitted to his taciturn nature and vulnerabilities.

Today, a majority of Muslims are born into Islam, the foremost reason for their being Muslims. I, too, was born a Muslim, but, sadly, grew up to be a Muslim who was not. I held the Quran, not knowing what Allah wanted to say to me. I carried the name of a person who was larger than life, yet I had no inkling of what he (peace be upon him) had achieved that was unsurpassable by all other men. I prayed (jibber-jabber, actually) and that was that. I celebrated Eid, not knowing exactly what I was celebrating, but I was a Muslim, or so I thought. It kills me to admit it, but I was play-acting like most of us are, these days. I wasn't a struggling Muslim, but a man who was struggling with life. I didn't know what Islam meant. The truth is, it didn't matter, and I didn't care, until the day my life skidded out of control.

There I was—no support, no friends, no hope, yet, life wouldn't give me a break. In my desperation, I turned towards my Allah. It wasn't easy. I was hurt, skeptical, and terrified of losing myself and the little shred of Muslim identity that had survived years in America.

I started to read the Quran with translation. When I was done with that, I picked up book after book on Islam, initially to quench my thirst for answers and later on to develop a better understanding of my faith. All my findings have been painstakingly turned into chapters in this book that run parallel with my life. I did not discover anything that hasn't already been discovered, but I uncovered truths that were not given to me by my parents. I understood Islam as if it were never taught to me.

Every single time I read, I felt a part of me change. My body sagged under its weight. My shoulders dipped more with each new discovery and the huge responsibility of conveying it to others. If that wasn't enough, I also carried immeasurable regrets.

My children, like me, were born Muslims and like me, understood little about their identities. I blamed myself entirely. But that wasn't all. I saw Muslims in transit everywhere I looked. I started to worry about the state of the Ummah, the Islamic community at large. Fortunately, I was never the kind to sit and sulk. I decided to give back.

Mohammed Qamruzzaman

AUTHOR'S NOTE

MOST OF THE people you will come across in this memoir bear their authentic names. However, in some instances, I thought it best to alter names to avoid personal embarrassment and undue pain.

Some close relations mentioned during the course of the book are;

Abba: father
Amma: mother
Apa: elder sister
Barhe Bhaiya: elder brother
Dadi: paternal grandmother
Nani jee: maternal grandmother
Nana: maternal grandfather

MUSLIM

In Transit

A LITTLE BOY GROWS UP IN PATNA, TRAVELS TO AMERICA
AND DISCOVERS THE ESSENCE OF ISLAM.

GROWING UP
PATNA, 1944–1946

اللهُ أكبر اَللَّهُ اَكْبَرُ

اَللَّهُ اَكْبَرُ اَللَّهُ اَكْبَرُ

اَشْهَدُ اَنْ لاَ اِلَهَ اِلاَّ اللَّهُ

اَشْهَدُ اَنْ لاَ اِلَهَ اِلاَّ اللَّهُ

اَشْهَدُ اَنَّ مُحَمَّدًارَّسُوْلُ اللهِ

اَشْهَدُ اَنَّ مُحَمَّدًارَّسُوْلُ اللهِ

حَیَّ عَلَى الصَّلَوةِ

حَیَّ عَلَى الصَّلَوةِ

حَیَّ عَلَى الْفَلاَحِ

حَیَّ عَلَى الْفَلاَحِ

اَلصَّلَوةُ خَيْرٌ مِّنَ النَّوْمِ

اَلصَّلَوةُ خَيْرٌ مِّنَ النَّوْمِ

اَللَّهُ اَكْبَرُ

اَللَّهُ اَكْبَرُ

لاَ اِلَهَ اِلاَّ اللَّهُ

"Allah is the greatest! Allah is the greatest!"

"Allah is the greatest! Allah is the greatest!"

"I bear witness that there is none worthy of worship except Allah"

"I bear witness that there is none worthy of worship except Allah"

"I bear witness that Muhammad is the Messenger of Allah"

"I bear witness that Muhammad is the Messenger of Allah"

"Come towards prayer!"

"Come towards prayer!"

"Come towards success!"

"Come towards success!"
"Prayer is better than sleep!"
"Prayer is better than sleep!"
"Allah is the greatest! Allah is the greatest!"
"There is none worthy of worship except Allah"

A S THE WORDS of the *muadhin's* call to prayer dissipated with the morning fog, I heard steady shuffling of *muttaqeen*, the cognizant believers, on the streets below, heading to the small, yet pristine, mosque situated just a few paces away from where I lived. I heard *Dadi*, my paternal grandmother, calling out to my sisters, and moaning as her fragile limbs protested against this early morning scuttle to the Sovereign's court. I stretched in bed, glimpsed the still dark sky outside my window and turned over to catch a few more hours of sleep.

When the sun came, up my entire room was drenched in light. There was nothing spectacular about it–just an ordinary room, bare except for my bed and a rickety old chair. My favorite feature was the big window facing the Ganges, not that I could see it. The street where I lived was dirty and congested. It resembled a badly chalked hopscotch grid polluted by adults and their belongings. Standing at the window, when I cared to look down, I would see a world that made me want to move to Ramzanpur, where *Abba*, my father, owned acres of land. But when I looked up, I saw a world that gave me second thoughts about leaving Patna.

Just across from our double story building was a beautiful house. The house didn't interest me as much as the young Hindu girl who lived in it. Every morning she would appear in her balcony with her *pooja thali*, the round, decorative plate used in Hindu rituals to venerate gods. She would light the candle, knowing that I stood at my window watching, and then she would do something that still baffles me today. She would look straight at me and rotate her *thali*. We would exchange smiles and then rush to get ready for school.

School was my least favorite place. Weak and a bit small for my age, I was an easy target for my classmates. Often I would find my stuff stolen, my books missing and my teachers annoyed.

I had decided that day was going to be my last one at the *maktab*. I simply couldn't take it anymore. Before leaving the house, I told my older brother, *Barhe Bhaiya* about my decision. He was not surprised, since bullying was a norm, but to cheer me up, he promised to get my favorite treat *baqar khani*, after dinner that night.

Bhaiya's cajoling pacified me; although, it did nothing to change my mind. On my way home from the *maktab* I found myself exploring the best possible ways to tell *Abba*.

What I lacked in stature, I made up for in brains. It would take some convincing, but *Abba* would concede eventually. He was a professor at Bihar National College and taught Persian and Urdu. He was also a man of principles. Father to six girls and three boys, he was very protective of his children, especially me.

As a child, I was forbidden to stay outside after dark, not allowed to go to the movies alone and hardly ever allowed to play outdoor games. That night, when we all sat down to dinner, I announced my decision to the family and waited for their reaction. While looks were exchanged, no words were spoken.

The next day I refused to go to school. Maybe it was something in my tone, or maybe *Abba* had glimpsed my resolve. He never questioned me or demanded an explanation, and that was that. Soon after, I was enrolled in another school and entered 4th grade. That's when *Abba* decided to take matters into his own hands. Every evening, he would summon me to the *dalaan*, the inner courtyard, and help me with my reading, one paragraph at a time. We read all kinds of books, delved into the history of nations and geography of the world, but we never picked up the Quran. It seemed my leaving the *maktab* had put an early end to my Quranic education.

QUESTIONS TO REFLECT ON;

- What builds our character? Is it the *maktab* and Quranic education, or teaching of good values at an early age? Or perhaps both?
- How important is it to teach children pure Islamic values?
- Do you think the *maktab* and Quranic education alone would build a child's character, if we don't pay any attention to teaching them Islamic values?
- Do you think a child who is given Quranic education without Islamic character will be able to succeed in this world?
- What is necessary for a child to succeed in the world?

2

FIRST OFFERING

What has reached you was never meant to miss you, and what has missed you was never meant to reach you. - Prophet Mohammed (PBUH)

ORE THAN SIXTY years ago, what failed to reach me was the meaning behind the words that still ring in my ears, five times a day. Today, I am convinced that those words were never meant to miss me. While I drifted between sleep and consciousness, the *muadhin* proclaimed his faith in the one and only Allah, the Greatest. He declared Mohammed (PBUH) His Messenger and beckoned the believers to come to *salah,* the ritual prayer, and to success. Then he implored, *salah* is better than sleep, but I slept on.

I don't quite remember when I woke up to my faith but I do remember my struggle. I recall that unquenchable thirst for answers that plagued me day and night for years. Initially, when I was drawn towards Allah, the first act of worship I offered was *fajr salah,* the prayer made before sunrise. Later, I found out the first obligation decreed upon the believers is performing *salah* five times a day. It is considered not just the foundation of Islam, but the most essential pillar after *tawheed,* the declaration of faith.

1985–1988 was the time during which I questioned my identity as a Muslim. What made me a Muslim? Kismet? Chance? Destiny? Take your pick. I was fortunate to have been born in a Muslim family; therefore, I was circumstantially a Muslim. Whether I was a good Muslim or a bad one didn't signify in my early existence. Like many, I was living the life of an ignorant fool until my wake-up call came.

They say, "Ignorance is bliss," and "What you don't know, won't hurt you." Wrong. My ignorance was torture, and what I didn't know was eating away at my *dunya* and my *akhirah*: destroying my worldly life and my Hereafter.

When I started offering *fajr salah*, I was clueless about the Islamic injunctions regarding prayers, thus *fajr* was my only *salah* of the day. I never felt inclined to take the next step forward until I started consulting books and memorizing chapters of the Quran. Then I took my first wobbly step.

Somewhere, sometime, I had heard someone declare, if a servant of Allah took a step towards Him, Allah took ten steps towards that servant. I was that servant, waiting for my Master to walk those ten paces.

While I waited, I read and pondered. My research on *salah* revealed its significance. I was unaware that *salah* was the decisive criterion between a believer and a non-believer, between a Muslim and a hypocrite. I was a Muslim; wasn't I born one? So did my negligence make me a hypocrite?

I started questioning every ritual Muslims performed, even *salah*. I was a thinking Muslim. My mode of education had taught me to question and seek answers before conceding. I knew Muslims inhabited every corner of the world. I knew most practiced their faith and offered *salah* five times a day, yet success didn't seem to come out of it. They were the most lamentable people, their conditions deplorable in east and west. It just didn't add up.

This creation of Allah had:

1. declared their belief in the oneness of God
2. accepted Mohammed (p.b.u.h) as Allah's messenger, and also
3. given proof of their devotion through worship

Then why were they suffering such a sorry fate? Why did Allah let His people suffer? What kind of a God was He? My mind kept throwing such questions at me again and again.

There were times when I was filled with doubt and felt abandoned by Him. There were other times when my entire being searched for a connection. My heart and my soul would yearn for something to ground me and not make me feel like a parched leaf drifting in the wind. I longed for Allah to notice me, and I realized that there was only one way to achieve that. I started studying the Quran with increased fervour. I prayed *fajr* with utmost devotion and consistency, and waited for Him to notice me.

QUESTIONS FOR REFLECTION

- Are you satisfied with your religious performance and believe Allah is pleased with you? Did you ever question your performance and think Allah may not be pleased? Are you a 'thinking' Muslim?

- Are you satisfied with the knowledge of Islam you have? If yes, write down what Allah (swt) has created us for as a beautiful reminder for yourself. If no, write down all the unanswered questions about Islam that you have in mind.

- Please try to find answers to all your questions, one by one, with the best of your knowledge and ability. Keep pondering until you are satisfied with your answers. It may take years but never mind, it will get you closer and closer to Allah.

3

LAUGHTER AND TEARS
PATNA, 1944–1947

And He is with you wherever you are. (The Quran, 57:4)

THE YEAR WAS 1944 and pre-wedding festivities were in full swing. *Barhe bhaiya* was getting married to my uncle's daughter and our entire family was going to Ramzanpur to bring home his bride.

The excitement was palpable and joy evident in each and every face. *Abba* was mostly home, having taken a break from his college. I would sit on his lap and observe the frenzy. I did not grasp the situation fully, but tiny arrows of anticipation would zing through my body whenever anyone mentioned *phuljhari* and *patakhay:* firecrackers and fireworks.

Dadi constantly complained about not having enough hours for all the preparations. It seemed as if things would never get done on time. My sister, *Apa* and my mother, *Amma,* would not be able to finish trimming the *dupattas*–those long, full scarves worn by South Asian women–with gold and silver lace in time. *Abba* would not be able to collect the bride's jewellery from the *sunnar,* and his sister, *Bu'a,* would not be able to finish making her special *Mithai* for *nani jee,* my maternal grandmother.

During the last couple of days, *Dadi* became so tense, she stopped speaking altogether. It was only when we were well on our way to Ramzanpur, did I hear her utter an audible sigh of relief.

The wedding was the happiest time of my life. It lasted for days. I was four and the joy and laughter completely swept me off my feet.

Every night, women of all ages flocked together and sang songs for the happy bride and groom. The old showered them with blessings and the young teased them mercilessly. Most nights I ran around claiming that the bride was mine, mine, mine.

After the wedding and the groom-thrown reception, *nikah* and *valima*, guests started departing for their home villages and towns. The magic ended with a poof. Soon after, we returned to Patna with the bride, and life quietly slipped into the same old routine. It would be two years before I returned to Ramzanpur again.

The year was 1946, and it was the mango season. Conditions all over the Indian subcontinent were tumultuous. The seed of hatred that had been planted by the *farangis*, a disparaging term by which Europeans were known, was now bearing fruit. Tempers ran high and blood ran cold. Hindus and Muslims who had been living together for centuries could no longer bear to breathe the same air anymore.

As conditions worsened in the city, I noticed that conversations hushed up whenever I walked into a room. *Abba*, who was the president of the Bihar wing of the Muslim League, religiously avoided discussing politics in my presence. I was a clever child, however, and picked up a few things on my own. I knew India was burning and innocent lives were burning with it.

Soon Hindu atrocities and Muslim retaliations became an everyday occurrence, and the breach between the two kept widening. At home, everyone was stuck in a state of nervous anticipation. Laughter disappeared and darkness seemed to envelope my family. When I heard that *Barhe bhaiya* was planning to celebrate *Eid al Adha* with his in-laws in Ramzanpur, I couldn't let him leave without me.

Bhaiya was almost like a second father. He was a professor and taught Persian. Although we had fourteen years between us, it didn't stop me from chasing him around. He made me feel safe and well taken care of, even when *Abba* was not around. I thought a trip to Ramzanpur with him would be a perfect getaway from the overcast skies of Patna. But, I couldn't have been more wrong.

—~m~—

We had just arrived in Ramzanpur a few hours earlier, and I was out walking with *Barhe bhaiya*, when we saw a man running towards us at breakneck speed. He collapsed when he reached us, but came around within moments. He told us to take shelter and that the end was near. I did not grasp the reality of his words until much later, but apparently *Bhaiya* did. He half carried, half dragged the man to the nearest house. There was a crowd already present there. We were told that all the neighbouring Hindu villages had joined forces against the Muslims of Ramzanpur. That was the first time I witnessed horror in the eyes of my elders.

Back in 1944, Ramzanpur was a small village in the state of Bihar in northern India. It was a Muslim-majority area, inhabited by less than a hundred men, women and children. The servants and the help were mostly Hindus. Since there hadn't been any Hindu-Muslim clashes in the past, the locals had given no thought to their protection. The entire village owned but a single gun and no other ammunition. Now, defenseless and surrounded from all sides, they were like sitting ducks with nowhere to run, nowhere to hide and no time to evacuate.

Quickly all the facts were laid down before the gathering villagers. Ramzanpur was the only Muslim village for miles. The Hindus from the surrounding villages would make a staggering force of 36,000 armed men or more. Since we were in no position to defend ourselves, we would be crushed. Everyone was in a state of panic. It would be a bloodbath.

When my elders felt the danger closing in, they decided to shift to another house. We kept moving from one place to another, looking for shelter, for safety. People kept coming together, very soon there was a throng of old and young, men, women and children, shuffling and jostling on the streets of Ramzanpur, all making their way to the strongest and safest houses.

Death was lurking on our heads and fear drove us forward. We were out on the streets when we heard the Hindu mob. The crowd panicked and picked up speed. Some people started falling behind. I turned to grasp *Dadi's* hand, but found her missing from my side. When I stopped to look for her I got separated from *Bhaiya*. I started searching frantically for both and soon spotted *Dadi*. She was twenty feet away, sitting on the curb, exhausted, her bad leg hurting her.

I ran to her, grabbed her hand and pulled her up. I wasn't leaving her behind. We started walking again, but our progress was slow. The street we were walking on suddenly seemed empty and foreboding. My eyes would dart, left and right searching for *Barhe bhaiya*. I was scared. Men who had worked for my grandparents and uncles, had served my family for generations, and whose families depended upon mine for support, were now thirsty for our blood.

Then they were upon us, like hungry wolves upon a flock of sheep. The empty street became a battleground within moments, and the Muslims of Ramzanpur were cornered and slaughtered before my eyes. My relatives fell left and right, while I stood shell-shocked, supporting *Dadi*. Soon we were conspicuous and alone, except for the bodies that lay strewn around us.

We had to get out of there. *Dadi* had almost given up, and I had to drag her with me. I saw another crowd approaching, and soon we were swallowed up. These were our people who swiftly deposited us to my uncle's house. But danger still lurked, just outside the huge stone walls.

My six-year-old mind that had never experienced fear was quickly becoming acquainted with it. I heard someone say that *Barhe bhaiya* was outside with a sword, keeping the Hindus from scaling the wall. I felt sick. I did not want to lose him.

There was a deafening roar outside, and the predators were upon us. Although uncle had locked us inside the house, the mob outside had broken in. We backed up into a room and barricaded it. There was no real protection left now and everyone started to pray. I heard people beseech Allah to save them and to send help.

The Hindus inside the house raided one room after another until they found ours. Finding it locked from inside they rammed the door, within moments it crashed open, and we came face to face with death.

—ᴍ—

I believe in miracles. I believe if it isn't your time to die, you won't. Allah will intervene, and you will live to see another day or as many as you are meant to. This was one such time. Death came for us in the guise of a bloodthirsty Hindu mob but was intercepted and turned away.

As we stood saying our last prayers, there was a shout and cry. The angry mob somehow dispersed, like animals fleeing from a forest fire. Allah had sent help. Outside the broken gates stood a contingent of the British forces, commanded by a Muslim officer. This officer's family resided in Ramzanpur. He was passing by with his troops when he saw thousands of armed Hindus advancing upon his village. He ordered his men to open fire, and the hunters became the hunted.

Within a few hours, order was restored. But by that time Ramzanpur was red with Hindu and Muslim blood. I wanted to go home. The news of the attack on Ramzanpur had reached Patna, and my family was worried. *Abba* was a resourceful man. He arranged for a company of British soldiers and came to get us on a big truck. When he reached us, it was already dark, and the mob was long gone. He decided to stay the night and leave with us first thing in the morning.

After dinner, I saw the British Army officer who had accompanied *Abba* hand him his gun and ask him to even the score. *Abba's* eyes were bloodshot. I was convinced he would take up his offer, but he refused and something settled inside me. The next morning, *Abba* boarded me, *Barhe bhaiya*, my uncle, his family and everyone else who wanted to leave *Ramzanpur* in the truck and drove us to Patna. I reached home and realized it was still *Eid*.

Following the announcement of the partition plan in 1946, all pandemonium broke loose in India. The plan for the creation of Pakistan, a separate Muslim state, and that of Hindustan, a separate Hindu state, was not received well by many Hindus. Muslims, who did not want to move from their homes, were forced to due to the unbridled violence that was unleashed against them. My uncle was

13

one of them. He left his home and kept moving as the boundaries of Pakistan kept altering, first to Calcutta and then to Dhaka, East Pakistan, where he eventually settled for good.

East Pakistan was a disaster in the making. Its impractical segregation from West Pakistan ensured that a third state would soon come into existence. In 1971, riots broke out among the Biharis and Bengalis. My uncle was killed, and his family fled to West Pakistan. On April 17, 1971, East Pakistan declared its independence and Bangladesh came into existence.

The Hindu-Muslim clashes changed my outlook on life. It was hard for me to accept that our own servants and workers would turn on us like wild dogs. They would claim our land and drive us out of our homes. Ramzanpur was gone. India seemed foreign. It was not the land where my father grew up in. *Nani jee* and *Nana* had also moved to East Pakistan and left Sheikhupura and India forever. We settled down in our house in Patna, and it became our only refuge.

The Hindu-Muslim clashes raised hundreds of questions in my mind about God, religion and our faith. Are we creations of one and only one God? If we are, then how come we are thirsty for each others blood? What makes us forget our relations and turns us into enemies? Does the suffering of other human beings please us? These questions would now follow me until I had found answers acceptable to my curious and inquisitive mind, and in the process, I would build my faith or lose trust in God and His religion; or I die.

Also, my mind did not stop to think; why am I still alive? I was so close to death, help came from nowhere and I am still alive. Why did Allah (swt) save me, is there any particular reason that I am still alive?

QUESTIONS FOR REFLECTION

- Do you ever wonder why Muslims are suffering all over the world?
- Do you believe Allah is testing us, or is it His wrath?

- If it is Allah's wrath then what did we do to deserve it?
- Do you remember any period when Allah tested the whole Muslim community of the world?

4

Identifying my Creator

Allah created all things, and He is the agent on which all things depend. (The Quran, 39:62)

TAWHEED AS WE KNOW IT

THE MAIN DIFFERENCE between Hindus and Muslims of the subcontinent was *tawheed*, and from that stemmed all the minor and major intricacies of faith. From the earliest times, man had sought out his Creator. I was doing the same thing, searching for my Lord and Master.

Who was He, the Creator of the Universe? I understood that all mortals knew Him, although by different names. Whether they believed in His omnipresence and supremacy was unclear; whether they identified Him with all His qualities was highly doubtful; and whether they worshipped Him or not was, in today's world, "None of my business." (This individualistic concept was proven entirely wrong, as I learned more about Islam, the Holy Quran and the way of the Prophet Mohammed, peace be upon him).

Don't get me wrong, I am not pointing fingers. All Muslims, including me, are aware that the universe was created by Allah, the Great. We know He has a hundred names and, therefore, a hundred attributes that only belong to Him. We, more often than not, follow His commandments and worship Him, too. We worship the way we have been asked to, or at least, we think we do. And this, for us, signifies our unshakable belief in *tawheed*.

IDENTIFYING ALLAH AS THE CREATOR

While I studied *tawheed*, I felt I was missing its essence in entirety. I knew the answer was there, staring me in the face, but I just couldn't put my finger on it. I had my facts right, yet the most important piece of logic seemed to elude me.

According to Ludwig Wittgenstein, "Logic has a way of taking care of itself; all we need to do is look and see how it does it." The Universe has logic to it. I realized a similar logic could be applied to everything under the sun.

Consider the Big Bang Theory: if the universe was a coincidence, the sun, the moon and the earth are the most remarkable flukes. We, humans are the perfect chance happenings. Our sustenance can be considered another very essential and timely accident of fate. Works perfectly, doesn't it? So if we need anything else, we can always ask for more flukes. But who do we ask? Nature? No. In the perfect world of the non-believers, things just fall into place perfectly by themselves.

I was glad to be a Muslim. I did not have to indulge in such idiosyncrasies. You can't have creations without a creator. It couldn't be done in the past, and it still can't be done in the modern age of technological wonders.

Being a man of practicality, I seldom waste my time with "What if," and rarely indulge in "What should be." With me, it's always facts, figures and derivatives. I have my own theory about the world. I believe the world is a big mainframe computer, programmed to produce a predetermined output to everything we put in. Neither we humans nor the computer has the ability to change that outcome.

My premise is the Supreme Law Giver and His universal laws. The world is designed according to corporal laws and physical directives, and the reaction to every action can't change unless a greater force is applied to overcome the laws or their effects—think miracles. Scientists tell us our planet is rotating at a high velocity around its axis and simultaneously revolving around the sun. They also predict imminent disaster if the world deviates, even by the smallest fraction. This makes one wonder about the entity holding the Earth in place.

Life on Earth is another big question mark. It is not just us humans on this planet. We share the Earth with 8.7 million different forms of life. The logical questions are: "How does life survive?" and "Who is providing the nourishment"? It can't be all there, simply waiting to be found and picked up. "What about the growing human population of the world?" We constantly hear that the global food production will fail to keep up with it. But the fact is, food production is also increasing, not at the rate that would soothe environmentalists, but nevertheless, it is.

Our existence on this Earth is not coincidental, because it can't be. We have sophisticated machines and technology that make our survival possible in today's times, but stop to think how that technology was developed. Who gave us that incredible brain power? The brain power which made it all possible. Just a cursory look at the working of the human body, the intricate system of nerves, muscles and tendons, the skeleton and the organs prove the existence of a Superpower and a much bigger mind at work.

Do you think human brain power and intelligence are directly proportional to human needs? I think not. Let's say you have a need, and you have an empty box. Can you draw whatever you want out of that box simply because you have a need for it? No, logic doesn't accept that. When you draw something out, however, you call it magic. It's something inexplicable and extraordinary. Therefore, unless there is a superior entity at work, you can't expect to keep pulling rabbits out of an empty hat, or needs out of an empty box, or even ideas out of your brain.

Other aspects which we conveniently ignore are the universal laws of nature: the law of cause and effect, and the law of action and reaction, just to name two. If it weren't for these laws, the world would not be running this smoothly, and we wouldn't be where we are today. It was not man who made these laws: the laws that decree fire to burn wood, man to freeze in sub-zero temperatures, a seed to germinate when it imbibes water and bees to pollinate our food sources.

The most significant discovery of the last century was DNA, the blueprint that holds all the codes and information for the reconstruction of cells and ultimately life. So if there is proof of storage and a design, logic contends the existence of a designer storing this data.

I am an engineer and guilty of thinking like one. I studied the design and the working of the world before concluding that it's perfect. We engineers conceive, model, develop, test and supervise. We apply principles of science and engineering, and create new paradigms. However, we fail to create a system that could match that of a human being, and the systems we create are never accidental.

The reality is: We humans are reasonable and even derisive when it comes to our lives, but we choose to be close-minded and irrational when it comes to identifying our Creator.

Although I believed in one God, my heart needed conviction. Wherever I looked, and whatever I chose to study, I felt Allah was leading me on, slowly opening my eyes to the signs that surrounded me. When I realized what I was doing, I felt ashamed for the first time. I was seeking verification.

Allah states in the Quran that men ask for signs when his veracity is evident in the secrets that He so generously revealed to us. I picked up the Holy Quran and found it brimming with signs, facts and validations. I studied verses where Allah, the Merciful, challenges mankind to bring forth something that matches His powers. Can man make the sun rise from the west? Can man snatch back what the bee takes away from him? Can man resurrect the dead? He urges His creation to think, to identify His signs and to submit to the one and only true Lord.

The more I read and pondered, the more I believed, and the smaller I became, in my eyes.

UNDERSTANDING TAWHEED FOR WHAT IT IS

La ilaha il Allah, Mohammed ur-Rasulullah
None is worthy of worship except Allah,
and Mohammed is the Messenger of Allah

Tawheed means asserting the oneness of Allah. Sounds easy, because we have been told that saying the declaration of faith, the *kalima shahadah,* fulfills its criterion. I thought the same thing. I believed I was Muslim. First, because my father was Muslim and second, because I had recited its declaration countless times.

I had been uttering these words since I was a child but never once reflected upon their meaning. As an adult, I still carried a child's perspective of *tawheed.* My God was One, and His name was Allah. Each morning after I woke up, I would declare my faith in Him. Then I would have the audacity to go about my own business, not considering the implications of my assertion at all.

But over my course of study, I learned that *tawheed* is not just a verbal testimony supporting Allah's oneness, but it is also maintaining that *tawheed* in all our actions, each of which should, directly or indirectly, seek Allah's favor, as He is the Absolute Ruler.

Tawheed is **declaring** and **maintaining** that:

- Allah is One, without a partner in His dominion and His actions
- Allah is One, unparalleled in His essence and His attributes
- Allah is One, unrivalled in His divinity and His worship

When I looked at *tawheed* in this new light, I felt a piece of the puzzle fall into place. These three aspects not just overlap but are inseparable. You can't believe in one and not the others. Simultaneously, you can't maintain one and not the others, and this is the true essence of *tawheed.*

I realized I had been reciting the declaration of faith but was nowhere close to fulfilling its dictates.

Declaring and maintaining *tawheed* means not putting anything before Allah's commandments: not your job, not your social life, and neither your family nor friends. For me, it meant developing and honing my belief to the extent where I could say the *kalima* and maintain it judiciously in my everyday existence.

When a man announces his belief in the Unity of Lordship, he accepts that:

- Allah existed before all else.
- He will exist when all else perishes.
- He creates and He sustains without any outside help.
- He is the sole and unrivalled ruler of the Universe and all its inhabitants.

Moreover, all that is good and all that is bad are predestined events, which are from Him as a test for us. Therefore, associating good fortune or bad luck with anything else means challenging *tawheed*.

I saw that in some events the cause and effect patterns were easily recognizable, while in others they were bewildering. A good deed was rewarded with goodness. But sometimes even good, honest men suffered atrocities that left me questioning Allah and His mercy. These were the times when I would remember the line from *Surah al-Baqarah*:

And Allah knows, while you know not. (The Quran, 2:216)

This would put me in my place. I still had a lot to learn. My knowledge and comprehension was nowhere near that of the Creator of the Universe? May Allah forgive my insolence.

Declaring and maintaining *tawheed* also means believing only Allah is capable of fulfilling your needs as the Supreme Giver. Depending upon, or asking others to take care of your needs and problems may fall under *shirk*. The truth is, it is only Allah, the Provider, who provides through different channels. This truth is often wrongly interpreted.

> *Say, 'Do you indeed disbelieve in Him who made the earth in two days? And do you set up equals to Him That is the Lord of the entire world? And He placed therein anchors of mountains rising above it and put blessings therein and ordained therein provisions for its inhabitants–all this in four days, complete for the enquirers.' This is the decree of the Honourable, the All Knowing. (The Quran, 41:9–12)*

Allah, the Lord of all worlds, created the world and placed blessings in it to fulfil the needs and requirements of all His creation. The verses clearly announce that Allah is our only sustainer and whatever provisions, or *rizq*, we are allowed in this world comes from Him and Him alone.

Tawheed is upholding the unity of Allah's being and essence. When we define traits of Allah, we cannot go beyond what has been permitted and outlined in the Holy Quran and practice of His Holy Messenger (PBUH). Allah cannot be called by names other than those that have been used by Allah Himself or His Prophet. Similarly, He cannot be assigned attributes and qualities that are used for His creation. For example, Christians often claim that God is a spirit or has a spirit. The truth is that the spirit is just a creation of Allah. Allah never refers to Himself as a spirit in the Holy Quran.

The third aspect of *tawheed* is maintaining Allah's unsurpassed divinity and right of worship. If one believes in the first two aspects, but refuses to uphold Allah's unparalleled status as the true God worthy of worship, then one falls short of implementing *tawheed*. In such cases, even if a Muslim recites the declaration of faith and accepts Allah as the true God, he is considered a non-believer and a *mushrik*, one who commits *shirk* or polytheism.

Worship is the most crucial aspect of *tawheed*. Allah alone is capable of granting men their wishes, as a result of their worship. However, there are those who feel the need for intermediaries between man and

Allah. The fact is that all forms of worship must be made to Allah alone. Sharing Allah's right of worship with a dead person, a saint or even a Prophet is condemned by both Allah and His Messengers. No matter what the excuse, praying to anyone other than Allah, calling out to angels, spirits or jinn for the purpose of getting closer to Allah, or for sending out requests through these intermediaries to Him is a form of *shirk* and completely unacceptable by our Lord.

Unfortunately, quite a few Muslims today depend upon saints and charms to achieve their goals and take their prayers to Allah's court. There are also those who would try black magic, astrology and fortune telling instead of asking Allah, the Merciful, to fulfill their desires. When this happens a believer is straying far from the path of *tawheed* and committing *shirk*.

WHAT IS SHIRK?

In the simplest words, the opposite of *tawheed* is *shirk*. The moment a person defies *tawheed*, he commits the unforgivable sin of *shirk*. *Shirk* means sharing or associating and in Islam it means affiliating a partner with Allah.

On occasions when *shirk* is discussed as the most reprehensible and inexcusable of all sins, most of us thank the Lord that we are at least safe from the big one. We quietly pat our own backs and heave a sigh of relief. Truth is, most of us are guilty of this one, too. We are simply blind to our own faults.

Nothing is more objectionable to Allah than *shirk*. Like *tawheed*, it can be divided into the following categories:

- Shirk by association
- Shirk by negation
- Shirk by humanization
- Shirk by veneration
- Shirk by idolatry

I believe it is imperative that we understand the different kinds of *shirk,* so we know what grounds we tread on and what transgressions we commit, intentionally or otherwise. What follows is a brief description of the types of *shirk* mentioned above.

Shirk **by association** means sharing Allah's status with man-made, lesser godly-beings, like saints, angels and spirits. It does not necessarily mean believing in a demigod with equal powers. Today, many are guilty of *shirk* by association, due to lack of knowledge and proper Islamic education. Negating the status of Allah as the true creator is also shirk by association.

Shirk **by negation** is denying the existence of Allah. Atheism and Pantheism belong to this category of *shirk.* Among Muslim Sufis, those who claim that all is Allah and Allah is all, they invariably deny the separate existence of Allah and therefore can be deemed guilty of *shirk* by negation.

Shirk **by humanization** is when Allah is made to look like, or is given qualities of man or any other creature. Thinking and believing that Allah has a spirit or a son is *shirk* by humanization.

Shirk **by veneration** is when man or any other creation of Allah is exalted and granted qualities or names of Allah. Moreover, when any creation of Allah is called a manifestation or an incarnate of the Almighty it is also *shirk* by veneration.

Shirk **by idolatry** is letting your love for Allah's creation surpass your love for Allah. This is a major form of shirk. When man turns to idols instead of Allah for help and rewards, it washes away all of man's good deeds. In the present times, we may not be worshipping stone idols like the Quraish of Makkah, but we are guilty of worshipping worldly wealth and desires.

Worship is love, and love demands surrendering one's will to Allah completely. When love for a person, thing or pursuit supersedes the love for Allah, then it constitutes as worship and falls under *shirk.*

Allah says in the Quran:

Have you not seen the one who takes his desires as his god? (The Quran, 25:43)

Change does not come easy, especially when one is comfortably settled. Nevertheless, changes are occurring all the time. Among the many things that have changed since creation, a few things remain unchanged. For instance, **man is still in a power struggle with his *nafs*, his personal desires. The only difference is that fulfilling one's desires and giving in to the *nafs* has become a cultural norm in our modern day society.**

In the early years of Islam, people of Makkah were engaged in a similar battle. They lost to their *nafs*, when they continued worshipping stone idols, then refused to give up their ancestral ways, even after accepting *tawheed*. Giving up wealth and status is the hardest when you are in the higher echelons of society. The Quraish of Makkah became slaves to their desires for the same reason. They committed *shirk* by ignoring the warnings of the Prophet and refusing to change for the sake of Allah.

Today, we worship our own demigods and are lost in the pursuit of the material world. We give more importance to ball games, parties, dates and business conferences than we do to the call of the *muadhin*. Even our charities have turned into despicable displays of wealth and munificence. Can we still claim that our *iman,* that our faith, is intact? Can we still think that our belief in *tawheed* is unshakable, and our lives are free from *shirk*?

The conclusions I made about myself left me despondent. Suddenly, my situation seemed hopeless. I couldn't figure out a way to set things right. I had dug myself in so deep that I felt there was no way out. I was on the road to discovery but had learned only a few facts about Islam. Reading about *shirk* had shaken me up. I was weak: a slave to my *nafs*.

I would never be able to win His favour! The huge task before me made me question my existence again and again.

I started wondering; if my nafs is my biggest enemy and I have to overpower it to get close to my Creator, then there must be a way, a way I still have to discover.

Also, I understood that Allah (swt) has created us with intelligence in order that we may develop wisdom. And wisdom is to know the Creator, to know ourselves, why He created us and what He wants from us.

QUESTIONS FOR REFLECTION

- Do you believe Allah (swt) is Just and Fair, and He will Judge all mankind on the Day of Judgment equally or would He be partial towards Muslims?

- Do you believe we would have God's favour on the Day of Judgment just because we are Muslims by name or because we are God fearing obedient people?

- Why has Allah (swt) created us with so many identifications such as DNA, hair, teeth, nails, finger prints, etc?

- How do you see our Creator? Why do you think He created us?

- Do you believe we are Muslim because we are born in Muslim families and recite Kalima Shahadah or do we have to do more? If yes, then what?

- Knowing that obeying our Nafs and giving in to our personal desires is Shirk, do you think we really believe in Tawheed?

5

MY FATHER'S SON
PATNA, 1950–1963

*Allah never changes the condition of a people, unless they strive to
change it themselves. (The Quran, 13:11)*

NANI JEE AND *Nana*, my maternal grandparents, were back in
Sheikhupura for a few months, and so was I. It was another
glorious Indian summer. The trees were heavy with fruits,
and the ponds were pulsating with fish. I spent my days chasing frogs,
mimicking Koels, and wooing Mynahs into my snares.

The days were easy, but the nights were tough. My grandparents had
lost most of their wealth during the time of partition. Their ancestral
home was destroyed, and their new house did not offer the protection
I craved. I would lie on the *charpai*, a traditional woven bed and sleep
outside. The first half of the night would be spent identifying all the
creepy sounds emitting from the dark and the second, gazing at the
blanket of stars that offered just a tiny bit of comfort. I would wait for
the first ray of light to touch the corn. Then I would relax and close
my eyes.

One day, when I woke up after another long night, the sun was
burning my forehead, and *Abba* was sitting next to me. He had arrived
earlier and planned to spend a few days with us. I was overjoyed; his
presence would chase away my fears. I ran to freshen up and came
back to see him lying on the *charpai*, a faraway expression on his face.
I asked him how long he planned to stay with us. My question startled
him. He sat up, his expression guarded, and his eyes focused on me.
I did not realize that *Nani jee* was right behind me. *Abba* thought the

question was on her behalf and that changed everything. He left the same day.

My father was an upright fellow, a scrupulous man who carried his own weight. He was self-effacing at times and never burdened my *Nani* and *Nana* unnecessarily. He neither overstayed his welcome nor took more than his due. Although he had jumped to the wrong conclusion this time, I could not convince him to stay.

---ᝩᝩᝩ---

I was my father's son in many ways. He doted on me, and I loved his attention. Whenever I fall sick, he would take my bedside and spend his nights with me. His concern grew when *Amma* was confined to bed after suffering third degree burns from a kitchen fire. She did not survive. In her absence, I grew closer to *Abba* in more ways than one.

Besides being a professor, *Abba* was also a landlord, or *zamindar*. We owned acres and acres of land, had an army of servants, and several cooks. The food mostly came from our own farms. There were trees of lychees, mangoes and bananas. Our estate was huge, and our hospitality renowned. Several of my cousins lived with us and pursued their academic goals. Although I looked up to these fellows, who were solely interested in books and degrees, we had very little in common.

I was a strong-willed boy, ready for challenges and hungry for adventures. I wanted to spend my days hunting the most ferocious tigers and elephants, but the only animals I was permitted to hunt were deer, ducks and fish. I wanted to play football, polo and go biking, but the only sport I was permitted to indulge in was chess. Abba could be very domineering at times, or maybe it was just me and my absurdities.

Sometimes I think I took up challenges simply to prove others wrong. I wanted to hunt tigers to prove to my classmates that I was brave despite being skinny. I worked hard to achieve good grades to prove my worth to *Barhai bhaiya*, despite having very little interest in books. I even planned to study abroad because I wanted to prove to *Abba* that I was capable of surviving on my own.

To look strong, I took up bodybuilding and running. It helped, and people started to think twice before making me the brunt of their jokes. Soon I was stepping into my teens, and *Abba's* overprotective ways started to come between us. That's when I began keeping secrets from him.

When *Abba* refused to buy me a bike, I secretly rented one. I would ride it everywhere, making sure to avoid places he frequented. I got into an accident once, but did not have the guts to tell *Abba*. He already knew; and when I was able to ride again, he bought me my first bike.

In India, I lived the life of a coveted prince. I was candid, daring and fun. I had money to throw around and not a care in the world. After school, my friends and I would hang out at a small restaurant, The Soda Fountain, located in the center of the city. The restaurant owner would always have a table reserved for me. Ram Piyara Lal, would be our exclusive waiter. He would stand around awaiting our orders for as long as we sat there.

In 1955, I graduated from high school and joined the Bihar National College in Patna to complete my Intermediate in Science (I.Sc.). College life was fantastic. I was popular, surrounded with friends and had the time of my life. It was all so new to me and all so thrilling. Partying, movies and eateries became an everyday indulgence. Books and studying took a back seat. The result was not surprising at all: I flunked my exams.

It took me three years, instead of two, to acquire an I.Sc. Then I decided to go for my Bachelors in Science. Patna University not only helped shape my career choice, but also helped me come out of my father's shadow. I developed preferences, gained a voice of my own, and decided to pave my own way.

Despite all that, I knew I was still very much my father's son, and always would be. We were alike on many different levels. I was not a teacher, but politics was a common interest. I was not a father yet, but knew how to shoulder responsibility. I was disciplined, stubborn, proud of my roots, and so was *Abba*.

While I was generous in my spending, I was not a fool. Friends were welcome to share my luxuries; however, none were allowed to take undue advantage. This was another trait of *Abba's* that I had adopted as my own. He had fed me with a golden spoon, but had kept me under the tiger's watch.

I was taught early on that no matter how rich I was, some things had to be earned. I was very active in Patna University politics and was nominated for the student union elections. I saw an easy victory, not realizing that politics was a dirty business. The opposition started dividing my supporters on the basis of religion, and things got messy.

I had one of the only two motorbikes in Patna, and I was always getting into fights. I was not a follower and did not take insults well. At Patna University, I had managed to accumulate quite a few enemies. One afternoon, when I was out riding my bike, I found myself surrounded by a bunch of hooligans from the university. They had been after me for quite some time, and today was their lucky day.

I was alone and a goner. I ran for my life until I was cornered, my only escape was a leap of twenty feet. It would break a few bones, but it would save my pride. I jumped. Then I sprinted home, while my enemies stood cursing on the other side. I still can't help grinning, when I think about that jump. It was impossible, and it did break some bones.

Once home, I cooked up a story for *Abba* and *Bhaiya*. I wouldn't say they bought any of it, but they did let me off easy, seeing the pain that I was in. My friends visited me at home. After that incident, I abandoned all fear. The results were bigger fights and bigger enemies. I was marked by several student gangs. A few of them hired thugs to finish me off. I retaliated, and my friends got together to settle the matter with them once and for all. After that they never bothered me again.

When exams drew near, the reprieve from politics gave me a chance to assess my situation. It was not good. My grades would never land me the job of my dreams, and I would be forced to abandon my opulent lifestyle. The problem called for a solution and the solution presented itself in form of "Amrica" –the land of opportunity.

That was it. That was my plan. I would go abroad and study engineering. Then I would return to India and wow everyone.

While I was going through the hurdles of life I was learning very important lessons:

- The bigger your goal, the higher your success.
- Life is full of struggle, take the challenges and beg for our Creator's help.
- Choose such friends who respect your values and dreams.
- Never refuse to help others, not to prove you are better but to thank the Creator who elevated you to the position that you can help.

QUESTIONS FOR REFLECTION

- Do you remember any events in your life that pushed you to think about who is Allah, why He created you and what He expects from you? What were they?
- Do you perceive Allah's hands taking care of you every minute, every moment?
- Do you realize how Allah is leading you to the straight path through the events of your life?

CREATION OF MAN

Then did you think that we created you uselessly and that to us you would not be returned? (The Quran, 23:115)

I GAVE UP, NOT once, not twice, but innumerable times. I considered myself a "revert," initially a Muslim by chance, but as I grew older, a Muslim by choice. Often, my questions and investigations would lead me to the precipice of faith. There were times when I had to close my eyes and take the plunge, hoping I would survive the fall with my *iman* intact. There were other times when I would see light and steadily climb up towards understanding.

I don't know what it was that pushed me towards Allah, while my heart whispered doubts and my brain kept questioning. It was as if my being was on a familiar path. It was on a road it had travelled before and knew where it would lead me. Sometimes when sins burdened my soul, my heart would sink into the abyss of gloom, and I would ask Allah why He created me.

THE STORY OF MAN'S CREATION

When your Lord said to the angels: "Verily, I am going to place mankind, generations after generations, on earth."

The angels said:

Will You place therein those who will make mischief therein and shed blood, while we glorify You with praises and thanks and sanctify You?

And Allah answered:

I know that which you do not know. (The Quran, 2:30)

Angels and *jinn* existed way before man. When Allah decided to create man, He chose clay, gave man his shape, and blew life into him. There is a story that before man, *jinn* inhabited the Earth. But they fought and shed so much blood that, ultimately, Allah sent His angels to eradicate them. He put an end to the destruction. Two thousand years later, when man was created, the angels feared a similar outcome.

The angels knew that **man was being created with desires** and would have to strive for sustenance. They also knew that once the desires became uncontrollable they would beget greed, mischief and intolerance on Earth. The aftermath would be violent and bloody. Perplexed, they asked Allah why He wanted to put man, another mischief-maker on Earth?

Allah answered, "I know that which you do not." Although man was given desire and strive to earn sustenance, **Allah also bestowed him with power to overcome and control both.**

Man was given the power of intellect, logic and reasoning plus the potential to serve as Allah's vicegerent. The angels were unaware that a testing ground was being prepared for men, to see if they were worthy of Heaven. **If mankind resisted all worldly attractions and maintained purity of their hearts, then there would come a day when they would return to heaven as victors.**

When the going gets tough many of us ask the same question: "Oh Allah! Why did you create me?" Allah answers that He knows what we do not know.

Adam, the first man, was made of clay; angels were made of light, while the devil, whose name is Iblis, was a *jinn* created from fire. After blowing His spirit, or *ruh*, in Adam, Allah asked all who were present to prostrate before him. This prostration was a sign of respect, not worship. All the angels bowed low, but Iblis refused outright, claiming he was far better than the one made of clay. Vanity kept him from fulfilling Allah's command. Thus he was banished from Heaven, disgraced and humiliated. But before he left, he asked Allah for respite until the Day of Judgement. Allah granted his wish. Instead of asking for forgiveness, Iblis told Allah he would lead men astray, he would attack them from top and bottom, from left and right, and after he was through with men, most would not be thankful to their Lord.

And Allah answered Iblis:

Get out from Paradise, disgraced and expelled. Whoever of them (mankind) will follow you, then surely I will fill Hell with you all.

This was the beginning of man, when the evil that questioned Allah's judgement became his worst enemy. What followed was predestined.

Adam was taught the names of everything by Allah, the All Knowing. He was taught to think and to perceive. Additionally, Allah granted him an insatiable thirst for knowledge and a desire to pass it on to his progeny, and therein lay his glorification.

The Prophet Mohammed (PBUH) related that after Allah created Adam, he extracted from his back all his descendants who would be born in the world, until the end of time. Then He stood all of them before Him, and took a covenant from the generations of Adam.

Allah asked: *"Am I not your Lord?"*

And the sons and daughters of Adam said: *"Yes! We testify to it!"* (*The Quran, 7:172–173*)

We stood before our Creator; we accepted His lordship over everything; we promised that we would not forget. The reason why Allah, the Most Merciful, took this covenant was to mark our souls with *tawheed*, so we may not deny the very knowledge of our Creator's existence on the Day of Judgement. **There comes a time when the child forgets, but the soul remembers. As the child matures into a strong and able adult, Allah the Most Merciful gives it clear proofs of truth and deception. These are *chances*, which occur in the life of all.**

Our souls were stamped with truth, even before we were born as humans into this world. So if my soul was driving me towards Allah it was simply answering to its *fitrah*.

Fitrah **signifies one's true nature;** it is human nature to accept Allah as Lord and Master of the universe. When a child is born, whether to a Muslim, Christian, Hindu, Buddhist or even an atheist, he is born knowing that only Allah is the true Lord. The soul remembers its pledge all too clearly. With time however, parental influences and environment lure it towards different faiths. At this stage, the child is weak and unable to resist negative pressures or assert its own path. **human beings belonging to any race or religion, to encourage them to turn towards Allah.** So begins the test of faith, which we have all been promised.

MAN: ALLAH'S VICEGERENT ON EARTH

Creation of man was a part of Allah's plan and so was man's touchdown on Earth. **Man was created unique. He wasn't of the angels because Allah bestowed him with intelligence and wisdom, with the ability to comprehend and identify, and the capacity to choose between right and wrong.**

Man was taught to excel. He was given potential, and his test was his striving for Allah's pleasure, then–after all he achieved or failed to achieve–his ready submission to Allah and His will. Angels and even Iblis worshipped Allah. Iblis disobeyed the Mighty Lord, but so did Adam when he ate the fruit from the forbidden tree, the main difference between the two was the act of repentance.

Adam was sorry and Iblis was adamant. Adam was forgiven and Iblis was damned.

Many people believe that Adam was punished too by being expelled from paradise and sent to Earth. The fact is when Allah decided to create man, He said to the angels:

"I shall make a vicegerent on the Earth."

Allah did not say "Paradise;" He said "Earth." **Adam was sent to Earth not as an offender, but as a dignified deputy appointed by Allah to act on His authority.** The All Knowing already knew what was to come. The experience with Iblis was a lesson taught to Adam and Eve before they descended to Earth. It simply said: "Watch out for Iblis and his minions. They would keep you from Allah's favour and not have you enter Paradise."

Man was given liberty to act as he chose, but his destiny was written and sealed way before his descent to Earth. The Preserved Scripture, or *Loh e Mahfooz*, is said to hold all of Allah's plans, plus the series of predetermined and inevitable events that would occur in the lives of all men and women.

Belief in destiny is an essential part of our *iman*. This does not mean that mankind is predestined to sin or that his struggle and choices mean absolutely nothing. We have freedom of choice, and what we experience is the result of the choices we make. Our disobedience to Allah is a consequence of our free will. It is the same free will that Satan attacks again and again, in order to tarnish our *iman*.

Allah has given man freedom to change his destiny. He knows what is to come, but He does not force things to occur. He made sure that we knew our status and His; then granting us free will, sent us to Earth. It is true that we are fated to succeed and fail. It is true that Allah knows which of us will be granted admission into paradise and which of us would be hellbound. But it is also true that Allah, the Benevolent, has left a tiny opening for His true believers, and this opening allows us to change what is written in the *Loh e Mahfooz*, but only if Allah wills it.

Allah's knowledge of what is and what is to come is absolute and perfect. He is the Doer of actions and we are the earners. We must not forget that He is Ar-Rahman (the All Merciful), Al-Mujib (the Responder to Prayer), Al-'Afuww (the Forgiver) and Al-Basit (the Reliever).

He taught man to think and act for himself. If man was not meant to think, then the Creator would not have blessed us with a brain. If man was not meant to walk, then we would not have legs today. If man was not meant to enter paradise, then Allah would not have sent messengers to set us on the right path.

Allah says,

Call on me; I will answer you. (The Quran, 40:60)

If man was not meant to change his fate, Allah would not have asked man to call on Him. The power of supplication, or *dua from a pure and obedient heart*, can change destiny. Allah, the Maker of Order, who has written and preserved the *Loh e Mahfooz* can also rewrite our fate, if He wills it. Allah, the Responder to prayers, can grant us our wishes. Allah the Forgiver, can forgive our sins and Allah, the Reliever, can relieve us of the undesirable dictates of fate. **To achieve all this, man needs to accept His greatness and His power over all and beg for His mercy.**

Abdullah ibn Omar relates that the Prophet Mohammed (PBUH) said:

For whoever the door of dua opened, for him the doors of mercy are opened (Tirmidhi)

At another place the Prophet (PBUH) said,

Dua turns away destiny, and good deeds lengthen age. (Tirmidhi)

Obedience to Allah and total submission to His law will reap wonderful results and earn man a place in heaven, but disobedience will only arouse Allah's anger and intensify the fires of hell.

If we remember the true nature of this world and the purpose of our creation, we wouldn't lose the path of the righteous. If we choose to wash our sins away—if we repent and ask for forgiveness—then we still have a chance, the same chance that Adam had. Allah forgave his sin and elevated him to the post of His Vicegerent, revealing that His doors are open to all those who repent.

REPENTANCE AND ITS CONDITIONS

Every son of Adam sins, and the best of those who sin are those who repent. (Tirmidhi, 2499)

Repentance is the creed of all believers. Since man is prone to mistakes, blunders and misunderstandings he is almost always committing sins or threading really close to them. Allah knows this and therefore, gives a lot of leeway to His believers, promising that His doors will always be open for sinners who turn back in repentance.

Most people today are led to believe that no matter how frequently they commit sins, if they repent regularly, then they are bound to go to heaven. Committing sins may include drinking alcohol, eating haram and doing all those things that have been prohibited by Allah and His messengers.

Another failing of man is that he is naturally inclined to take the easy way out. If someone tells him, "It's okay to drink first and repent later, you will be forgiven eventually," then man will readily and gladly accept it. But if someone tells him, "If you drink and repent, it is only okay if you do not touch alcohol ever again," then man will have a much harder time repenting.

The truth is, repentance is a return journey to Allah. When you plan this trip you make preparations by:

a. Giving up the sin

b. Hating it and not going near it again

c. Regretting in falling short in obedience to Allah.

Now, if you simply say, "Sorry," to Allah and temporarily muster the emotions of remorse in your heart, knowing full well that you will commit the same sin again, you are just planning your trip, but you are not intending to ever take it. Unless you actually take the trip, you are not any closer to getting yourself off the hook.

Sin helps man to realize his mistakes. He fitted *nafs* inside man. **Nafs is neither spirit nor soul.** Yet it resides inside the body as a part of the physical self; although, it is not the physical body. **It possesses desires, sentiments, tendencies, hereditary characteristics, experiences, and a conscience.** So, whenever man takes a false step, his *nafs* berates him.

It is crucial to listen to one's protective *nafs*. When man stops listening to it, his indifference steadily pushes *nafs* over to the dark side, where it loses its purity and turns into a self-pleaser. It realizes that if man doesn't like its suggestions, then he will not act on them. So it starts to tell man only what pleases him because then man obeys. Hence, *nafs* turns into a self-serving Commander.

Allah created something beautiful inside man to make sure he would keep returning to Him, but man seems to have forgotten the true path that leads to Allah. This true path requires sincerity, a condition that is a must in every act of worship. It requires true remorse and permanent abstinence from sin. If the sin has been neglect, i.e., in performing salah, it should be rectified. If it involves a relationship or human rights, then pardon must be gained from the person and Allah.

If a man means to return to sinning after seeking forgiveness, then his repentance, or *tawba*, becomes invalid. However, if he truly repents but later is unable to restrain himself, not because of lack of trying, then he still stands a chance. But, it is crucial that he grieves over his relapse and renews his *tawba* at once.

They say there is a time for everything, there is also a time for *tawba*. Allah has given us our entire lives to repent but there are two instances in which *tawba* is worthless, even if it is true.

    a. The time of death

    b. The time the sun rises from the west.

Allah does not like to be taken lightly. If you have spent a lifetime pleasing yourself, secretly comforting your inner voice that you will repent when you are old, be warned, your repentance will not be accepted at that time. There will also come a time, before the Day of Resurrection, when the sun will rise from the west; this will be a sign from Allah, and all doors of repentance will close. The believers and nonbelievers will bow their heads in submission to Allah's will, but it will be too late by then.

A true believer must remember that sincere and timely repentance will wash away his biggest sins and earn Allah's favor, but ill timed and insincere apology will be of no consequence whatsoever. As Allah declares in Surah An-Nisa:

But there is no repentance for those who continue to do great sins— until, when death approaches one of them, he says: I do, indeed, repent now! Nor is there repentance for those who die while they are disbelievers. For such as these, We have made ready a most painful torment. (The Quran, 4:18)

When Adam repented, he was filled with pain, sadness and shame. He was so disgusted with himself that he couldn't even face his Lord. Ibn Asakir reported that Adam wept for 60 years for his loss of paradise and 70 years for his mistake. Allah accepted his repentance and made him His first Vicegerent on Earth. He had erred, yet the Merciful honored him after his true repentance.

MAN AS A VICEGERENT, OR *KHALIFA*

A vicegerent is a second in command or a representative of a higher authority. When Allah says that man is His *Khalifa*, He lays down three basic facts that set the premise for man's life on Earth. The declaration also answers three critical questions about man and his existence:

Questions:

1. *Who is man?*
2. *Why was he created?*
3. *Why was he sent to Earth?*

Answers:

1. *Man is Allah's appointed deputy.*
2. *He was created to follow Allah's commands.*
3. *He was sent to earth to establish the laws of the Creator.*

Allah appointed man His *Khalifa*, binding him to His authority meaning:

a. Man is not his own master.

b. Man is not free to do as he pleases on Earth.

c. Man has no authority to overrule the laws of Allah.

As Allah's deputies, men have been sent to Earth to propagate and establish the decree of Allah, the Great.

To carry and fulfill the huge responsibilities of a *khalifa*, Allah blessed man with the necessary tools: he was equipped with a brain to make calculated decisions; he was provided a heart to discern what mystified the brain; and He was given a soul to remind him where he came from.

With all that, he was granted drive, executive skills and a strong mind. He was also provided a manual for success–the Holy Quran. Furthermore, hundreds of messengers were sent since the beginning of time, to guide him and remind him of his oath to the Creator.

Man holds the honour of being the best of Allah's creation on Earth. In this age of intelligence, he propagates independent thought, liberal views and deludes himself into thinking that he is answerable to no one except himself. He considers morals and values the products of modern progressive societies. When in actuality, it was Islam that gave him morals and taught him to value human life.

Man is the only creation of Allah who is endowed with the power to bring about massive innovative developments, and unimaginable destruction. He can touch the sky and penetrate space but he is also capable of delving into the lowest pits of morality. He is a sinner and a saint. **When he acts as a servant, utilizes his powers according to the Creator's set limits, propagates what is right and destroys what is wrong, then he serves humanity as he was meant to; but when he abuses Allah's given authority, and uses it to serve his own base desires and worldly goals, he becomes a transgressor.**

IBLIS: THE BIGGEST TRANSGRESSOR

Before Iblis became the biggest transgressor and man's worst enemy, he was among the honourable and favoured creatures of Allah. In the times of Prophet Mohammed (PBUH), some said that Iblis was the head of the angels. Others said he was the most learned and virtuous among *jinn*, the keepers of Paradise. Then there were those who believed that prior to turning into the Accursed Satan, or *shaytan*, Iblis was one of the four eminent possessors of wings.

Shaytan means "opposed to good." It all began when Allah moulded Adam out of clay and gave him the shape that we possess today. For as many as forty years, Adam's statue stood soulless in the court of the Creator. The angels never lingered around him, being fearful of this strange presence. But the being that feared Adam the most was Iblis. Whenever he chanced to pass by, he would look upon the statue, mesmerized, and murmur, "You have been created for a great purpose."

Then when Allah blew His Spirit into Adam and asked the angels to prostrate before him, Iblis refused, claiming he, the one made from fire, was a great deal better than the one made from clay. He compared himself to Adam and reached a conclusion by reasoning. He felt he was superior to Adam, when in fact, he was just vain and acting out of jealousy.

Iblis's pride caused him to disobey Allah. He could not accept that a man of clay had been given precedence over him. He mocked Adam and tried to justify his refusal to prostrate by claiming that fire was better than clay, when the truth is that only Allah knows which is better. As punishment, Allah ordered him to leave paradise.

Expulsion from paradise enraged Iblis even more, and he asked Allah for respite, saying he would mislead mankind and prove them unworthy of His honour.

Iblis also blamed Allah for leading him astray and retaliated, saying he would lead mankind astray. He further said that he would wait for mankind on the "straight path" and attack his *iman*, and then they would not be grateful to their Lord, except a few.

See? Those whom You have honored above me, if You give me respite (keep me alive) to the Day of Resurrection, I will surely seize and mislead his offspring (by sending them astray) all but a few! (The Quran, 17:62)

And Allah gave Iblis what he wanted.

From then onwards, Iblis turned into man's sworn enemy. He held man liable for his banishment and vowed to destroy his life in this world, as well as in the next.

Allah could have finished Iblis off, then and there, but we witness that freedom of thought again: first when the angels had questioned Allah about man, and now when Iblis wanted to prove the unworthiness of man and wanted reprieve until the Day of Judgment. Although, Allah consented to let Iblis off, He told him that He would forgive man as long as he chose to return to Him.

This shows that Allah is Merciful and demands willful obedience. Later, Allah asked Adam and Eve to dwell in paradise and enjoy its bounties.

FIRST DECEPTION

Iblis deceived Adam and Eve into thinking that he was their sincere friend, before he led them to disobey their Lord.

Adam and Eve were warned not to go near a particular tree or eat of its fruit. When Iblis found out about this he planned out his first deception.

To entice Adam and Eve, he whispered promises of immortality in their ears while simultaneously convincing them of his goodwill and friendship. Then he fed their desire for the fruit, day after day, until they could think about nothing else.

A day came when Adam and Eve forgot Allah's warning about Iblis and ate the forbidden fruit.

Their Lord called out to them saying;

Did I not forbid you that tree and tell you, 'Verily Satan is an open enemy unto you'? (The Quran, 7:22)

Then, Allah sent both man and Satan to Earth. Adam had learned his lesson well. He understood that mankind had weaknesses, and Iblis would attack him through them.

When Adam left paradise and stepped on Earth, life changed dramatically. Now he had to toil and struggle, as well as protect himself and his family from Iblis. As for Iblis, he never left Adam alone, he continued his game of deception; until one day, he persuaded one of his son's to commit murder. This was the first murder on Earth, committed by one brother of another, out of jealousy.

WARNINGS AGAINST SATAN/SHAYTAN/IBLIS

Allah warned Adam about Iblis and his enmity immediately after he was created. He cautioned Adam again, after he forgot Allah's warnings and tasted the forbidden fruit. Then, although Adam and Eve were forgiven, their lack of judgment in regard to Iblis instigated a chain of events that hastened their descent to Earth. Seemingly, Allah had planned it this way to teach Adam never to fall for *shaytan's* ploys again and to always remember the perpetrator who led him to disobey the Creator.

If the sole purpose of our lives is to maintain *tawheed* on Earth, then the sole purpose of Satan's life is to mislead and distract us from our goal. Man is forgetful and not as cunning a creature as the one who is driven by infinite hatred. Allah therefore sent messengers with commandments and reminders to man to be wary of Satan. The Quran mentions Satan 88 times, forewarning its readers of his treacherous nature.

TRAPPINGS OF SATAN

Allah created a wonderful world for man. He made light, so we may identify darkness. He made evil, so we may appreciate goodness. He filled the world with marvels and filled our hearts with desires. As a result, we are attracted to everything that is good in this world, and it is okay, because Allah made it so. It is alright to enjoy the blessings Allah sends: riches, big houses, and luxury cars. But it is not right to lie, cheat, rob or kill in order to get them.

Allah placed attractions in this world, but the mind and heart of the true believer does not let these attractions distract him from the right path. For him, the luxuries of the world are transitory, and his true goal is paradise. What makes things complicated is the part Satan plays in fanning man's desires.

The devil whispers into the ears and hearts of the believers. He talks to the brains and uses rationale as a tool to lure the thinking man into his trap. It is not easy to encompass his cunning and perfidy in words, or his revulsion for man; but it is necessary to understand his worldly goals.

Satan made four promises to Allah regarding mankind.
He said:

"I will lead men astray."
"I will give them false passions and desires."
"I will order them to deface Allah's Creation."
"I will order them to slit the ear of cattle," i.e., make the permissible forbidden and vice versa)

These dark promises have become a darker reality for man today.

Iblis is constantly recruiting non-believers and polytheists into his army. He presses men to commit *shirk*. When they do they become his advocates. However, if he fails, he tries to lure them into *bidah*, or practicing something not ordained by the Quran or hadith, while performing it as such. If he fails, yet again, he attempts to entice men into performing major sins, and then minor sins.

Satan never gives up on anyone. He knows even the tiniest sins can collect and form a mountain one day; enough to banish a man to hell. If he is unsuccessful in ensnaring a true believer, then he strives to keep him from greater deeds. He turns families, friends and even strangers against the believer to prevent any goodness from escaping him.

What's more, Satan empowers the corrupt to help him in his cause.

TRICKS AND TREATS: PLOYS OF SATAN

Satan would open seventy doors of goodness for man, if he could keep him from one deed that is greater than those seventy or lure him into one sin through those seventy deeds. The cunning schemes of Satan are beyond man's comprehension. His attacks are subtle and he exploits men by taking over their thoughts and desires.

Satan uses tricks to deceive man while treating them to their own vulnerabilities. He tempts man with false passions, convincing them that it is human nature to want more and seek satisfaction. Carnal desires and fornication are examples of such ghastly human conduct, which turn man into a self-serving animal.

In Islam, the union of man and woman is spiritual. Today in some societies, if a girl is still a virgin after sixteen years, she is considered not normal, an aberrant and a strange fish. Appalling, but true. It is not much different for boys. The value being attached by humans to humans who guard their purity is disturbing. It is also the second promise of Shaytan. While Islam celebrates man as the best of Allah's creation on Earth, Satan makes man stoop to the level where the line between man and animal is hardly discernible.

PRIDE: A TRAIT AND A TOOL

One of the most effective tools of the Devil is false pride, which he instills, to distract and mislead true believers. The same pride that caused Iblis to challenge the command of Allah, is enough to neutralize the good deeds of man. On the other hand, humility is favored by Allah, because it is a trait possessed by believers who realize their true worth.

The arrogant forever carry an air of superiority and have a way of making their good deeds look bigger and their sins seem paltry and of no consequence. Yet they do not gain Allah's favor no matter how much good they do.

Pride and arrogance are traits of the Devil and are abhorred by Allah, the Merciful. Although the Devil understands that pride can make a disbeliever out of a believer, most men don't.

WAR AGAINST SHAYTAN

While the Devil declared open war against man in Allah's court, man is yet to declare war against him. Early Islamic education is crucial to train children to recognize the Devil and his ploys, and to teach them defense tactics against him.

The Prophet Mohammed (PBUH) has said:

Every one of you has been assigned a companion from the jinn. (Muslim, 2814)

It is this jinn or devil that constantly tries to divert man from the straight path. While man may know this fact, there may be times when he forgets – out of sight out of mind, but the Devil never forgets. He waits patiently for the perfect timing before he attacks. Sometimes man may become so weak in his *iman* that the whisperings of the Devil may seem like his own.

The first step towards defeating the devil is knowing him. Know the invisible Satan that flits from heart to mind, and from mind to heart. Know this enemy who plays with man's desires and weaknesses. Know this enemy who will not rest until he warrants a place for man in hell. Know him and understand his goals, in order to trounce him.

If man has enemies, he has friends, as well. Allah and His messengers warned him against the Devil so he may stand guard against his tricks. Man is weak and prone to stumble. But, Allah is Merciful and Generous. Therefore, Allah provides man with numerous opportunities to repent and earn rewards for their good deeds.

ZIKR ALLAH/REMEMBERING ALLAH

Remembering Allah is the most effective way for warding off *shaytan*. In the day to day life, the believers remember Allah through prayers, worship and good deeds.

An example of worship is when man indulges in *zikr* of Allah. Zikr is the remembrance of Allah, through praise which glorifies Him, and the recitation of the Quran.

Good deeds are anything and everything that man does to earn the pleasure of Allah. These could be charity, kindness towards parents and others, helping the needy, teaching the ignorant, giving the Islamic greeting of peace, staying away from sin, curbing anger and thanking Allah, etc.

Once man is on the path of goodness and veracity, he should never forget that Satan is right there with him, trying to make him slip and lose his ground. One way to avoid falling into the Devil's trap is through constant *zikr*.

EARLY ISLAMIC EDUCATION

Early Islamic education is an effective way for honing and sharpening instincts against *shaytan*. Teaching children early on, to guard their characters and chastity against *shaytan,* will raise strong and resilient adults. Islamic education helps them identify the dangers of falling prey to Satan and equips them with the right weapons to fight him off.

On the contrary, giving in to every immature demand and raising children who are naïve and ignorant about their purposes in life, who can't identify their real friends or foes, who haven't the slightest idea about the disguises of Satan or his ploys and who are confused about what side they should be on, is highly irresponsible.

Islam is all about striving and trying in the face of adversity. It is about getting up every time you fall, because if you don't fight for a piece of heaven, you may not get one!

QUESTIONS FOR REFLECTION

- Why was mankind created with desires, and what is the difference between desires and greed?
- Why did the Angels think that man's desires would become uncontrollable? What was it that Allah knew but they did not?
- What will make a man victor when he returns to Allah?
- What names was Adam taught by Allah?
- What covenant did Allah take from the generation of Adam?
- What is *Fitra*? What does a child forget, but the soul remembers? And what are the chances, which occur in the life of all human beings?
- In what way was man created unique, and how is man different from the angels?
- In what capacity was Adam sent to earth and for what reason?
- Can fate be changed? If yes, then how?
- What makes us lose the path of the righteous?
- What is *nafs* and what does it do when we take a false step?
- What makes us transgressors?

- One disobedience got the Devil kicked out of Heaven. What makes us believe we deserve Heaven even though we disobey Him day and night?

7

SAILING TO "AMRICA" PATNA, BOMBAY, GENOA, NEW YORK, 1964

And He found you lost, and guided you! (The Quran, 93:7)

I WOULD HAVE TO fight for my piece of Heaven. So said Ram Balishwar Babu. He was a close friend of *Barhe Bhaiya* and a professor of Logic and Astronomy. He was also a renowned *jyotishi*, more commonly known as a fortune teller. Many people consulted him on a variety of matters ranging from first love to first child and everything in between.

Word must have gotten out about my conflict with *Abba* over Amrica, because Ram Babu came to see me one day. He said Amrica was simply not in the stars for me. At this stage in my life, I was not one to take this lying down. No stars and no man would chart my destiny.

I found out about a place called USIL in Patna and went to check it out. There I discovered that USIL was actually the United States Information Library. I was the happiest man in Patna that day.

USIL was information galore. I filled my pockets with registration forms and catalogues and brought back as many as I could. The next few days were spent filling out forms and sending inquiries to almost a hundred universities in the United States. Then began the wait.

Every day I would return from college and check to see if I had received a reply. I would even walk to the post office to make personal inquiries, but there was no mail for weeks. *Abba* knew about my applications and was waiting with me. As days went by, both of us tried to keep up appearances for each other's sake. While he tried to act indifferent to my growing trepidation, I tried to act as nonchalant as possible.

A month passed. *Abba's* concern for me grew tenfold. I couldn't keep up the drama anymore. The wait had sucked the blood out of me. One morning while I sat at breakfast, quiet and lost in my own thoughts, the bell rang and a voice called, "*Daakia, sahib jee!*" The postman was hailing us, and the letters came pouring in! When I saw the smile that lit up *Abba's* face at the postman's announcement, I knew our battle was over and I had won my case.

Choosing Howard University in Washington, D. C., was easy. Howard offered me the maximum number of credits equivalent to two years of study. In addition, it was the least expensive option. Once my admission was confirmed, I got tickets for a train journey to Calcutta, Bengal. Since the visa, passport, and foreign exchange offices along with the Reserve Bank of India were located there, I would have had to take that trip sooner or later. I chose sooner.

At this time, the Indian and Chinese forces were at war on the border, and there were recurrent Hindu-Muslim clashes, but thankfully, my train journey was uneventful, and I reached Calcutta in one piece. Hiring a rickshaw, I went straight to the Reserve Bank of India to procure my visa and permission form, but I was refused entry.

I tried again the next day and was rebuffed one more time. The war with China was complicating things for me. However, after many arguments and a lot of persuasion, I was eventually given an appointment with the director of the bank. His first question was about the feasibility of my plan. He said since Bachelor's in Engineering degrees were available in India, I had no reason to go to Washington to get one. He was wrong. I did have a reason: Howard University had offered me a place; whereas, the universities of India had refused.

The director was taken aback by my ready reply. He had just one choice left. I returned to Patna on cloud nine. My family was a picture of disbelief, but that soon changed to awe and admiration, when the acceptance letter arrived from the Reserve Bank of India. I finally had everything I needed and was ready for Amrica.

A month before my ship was meant to leave the port of Bombay, *Abba* had a severe stroke. It left him partially paralyzed. This sudden turn of events brought back the words of the jyotishi. For a while I was thrown off track, but it was *Abba* who took the decision for me. He pressed a blank check into my hands and closed my fingers around it. This gesture and the look in his eyes kept saying go – just go.

I knew what I had to do. I took the permission and returned the check. I would go to Amrica on my own terms. Although, I realized later that *Abba* was trying to kill two birds with one stone: he was giving me a go ahead and simultaneously trying to ease his concern regarding me. I did not understand his motives at the time and had a hard time living with my decision afterwards.

Refusing the check because I believed that my siblings had an equal right to my father's wealth was an honorable act, but refusing the wish of a dying man was anything but. I wish I had had the wisdom to reflect and act accordingly. Sometimes, the right thing is giving in not because you are wrong, but because sometimes wrong is the right thing to do.

Abba passed away and our spirits left our bodies at the same time. His travelled to another realm marking the end of a journey and the start of a new one. Mine simply got lost. It took me an entire year to coax life back into my body. The healing had finally begun.

—ww—

I threw myself into preparing for my journey. I had opted for a sea voyage, because I needed time to collect my bearings. America still seemed like a faraway dream, and I was unsure if I would be able to survive it.

The excitement surrounding my voyage barely gave me time to reflect. There was a huge farewell party given in my honor, and all my friends and relatives collected to shower me with blessings, poetry and goodbyes. Their love overwhelmed me, and emotions threatened to inundate me. I kept a straight face until the end of the party and cried my heart out on my train journey to Bombay. I cried for *Abba*, for *Barhe bhaiya* and for India.

There is something about Bombay; it keeps you on your toes. Somehow the city has always reminded me of the black faced Asian monkey, *langur*: dark, puckish and up to no good.

When I arrived at the port, it took me a few minutes to take in everything. I asked a porter for directions to the ship leaving for America and found myself directed towards a giant called the Roma. This was a passenger ship, boasting cabins for 287 people and dormitories for an additional 684.

When I tried to climb aboard, I was asked to show my visa for Genoa, Italy. I got into a heated argument trying to explain that I was heading to America, not Italy. But, the Italian captain would hear nothing of it. He told me that the ship would harbor in Italy for three days and I had less than twelve hours to procure a visa if I wanted to sail with him.

The thought of returning to Patna put spurs on my shoes, and I practically flew to the phone booth. I located the number of the Italian consulate general and called him up. It was a miracle that he answered, and it was another miracle when I somehow convinced him to see me in his office.

The hour was late and the sun had already set when I arrived at the consulate. The consulate general was very accommodating and went out of his way to help me. He required three passport size photographs to issue my visa; which I did not have at that time. He issued the visa anyway, in exchange for a promise that I would get the photographs taken immediately and mail them to the Italian consulate without delay.

I kept my promise, mailed the photographs, and returned to the docks.

Early the next morning I boarded the Roma. The ship was bustling with passengers from all walks of life, foreigners and natives of India. It was a luxury vessel packed with everything a man could think of. There were restaurants, swimming pools, night clubs, movie theatres and even tennis courts. Food was served every two hours and a man travelling on his own had plenty of amusements to indulge in. I had no complaints, but even in this lap of luxury something seemed amiss.

I would like to say that when the ship set sail for Genoa, I left behind my worries on the port of Bombay. But that's not what happened. I carried the burden of my decision on the tip of my nose. I held it high and carried the weight all the way to Italy.

I spent most of that time inside my cabin, since the incessant rocking of the ship made me nauseous. Plus, my heart was still mourning its loss. I think it was probably my sea sickness that caused me to regret my decision. Alone in my cabin with no servants to look after me and no family to mollycoddle me, I was entirely on my own for the first time in my life. Loneliness was killing me.

Sometimes, we have to step off the beaten track to discover who we really are. I discovered that I was a man who valued family ties, and cutting them off even temporarily was crushing me. America was another country; for all I knew, it was another planet. Everything from people to food to culture to language would be alien to me. Would I be able to survive the unknown on my own? Only time would tell.

As I got used to the sea, my condition started improving and with that my spirit. I decided to take matters into my own hands. The first thing I did was quit eating Indian food. It was terrible, and that's putting it politely. Next, I decided to take a leisurely walk on the upper and lower decks to explore my options. It didn't take me long to realize that the paltry $8 in my pocket would not let me avail much of what was offered on board. Besides, I was saving that money for a quick trip to Maple, to check out some historical sites.

When the Roma dropped anchor in Genoa for three days, I couldn't wait to set foot on land. But once again, problems arose. I had no money, no contacts and no place to stay. When I tried talking to the seamen, they retorted in Italian, which was all gibberish to me. I decided to talk to the captain of the ship. It was fortunate that he knew English and I explained my plight to him.

The captain was a loud, jovial fellow and he presented me with a proposition. He said he would call up his friend, a hotel owner in Genoa, and arrange for my lodging–if I agreed to carry two bottles of liquor for him through customs. I accepted, although reluctantly. Then gathering all my courage, I walked out with the heaviest liquor bottles in the whole of Italy. I was terrified and kept thinking I would be caught and then deported. But my fears were baseless.

As soon as I was through customs, I handed the bottles to the captain and walked out with his Italian friend who had come to pick me up in his car. He drove me to a small hotel and charged a very nominal sum for accommodations.

The hotel was located in a busy part of the city and all day I would hear Italian, a bit of English and more loud Italian. I fell in love with the people whose hands moved constantly to support their tongues. Italians don't speak the language, they sing it and they sing it beautifully.

I would spend my days outside on the streets and sometimes come in to ask the hotel owner what certain Italian words meant. He was always keen to help and offered to give me a few quick lessons.

I learned that *magari* means, "I wish." *Grazie* means, "Thank you." *Sale e pepe* is used for salt and pepper. "*Mi prendi in giro,*" is what he said every time I complimented his wife's cooking. I thought it meant, "Our pleasure," or something close to that, but it actually means, "Are you kidding me?!"

Every day, the good man would bring a tray piled with food up to my room and sit with me while I ate. At that time, I was not a fan of Italian food, so when he offered me his wife's Indian cooking I was over the moon. However, when I tasted what they called Indian, I dropped back to Earth and asked for Italian again.

After three days, I thanked my hosts and left Genoa on a ship named Constitution. This was a much bigger vessel and offered a lot more entertainment than Roma. Every passenger had their own reserved dining table. Since I was on my own, I shared a table with a German-American family–a mother and her two adorable kids. The mother introduced herself as Christina, a German, going to America to join her husband, who was a professor. We all got along very well and spent the rest of the voyage together.

Finally, after days at sea, the Constitution reached America! I was still jittery, although much better informed about American culture than I was before starting out from India. I thanked Christina for instructing me in American ways, and we parted after exchanging addresses.

When I stepped on the American turf, the first thing I acquired was an 'e' in my Amrica. Practicing the new pronunciation under my breath I made my way to customs one more time.

Customs have a way of scaring the daylights out of me. I knew that my nerves would only settle once I was cleared and out of the New York port. While I waited to get my documents, I gazed out at the concrete jungle, wondering ...fearing ...and doubting ...my dreams.

My life events are my teacher. They taught me:

- **Pay full respect to others**
- **Be honest, sincere and keep your promises**
- **If you have confidence in yourself and trust Allah, you will be successful at every step of life, In Sha Allah.**

What have your life events taught you?

8

OF HEAVEN AND HELL;
OF MAN AND HIS WORLD

I have prepared for my servants what no eye has seen and no ear has heard, nor has it occurred in a human heart. (Bukhari, Muslim and Tirmidhi)

G OALS KEEP US alive. They get us out of bed each morning. When I failed my family and friends and when they failed me, I started to search for love elsewhere. I found a much greater love, that of Allah, but I did not understand it much. It just worked like a magic balm on my abrasions and gave me a reason to go on. I could fall back on His love again and again and He would never shut His doors on me. That is what kept me returning to the Quran. I was searching for something which I could not name. Perhaps, for a little piece of heaven on earth. And then I discovered why that was an impossibility.

Fighting for a piece of heaven becomes plausible only when a believer understands the concepts of both heaven and hell, and that is only possible, if one understands the magnificence of Allah. Man is limited. Allah is not. Our thoughts and mind might take us to the brink of the horizon, but can they bring us back from the point of no return? Can they reverse the power of a single black hole, let alone the known 4.3 million that populate the universe?

At the point when our rationale goes haywire, and our brains refuse to answer–at the point when our faculties pronounce the word, "impossible," because there is no better or intelligent explanation, that is where one can start to get an inkling of the true nature of the one and only Allah. There are no words to describe His power and none that can do justice to His mercy or His wrath, except His own words.

Heaven and Hell were both created before man and both are beyond man's wildest imagination. There is only so much that man is capable of imagining, and beyond the fields of his imagination, is Allah. If a man thinks Allah is Great, Allah is so much greater, but man, within his limits, is incapable of grasping His majesty.

PARADISE/JANNAH

Heaven on earth is nothing more than a mellifluous paradox. There can be no heaven on earth. Period.

Paradise, *jannah*, or heaven is a world beyond earth and its laws, a place of eternal bliss created by Allah. Can man fully comprehend the wide expanse of *jannah*? Absolutely not! But we do understand that it is a reward for those who remember their pledge of loyalty to Allah and who stand by it, despite temptations, threats, and hardships of the worldly life.

The Quran describes *jannah* as the permanent abode of believers who stand their ground in the face of adversity and struggle against all evil. The heavenly gardens of *jannah* will make such men forget the pain and hardships of the transitory world. All their wishes will be granted and all their desires will be fulfilled. Man will be blessed with serenity and everlasting peace.

But *jannah* is reserved only for the loyal servants of Allah and there is a reason why the Prophet Mohammed (PBUH) said:

No one of you will enter Paradise by his deeds alone, not even me, unless Allah covers me with His Grace and Mercy (Bukhari and Muslim)

Now why would the Prophet (PBUH) say that? Aren't there enough hardships in a believer's life to earn him a piece of heaven? Doesn't an obedient servant of Allah deserve *jannah* as compensation for rejecting the forbidden temptations of this world? What about Prophet Mohammed (PBUH)? Surely he deserves heaven more than anyone else?

Man, with his limited understanding and hasty nature, frequently jumps to the wrong conclusions. Jannah is a manifestation of Allah's mercy and grace. It is His benevolence and His greatness encapsulated. If heaven had a price attached to it, then no man would be capable of paying it, no matter how hard his life, how good his deeds, and no matter how big his trials. Therefore, it is only through Allah's mercy that man will enter paradise.

Allah says in the Quran:

Allah has promised to the believers—men and women—Gardens under which rivers flow, to dwell therein [forever], and beautiful mansions in Gardens of everlasting bliss. But the greatest bliss is the Good Pleasure of Allah. That is the supreme felicity [or success]. (The Quran, 9:72)

Today, most Muslims think heaven is within their grasp. Some are even naïve enough to believe that reciting the declaration of faith, *kalima tawheed*, guarantees their place in heaven. Others believe being a Muslim is all that matters, and not how you live your life.

Man has failed today, because the words of self-proclaimed scholars of Islam have taken precedence over the words of Allah and His messengers. The sad reality is most prefer being spoon fed easily digestible views that make little or no sense than take on hard facts about Islam.

If acquiring a piece of heaven was this easy, why did the Quraish not accept Islam and get it over with? In the Quran, Allah constantly addresses His creation, urging them to think and reflect. How hard is it to pick up the Quran and find out for yourself what Allah wants from you? For the benefit of those who are being misguided and can't decipher the truth on their own, here is a quote from the Quran:

Allah says;

Do the people think that they will be left to say, "We believe," and they will not be tried? (The Quran, 29:2)

How is man tried? Everything that approaches man has a purpose. Good days and bad days are a test. Life has a purpose and there is nothing random about it. Popular concepts and hedonistic theories only serve to make us self-indulgent and self-gratifying, but the wise among us can see them for what they are, ploys of Satan. They know Islam does not endorse the self, or *nafs*. Islam is about total submission to Allah.

How a person deals with others is a daily test, how a person conducts business is a daily test, and whether a person submits to Allah's will or his own, or that of the world, is a daily test. Unless we pass it, and prove ourselves worthy of His mercy, it is the height of absurdity to expect a piece of *jannah*.

Satan may leave the non-believers alone, but never a believer. Consequently, the biggest hurdles and the biggest trials in this world befall the one who strives for the pleasure of Allah. It is ludicrous to think that a person who struggles his entire life to keep his *iman*, intact, will be on equal footing with someone who sells his *iman* every day under the pretense of being a Muslim. Remember, Allah cannot be deceived; man only succeeds in deceiving himself.

And of the people are some who say, "We believe in Allah and the Last Day," but they are not believers. They [think to] deceive Allah and those who believe, but they deceive not, except themselves, and perceive [it] not. (The Quran, 2:8)

HELL/JAHANNAM

He loves me, He loves me not! With good news there is bad news. While Allah describes heaven to give man hope and incentive, He also describes hell and warns the non-believers of His wrath. The prophets and the divine books describe hell as the opposite of *jannah*. If *jannah* is eternal bliss, then hell is eternal suffering. It is a place prepared by Allah for transgressors who not just deny His Lordship, but also reject His messengers.

Like heaven, hell is an actual place and the pain, horror, humiliation and punishment it will inflict on its dwellers are as real. There are no deaths in hell only everlasting anguish. When the fires of hell will lick the non-believers and polytheists they will cry for mercy, but there will be no one to help them. It is said there are nineteen keepers of hell, each one with enough power to subdue the whole of humanity on its own.

CHOOSING TRANSITORY BLISS OVER ETERNAL HAPPINESS

The modern Muslim is a comfort seeker. He avoids risks and thrives on security. Even the very thought of pain is enough to make some confine themselves to their homes. Such people steer clear of painful discussions and controversial issues, including certain aspects of religion. Talk of Hellfire and wrath of the Almighty may be real in their books, but is never allowed to surface in their lives.

Such people understand disobedience to Allah will lead to punishment in hell, but they never want to think about it or hear about it. These people live in a state of denial and are afraid to step out of their comfort zone. As a result, Islam is turned into his-lam, her-lam, my-lam and their-lam.

Islam is not a joke and yet people make a mockery of it in their daily lives. Let's get the basic facts right. You can't practice Islam by staying within your comfort zone and using it whenever convenient. Islam is law, not desire. For Islam to be real, *tawheed* must be lived in its fullness. Choosing what we like and rejecting the rest is nothing but pretense and duplicity.

A Muslim does not have double standards. Those people who accept messages and false hadiths that make them feel good about themselves, and promote a surreal sense of God and Godliness are lost.

We take Islam for granted. We think it is not our duty to inves-tigate, but that of the Muslim scholars. This may be true, but it is only half truth. **It is our duty to accept only what is authentic and for that we need to have sufficient knowledge about Islam.** However, if we don't, then we must seek the means to gain that knowledge. Excuses do not work in Islam, and if it did, then laziness is not a good enough excuse, and ignorance is no excuse at all.

Hell and heaven are two sides of the same coin. Without one, the other loses its influence over man. We can't accept one and reject the other. Keeping our eyes tightly shut will only block out the light, it won't save us from punishment. Keeping our fears at bay may give us a good night's sleep, but it won't douse the fires of hell. Keeping an eye on the rewards and shunning the reality of retribution may give us hope, but it won't make us better Muslims.

ALLAH'S CREATION: MAN AND HIS WORLD

Allah is the uncontested Creator of every particle, molecule and fragment that has an existence. He is the creator of energy and the destroyer. He is the creator of heaven and hell, earth and man. Whatever man created, creates or will create is just a spin-off of what already exists.

Heaven is a place over which Allah presides on His throne. We have different theories about what actually happened when man was created, but the gist is that **heaven was created as the best for the best of Allah's servants.**

Allah molded man and called him a creature of haste–a failing that man was born with. Allah also created man thirsty for knowledge, and that explains his natural aptitude for the lessons that he received. However, there are certain lessons which he must learn on his own, through experience and failure, before he can return to Paradise.

Allah wanted recognition and submission from mankind, but of their own accord. He wanted man to identify his Lord in His creation, accept Allah's authority over all and understand that not a leaf moved without His will. Moreover, He wanted Adam and his progeny to acknowledge Him willingly, as the sole provider and sustainer of the world and hereafter.

Consequently, a track was designed for man with a start and a finish line. Getting to the finish line was not the goal, but the journey itself. This track was the *dunya*—the life of this world—which was littered with signs from Allah. Then its reality was shrouded behind a colorful façade of finery, comfort, provisions and worldly passions. It was turned into a temptation for man whose test was to walk through it without letting it steer him away from the true purpose of life. **The purpose was solely to prove himself worthy of Allah's benevolence, and therefore the test.**

When Allah decided that Adam was ready for Earth, He said:

Get down (upon the earth) all of you from this place (Paradise), then whenever there comes to you Guidance from Me, and whoever follows My Guidance, there shall be no fear on them, nor shall they grieve. But those who disbelieve and belie Our Ayah (proofs, evidences, verses, lessons, signs, revelations, etc.) such are the dwellers of the Fire, they shall abide therein forever. (The Quran, 2:38-39)

At another place in the Quran, Allah disclosed the nature of the world and the transience of man.

Everyone shall taste death…The life of this world is only the enjoyment of deception (a deceiving thing). (The Quran 3:185)

In Holy Quran, 18:7, Allah declares:

Whatever is on the earth Allah, has made them to decorate the earth, but they are also made attractive to human beings so that they may be tested who are best in conduct and who fall for the glitter of the earth. (The Quran, 18:7)

UNVEILING THE DECEPTION

The entire essence of Islam is summed up in the above verses. Allah created the world in a matter of six days, and He calls it a mere deception. The world might appear to us as an obvious fact, but the maker says it is just a sham, something that has been created to trick, deceive and mislead mankind. The question is, how is the world a deception? We are notified beforehand of its true nature.

The answer takes us back to the Creator. The Entity that created us, the world, and the universe, knows that man has shortcomings. If Allah created a deception, then it will have the power to deceive, but, then again, when Allah equips man with tools to not just see through the sham, but also to overcome it and get past it, then those tools will have the power to get man through the worldly journey.

Allah did not just create man and leave him to fend for himself in this world, but promised and guaranteed sustenance for as long as he lived:

There is not a single moving creature on the Earth, but Allah is responsible for providing its sustenance. (The Quran, 11:6)

Rizq does not just denote food, but everything that makes life possible on Earth: the very air we breathe, the solid ground below our feet, the needs of our body and that of everything we depend upon for our survival. Then Allah asks man to call on Him, and He will answer—bestowing upon man more than he deserves. In return, He asks for submission and obedience, voluntarily. With all that, He makes sure that man has all the guidance and help he needs to fight his biggest enemy, *shaytan*, and pass unscathed through the world of deception.

Many things are not as they seem, and the world is one of them. Allah uses many descriptions for the world. Some of them have several meanings in turn. One word that is used is *laa'ib,* which signifies fun, game, sport, joke, prank, jest and play. Another word used is *lahw,* which means diversion or pastime, especially the kind that makes man frivolous, indifferent and vain.

The word *zina,* when used for *dunya,* turns the worldly life into finery, show, pomp and decoration, but nothing substantial. Allah also calls it *tafakhurn* a place where men contend for supremacy over each other on the basis of reputation, distinctions, awards, parentage, wealth, rank and even children.

One more description used for the world is *mataa al-ghuroor:* a place where all provisions are deceptive and illusory; they may serve a purpose, but they mislead many into believing the world will go on forever. All the supplies of the world can be used to achieve the best of *akhirah*–the Hereafter–but on their own, they are pure enticements to lure man away from his true goal.

The Quran has used five hefty metaphors for the worldly life. There are revelations within them for those who think and reflect. When Allah says the world is a game or sport, and we start analyzing our lives that way, it turns into a stark reality.

Let's take baseball, for instance. The diamond is the world. When a child is born, a player steps up on the first base holding a baseball bat. When he grows up and becomes an active participant in his life, he starts hitting the ball thrown by the pitcher and covering bases; which is a metaphor for whatever life throws at him and his reaction to it. Covering bases is an allegory for progress that man makes in his life. One doesn't necessarily have to be a player, one can be a spectator watching from the bleachers. What matters is the degree of involvement in the game. We become so utterly absorbed in the world that we forget the real purpose of our descent to Earth.

We wake up each day and follow the same routine, breaking away from it only because we are bored, not because we have found a higher purpose. It is then that the world becomes a diversion and a pastime–a place where we kill time for the fun of it. We indulge our desires and go after our worldly dreams without stopping to think about our final resting place.

A weekend diversion gears us for another five days of work. We work to earn and spend. We meet our friends and tally scores. This is when the world becomes a place of pomp and show. What you are wearing and where you are eating tells us more about you than your dealings with others. That's where the world becomes a competing ground for our desires. We lose our straight path and become so engrossed in the world and its paraphernalia, that the transitory delights become our permanent sustenance.

We lose ourselves in the pleasures of the world and allow Satan to lead us a merry dance–all because we become participants in the game of deception. We become so engrossed that we forget that time is ticking. The aspect of winning, gaining and achieving more than anyone else, makes us forget the Divine warnings. Eventually, we lose ourselves to the euphoria and exhilaration of a great win. We win the *dunya* and lose the *akhirah*!

Allah mentions the fate of such people in Surah al Baqarah when He says:

> *The worldly life has been made attractive to those who have denied iman. Such men ridicule the men of iman but the pious shall rank higher than them on the day of Resurrection. As for worldly livelihood, Allah grants it to whoever He wills without measure. (The Quran, 2:212)*

However, all is not lost for those who heed the words of Allah and His messengers. They stand a chance against the enticements of the world and the trappings of Satan. They remember the words of the Prophet Mohammed (PBUH), who said that for a believer the world is a confinement and for a non-believer the world is a carnival, funfair and a place of exotic delights. In the end, the believers who let the words of the Prophet (PBUH) be their guide and strength, are the ones who succeed.

THE THINKING MAN

Allah created Adam and blew His wisdom into his heart, He created a thinking man, a creature of rationale, fitted with a heart, possessing a soul and a conscience. Only Allah knows why man was granted free will. It would have been so much easier if men were more like angels and submitted to Allah without thinking twice. But then again, the bigger the test and trials, the bigger the rewards of success.

If it is Allah's right to be recognized as the sole Creator of the Universe, then it is man's calling to recognize his Lord as one. Man has been blessed with intelligence and with all the power of thought. If man still does not recognize Allah, then he has failed miserably.

Man, in this world, needs to recognize that Allah's mercy makes every day possible. When he wakes up, it is a blessing. When he finds food on his table, it is a second blessing. When he has the motivation to work, move, and live, it is a third, fourth and fifth blessing. If a man decides to spend his day penning the blessings of Allah, then he would run out of hours. But not out of Allah's grants. Therefore, man is eternally indebted to Allah. He is obliged to thank his Lord, to accept His Lordship, and to do His bidding without questioning His authority.

Man at his lowest is a fickle creature: self-centered and pathetic. Man at his greatest is stalwart, compassionate and *ashraf al-makhluqat,* the best of Allah's creation. No two men can be judged using the same scale. Every individual has different physical and mental capabilities, but it doesn't end there. Each individual lives in a particular environment, deals with different conflicts and reacts according to his unique capabilities. Since no two lives can be identical to each other, no two men would be judged the same.

If a man enters *jannah*, his hard work and sincerity in pleasing Allah will play a major role in turning the scales in his favor. However, Allah's mercy will be the deciding factor on the Day of Judgment.

MAN'S COMPONENTS: SOUL, HEART AND BRAIN

Human body is a marvel. All its components work around the clock, from the biggest organ to the tiniest cell. Numerous systems work as a whole to project life into the human body. Although a body is divided into components, which together make a whole; we can't separate the mind, heart or soul from the body, or from each other.

Each one is crucial for the existence of the other, and together they are vital for man's survival.

A man's body can be reduced to the status of a machine, but factually it is not one. It may be called a system. Machine and man are both moving devices developed or created to perform a task, but that is where the similarity ends. Man performs, but he also possesses free will and choice, which a machine does not.

THE PHYSICAL BODY

Creation of a human body and its development from a clot of blood is one of the countless miracles of Allah. The process of how life takes shape in its initial stages: how it grows into a discernible form, how it acquires a brain and a heart, then finally, a soul, while still inside the womb overwhelms and makes one capitulate before the greatness of the Creator.

Allah has provided the human body with intrinsic wisdom, to help it create, replace, repair and defend itself. Crucial knowledge is continually exchanged between cells to help construct and operate complex systems of tissues and organs inside the human mold. This sophistication of design and functionality within each cell is no chance-happening. There is not a single man-made machine that can match the consistent verve and dynamism of man.

Plus, man is born with innate wisdom and immense potential. His defining characteristics are his heart, soul and brain. Remarkably, all three have the power to bend and shape his world and his afterlife.

THE DECISIVE BRAIN

Although intelligent and wise brain is often the dupe of Satan. Its main function is to process and analyze information, and take decisions and dispatch orders to the rest of the body. The speed with which it performs and delegates orders is incredible, yet certain decisions remain pending for decades. The reason behind such tardiness is that the brain refuses to acknowledge the urgency of certain situations.

When the mind is pressed to dispatch certain orders to the rest of the body–by internal desires or external requests–it executes without questioning its religious or moral standing. The mind or brain evaluates the action in terms of its value to the individual. It is often seen as calculative, basing its decisions mainly on the probable results. If the result seems profitable then it exerts all efforts to achieve the goal successfully, otherwise, the command is ignored completely. On the other hand, if the mind's assessment of the action is questionable, sometimes the action is performed but lacks commitment.

When a person hears a commandment of Allah, or reads something in the Holy Quran or teachings of the Prophet Mohammed (PBUH), his brain immediately decides whether to perform that action or not. This decision is based on the value system of that particular individual. The brain pits the value of the Quran and Prophet's teachings against the individual's:

- Strength of belief;
- Perimeter of comfort zone, i.e., whether the task can be performed from within it; and
- Worldly desires, i.e., whether the task interferes with his worldly goals.

The stronger the belief in Allah and His Prophet (PBUH), the stronger is the inclination to perform the action. Similarly, if the person is a true believer, he would care more about his good deeds than his comfort zone, so either the comfort zone would not exist or would be ignored by the individual. Again, worldly desires are of little or no consequence for a true believer; therefore, he would not allow them to come between him and his Lord. Consequently, the brain would receive a positive signal, and the action would be performed.

On the contrary, for a person whose *iman* lacks strength, his comfort zone would keep him from taking unnecessary risks. Plus, his worldly desires would stand between him and His true call. In such cases, the brain would receive a confused message, and the action would not be performed.

The brain allows man to make rational decisions, but it can also be turned into a vile scheming pot for achieving our base desires and worldly dreams. It is hard to imagine the same brain as a crucial and beneficial organ that not only keeps us performing on a daily basis but also assisting in our progress.

Today, if man is planning vacations on the moon, it is because his brain gave him power to think and make it possible. The brain has the capacity to make a lot of other things possible as well. Ego, greed and materialism also reside in the brain. Plus, it is the easiest target for Satan who plays with man's thoughts, until he twists them to serve his own purpose. Sadly, man can rarely tell the difference between his own thoughts and those introduced by the devil.

THE PURIFYING HEART

Heart is the best component of the human body. When a child is born, its heart is pure and it stays pure as long as it stays on the path of goodness. When the same child is asked to choose between black and white, wrong and right, it is the heart that guides the child and encourages him to choose right. However, if the child chooses the path of darkness, it is because the heart fails to convince its owner and is overpowered by the youthful brain.

A pure heart is often the brain's biggest opposition. When the heart is God-fearing, the brain and its materialistic prompts are easily ignored. However, when the brain's selfish schemes are frequently given precedence over the heart, the latter weakens and gives up on the body, which soon becomes the hub of Satan. Then the body is forced to walk the path of worldly desires, which discolors the heart and tarnishes the soul.

On the other hand, when the brain is allowed to develop in the environs of a pure heart, it reaches a point of extreme self-awareness, where it sees through the ploys of Satan. Then, when confronted with desires and lust for money, power and flesh, it stands its ground and throttles the forces of evil together with the heart and soul.

THE SPIRITUAL SELF

While the brain recognizes intelligence and reaches a conclusion by default, i.e., life exists, and if I didn't make it, then someone else did. The *ruh,* or soul, works differently. Since it already pledged its loyalty to Allah, it retains a memory of that promise and accepts His Lordship without much ado.

Zikr serves as nourishment for the soul. The more a person remembers the Lord, the healthier his soul is, and vice versa. A healthy soul has the power to rescue the conscience of a dying man; however, if the soul is ailing, it means the conscience is lost and will suffer with the body till the day of resurrection.

To succeed in the afterlife, it is crucial for man to understand the relationship between the body and its components. Through understanding their power, man can exert the influence of one over the other, and achieve equilibrium in this life and success in the next.

The events of my life taught me that if I want a piece of Heaven I can't trust the self proclaimed scholars whose teachings are most misleading. Instead, I have to work hard to get close to Allah.

The more I studied the Quran, the more I grew in my belief; Salat and Zakat are essential requirements in Islam but if they fail to build our character they have no value on the day of judgment.

QUESTIONS FOR REFLECTION

- **Do you know where your lifestyle will lead you? Are you struggling for a piece of Heaven?**

- Do you believe this world is a testing ground and we have to struggle for a piece of Heaven? Or,

- Do you believe it is only through Allah's Mercy that man will enter paradise and it is through Allah's will and grace that man will earn His pleasure?

- Do you believe that every moment of our life is a test, including how we deal with others, such as family, friends, neighbors, strangers, and even plants, birds and animals, etc?

- Why do you think Heaven and Hell were created, if they were not meant to keep us on the path of righteousness?

- Can we truly be obedient slaves of Allah without sacrificing our comfort zone?

- Fighting for a piece of heaven is a serious matter. Do you think we should make every effort to acquire it, or should we totally depend on our sheikhs?

- What is the essence of Islam?

- Is this world a deception? If it is, how can we get through it and pass the test?

- Has Allah (swt) created us weak so we would fall for the glitter of the earth?

- What are the tools Allah equipped us with to enable us to not just see through the sham, but also to overcome it and get past it?

9

LEARNING THE ROPES
NEW YORK, 1964–68

You have to learn the rules of the game, and then you have to play better than anyone else!–Albert Einstein

I WALKED OUT OF the New York Port a fledgling, barely able to fly, but curious and ready to explore. My eyes darted around, taking in the people, buildings, cobblestoned streets, and the people again. I had a feeling that my subconscious was searching for a familiar face. My heart was thumping like a new machine inside the same old body, and I had a big eager smile pasted on my face, which was starting to hurt a little.

Then I saw them, a noisy bunch of girls and boys close to my own age, in denim and corduroy, holding placards. What caught my eye was the name Mohammed Qamruzzaman on one of them, another one read "Welcome to the Big Apple," which confused me at the time, but nevertheless my name in bold was just the invitation I needed. I walked straight up to them and introduced myself. It took them a moment to understand my broken English, but when they did, a loud cheer went up and I was pulled with them to the waiting taxis.

I noticed I wasn't the only foreigner among the group; there were six more but none from India. The boys with the placards introduced themselves as the welcoming committee of I-House, (International House, New York), where I would be staying for a few days.

On reaching the building, we made our way towards the main entrance and there the words of John D. Rockefeller, Jr., "That Brotherhood May Prevail," welcomed us with open arms.

The brotherhood that brought me to the building disappeared as soon as I was shown to a room, and from then on I was left to my own devices. I would spend my time looking out at Riverside Park. Sometimes I would even find the courage to venture into the piazza, which opened onto the Sakura, another park, but mostly I cherished the four walls of my room and the quietness of solitude.

I knew I would have to fly soon, but I wasn't ready to spread my wings just yet. I was afraid of the sheer size of the American sky, uncertain about its vastness, and the freedom that might devour me.

I had to get on a bus to get to Washington, D.C. One day, I surprised myself and left the grounds of the I-House immediately, without overthinking and overanalyzing, and that is how I discovered the bus station. The bus would drop me at the Greyhound Station and then I would have to plan my next step.

I decided to write to the Foreign Student Advisor of Howard University before leaving. My note was short and to the point. I told them that since I was a foreigner in America it would be best if they arranged for someone to pick me up from the Greyhound Bus station.

The next day, I took the bus to Washington, D.C., and got off at the Greyhound station. I hoped I was on time and hadn't kept my ride waiting. But when I looked around there was no ride. It did not cross my mind that Howard might not be sending me one.

I waited and waited before finally concluding that the ride was not coming. By that time, the sun was exactly over my head. I was not just hot, I was also very hungry and highly distressed. Just when anger was starting to replace my anxiety, a car pulled up in front of me.

The driver was a well-dressed man, in a shirt and tie, and the words "Diplomat Cab" were painted on the side of his car. I knew what a diplomat was, thank God for that, and quickly accepted his offer to drive me wherever I wanted to go.

The diplomat was all kindness and humility. He even got out of the car to help me with my luggage, but there is something called "Indian courtesy," too. I did not let him touch my bags and insisted he go back and sit down, while I struggled to load them on my own. He was doing me a huge favor, and I did not want to seem ungrateful.

The diplomat drove me to the Howard University campus. I enjoyed the ride immensely, thinking how beautifully things were turning out for me. When we entered the grounds of my new University, I got out and thanked him profusely. Then again, insisting that he keep sitting, I once again struggled with my luggage. When I had everything, I turned around to wave goodbye, and it was then that the diplomat demanded his fare.

I was dumbstruck for a second or two. Then I made him repeat himself, before I grudgingly handed him the money. I couldn't believe the diplomat would charge me!

Shaking my head, I turned around and started walking towards the nearest building. I wanted to get to the Foreign Student Advisor's office and ask for help. I needed to locate my dorm, get the keys and deposit my luggage. As I walked I kept turning around to take in the vast grounds of Howard and the magnificent building located on top of the hill. It was then that I stumbled and decided to sit and catch my breath.

While I sat atop my suitcase, I saw an Indian walking towards me. I had to stop myself from jumping up and engulfing him in a bear hug. He introduced himself as Gupta, a Ph.D. student of Physics, and offered to help me find my way around campus. Gupta took me to the Administration building, showed me the Louis K Downing Hall, the school of Engineering, and left after helping me move into my dorm.

Now it was time to spread my wings and take my first flight. Excited, I dumped my bags and walked out to get a feel of my new home and to find some food. I had walked just a few blocks when two guys approached me, asking for a match. I did not have one, since I didn't smoke and tried explaining it, but somewhere in the middle of my explanation, they grabbed me around the waist and the next thing I knew I was on the pavement. While one of them held me down, the other frisked me for cash.

I screamed. I actually screamed but nobody came to help. There were people walking up and down the road but it was as if the three guys scuffling on the ground were invisible. I realized I would have to be my own hero. I rammed my knee into the stomach of the guy searching my pockets and bit the hand holding me down. Then, I ran all the way back to my dorm.

Once inside my room, the first thing I did was check my back pocket, and the next thing I did was thank the Lord. My money was all there. I would not have to wait for my bank draft from India, and I would not have to starve.

That night, I had to do with grilled cheese. Early the next morning, I walked into a room full of naked men and received my second cultural shock. I double checked to make sure that it was the showers and walked out as fast as I could. This was something completely unacceptable. I immediately requested permission to move out of the dorm and live off campus.

I was told that since I was underage, I would need a guardian. Dr. Gupta came to my rescue again. He offered to fill the position for as long as it was required. Then he helped me move one more time.

Although I was packed, I hadn't the slightest idea where I would go. I was hoping Dr. Gupta would offer me a place, but I didn't want to force myself on him. As we were walking out, I ran into someone I hadn't thought about since I left India–Khalil ur Rahman, my partner in crime.

Khalil means a friend and Khalil ur Rahman means friend of the Compassionate. True to his name Khalil turned out to be my savior. His arrival meant we could both rent an apartment together, and that is exactly what we did.

Khalil and I had both studied together at the B.N. College and at the Patna School of Engineering. When I had decided to leave for America, I had tried convincing him to come with me. But Khalil wasn't too keen about studying abroad. His excuse was that his folks would be unable to afford the heavy expenditure of travelling and foreign education. I told him that we would be in the same boat, and promised we'd work together to support ourselves and even pay our own tuitions. I did not stop there; I went on and on about America being a land of opportunity where dreams come true, and where Indians like us became millionaires. When he still seemed unsure, I told him he was an idiot to let such an opportunity pass by.

My efforts had apparently paid off; he had changed his mind, and now he stood in front of me like a ghost from my past. He told me he had flown to America, and that he was a newly married man.

I could not believe my ears. Married! Khalil! It all made sense, though. Indian Muslim parents, who send their sons to America, do not want them returning with *gori mames* (white girls) on their arms. So getting them married before sending them off is a precautionary measure.

I laughed in delight. I was happy that Khalil was here. No, I was ecstatic. It was as if he had brought with him a slice of India. His story, however, made me think of kites and strings. I imagined Indian parents flying kites on rooftops, and imagined us on the other end of the strings, being tugged and pulled. Khalil asked me what I was laughing about, but I just shook my head and hugged him tighter.

We moved into our new apartment, and experiencing all the new firsts was exhilarating. We were as compatible as a newly married couple and almost as happy. Khalil was a good cook, so I left the kitchen to him and took up the cleaning department. Together, we were an excellent match.

Living together simplified life and saved us both a lot of time and money. While the new school and the newly-acquired wife kept my friend focused on books and writing letters back home, I was often on my own and ventured out looking for Indians.

We needed a job. I asked around and discovered that the Washington Post was offering Indians part time work. We both applied and were hired instantly for a minimum wage of $1.25 an hour. At the Post, we met two more Muslim boys from Pakistan, Azeem ur Rehman Khan and Abdul Nabi Memmom.

Meeting someone who understands your language in a land where the majority doesn't, is an inexplicable experience. You immediately feel validated. You want to talk more, laugh more, and hang on to them for as long as you can, and when you have to leave them, you look forward to tomorrow, because you hope to meet them again, and feel validated one more time.

In my earlier days in America, meeting an Indian or a Pakistani, with whom I could talk in my own tongue, without stopping to consider the rules of grammar or having to repeat myself twice, was a novelty. The experience was like cycling downhill without having to pedal.

Azeem and Mammon showed us the mosque in Washington, D.C., which was the first in America and probably the only one at that time. We took to going there quite often for prayers. The mosque was not just a place of worship, but a place of communion for all the Muslims who lived in the surrounding area. I made lots of new friends.

Six months later, one evening when I reached the Mosque for *Isha*, the night prayer, the mood there was almost festive. I discovered that the Muslim students from Baltimore and Washington had decided to form an organization called the Muslim Student Association (MSA).

Within minutes, the organization had enlisted thirty members. I also got caught up in the excitement. I was a people-person, interested in anything and everything that had to do with politics and elections. When my friends spotted me, they started insisting that I run for the Public Relations office. I knew I wanted to, and I also knew that a majority of them supported me. I saw an easy win and quickly gave my name.

I lost by one vote. It taught me two lessons, a) that politics is a dirty business and b) that failure is the first lesson in success. It was Zaeem, a Pakistani, who had come out against me. The reason being the longstanding hostility between India and Pakistan, where one can't stand to let the other succeed without making a few waves. That's all he did: passed a note asking his fellow Pakistanis not to vote for an Indian. In spite of that, there were quite a lot who voted for me; otherwise, I would have had an empty ballot box.

I was shocked and hurt. Zaeem boldly admitted what he did and called it "pure politics." If this was what politics would be like for me, as an Indian, on foreign turf surrounded by Pakistanis, then my prospects didn't look too bright. That day, when I left the mosque, I kept thinking why Muslims couldn't unite and function under the banner of Islam. When Islam transcended borders, why did we choose to divide ourselves on the basis of nationality? I wondered if I would ever be given a fair chance to prove my mettle in more such organizations, before being cast aside as an Indian Muslim.

Khalil and I ate fish and vegetables every day for lunch and dinner, but we weren't prepared to live on it for the next three years. The food we survived on was bland and American. And although I had developed a taste for grilled cheese and scrambled eggs, my palate craved the tang and smell of Indian cookery.

The issue of *halal* and *haram*, permissible and impermissible, had to be solved quickly. One morning, Khalil decided to drag me grocery shopping. That day we explored a major part of Washington, hunting for turmeric, cumin, coriander powder, garlic, cloves and allspice, but with no luck. By late afternoon I had almost given up, when someone directed us to a Spanish grocery store. It is hard to believe that there were no Indian grocers back then, only Spanish, who were later put out of business by the Indians.

The Spaniard at the counter was a cold fish, despite the fact that 70% of his customers seemed to be Indians. When he saw us coming through the door, he started muttering in Spanish. I went up, said, "Hello," and spent the next fifteen minutes trying to make him understand what I needed, at the end of which Khalil showed up with a basket full of Indian goodies. He paid the man, who demanded his money in perfect English. It was my turn to start muttering now. I switched to Urdu and walked out cursing under my breath.

That night we dined like *rajas* on onion *pakoras*, fried vegetable snacks; fish *biryani*, a rice dish; *raita*, a vegetable and yogurt salad; and homemade *gajar ka halwa*, a sweet carrot dessert. However, for the next six days, Khalil refused to serve me *chapati*, wheat flatbread; *qorma badami*, the Indian almond curry; or *gulab jammun*, a sweet of fried milk balls. He kept shaking his head at my outrageous demands and giving me a look that said, "Are you out of your mind?" Eventually, I stopped pestering him.

Six months later, I had my first taste of *halal* meat in America. The year was 1964, it was December, early winter, and wetter than I had anticipated. We Indians love rain, so it was surprising to see it have such a dampening effect on the Washingtonians. When I saw people running for cover, withdrawing not just from rain but into themselves, and coming out angry and irritated, because it was "raining again," I couldn't help but reminiscence about rain in India.

Rain in India is always announced by the sweet smell of wet earth and the delighted shrieks of wetter children. It pulls life from the dull and mundane and cheers up the bleakest hearts. Indians have songs that celebrate the rainy season and even special delights that are a must for rainy days, like *anarse key golian*, which are fried dough balls rolled in sesame seeds, and *gulgulay*, fried Indian doughnuts made from rain water.

Once or twice, when I was caught outside on a rainy day in Washington, I could not believe my ears when I heard children singing songs like: *"Rain, rain, go to Spain; never show your face again!"*

At such times, I felt a lump in my throat and my brain instantly conjured pictures of Patna, where I knew the children would be singing;

"Allah mia barish dey, so baras key barish dey!"
Oh Allah, give us rain, give us rain for a hundred years!

Eid 1964 in America was a complete antithesis of Eid 1946 in Ramzanpur. I had a whale of a time trying to relive and make amends for the past that I could not change.

Eid is a time for joyous celebrations, and I was determined to have it all my way, regardless of the American culture. On Eid morning, I woke up early, showered and dressed up in my traditional garb: a *sherwani*, a long sleeved, closed fitted, knee length coat, worn over a shirt by men in India and Pakistan; and *tung pajama*, fitted pants; then, putting a *topi*, a lightweight hat of the subcontinent, on my head, I left for the mosque.

For Americans I was a sight to behold. As I walked to the mosque, my head held high and every inch of me emitting pride for my heritage, people stopped in their tracks to stare, but I couldn't care less. It was Eid, I was happy and on my way to meet my Muslim brothers, but when I reached the mosque I was surprised to see it empty except for a few unknown faces. I ended up making a few more friends and left happier than I had arrived.

For the Eid dinner our entire MSA association was invited by another association, formed by the wives of all Muslim ambassadors residing in Washington. It was a grand gesture by all the heads who arranged a fabulous dinner for overseas Muslim students. The dinner was lavish, the food was halal, and our hosts were generous. We ate all we could and were later asked to take home as much as we wanted to, and that we did.

Three years later, in 1967, I got my second chance to run for office, this time for the Indian Association of Howard University. The elections reminded me strongly of my first try. One more time, I was a part of the minority, Khalil and I being the only two Muslims, among Hindus and Sikhs of India. Again, there was a lot of ill will and bad mouthing against my religion and Muslim background but despite that my Indian friends remained loyal. I won by a comfortable margin and was elected the president of the association.

The Indian Association of Howard was a much bigger and better organized society consisting of over 200 members. This also meant that the responsibility bestowed on me wouldn't be a small one. I gave it my all and kept busy for the rest of the term organizing events, dinners and talks. I also formed an umbrella organization to connect all the Indian associations of Washington. Plus, I made sure that the association I presided over was a part of all the events that took place in Howard University. I was determined to leave a legacy behind and worked hard to achieve my goals.

The same year, India donated a statue of Mahatma Gandhi to Howard. I heard that Baby Nanda would be coming to present it to our dean. Baby Nanda was a famous Indian movie star and my all-time favorite. The entire Indian student body was buzzing with excitement. A function was being arranged in her honor, and I couldn't believe it when I was invited to host it. Later, I was also given the duty of entertaining her and escorting her to places in Washington throughout her stay. It was a fantastic experience for me. As for Baby Nanda, she received a lot of publicity back in India.

My efforts paid off when I gained recognition as the leader of the Indian community in Washington, within a year. In 1968, another prominent Indian was coming to New York. This time it was not an actor but the Prime Minister of India, none other than Indira Gandhi.

When Indira Gandhi arrived, I was one of the two Indian leaders who were invited to meet her. The Indian Embassy made all the arrangements and I travelled with the ambassador in his car to New York. There I got my thirty minutes of fame, when I talked to the Prime Minister and discussed pertinent issues regarding Indian students in America.

The chat with the Prime Minister made me take my role as president of the Association more seriously. I would run into Indians every now and then, but I discovered there were only two Muslims from India, and I was one of them. However, I knew quite a few from Pakistan and other Muslim states. They were all ambitious, motivated and good people, but lacked direction when it came to preserving their identity. I decided to bring them together and educate them. I felt there was a serious need for a Muslim Association that would exclusively support the Muslim community.

First, I took up the idea with my friends, and when they approved, I took it to the university officials. Within days we had The Muslim Student Association. The aim of this body was to educate Muslims and non-Muslims about Islam, and to organize Islamic events like Ramadan and Eid.

—⁓—

Life in Washington was a far cry from life in India. I had lived like a prince in one and had been reduced to a pauper in the other. While I studied, I carried the burden of my everyday existence. When I couldn't deliver any more papers, I started looking for another job. I found one at a drive-in restaurant located in Alexandria, VA. It seemed an improvement over my last job but it was an hour's bus ride away from my apartment.

After classes got over at school, I would head to work and return as late as 2:00 A.M. Often, the owner would make me stay back and clean up, and I would miss the bus. Then, I would sit on the curb and wait for the next one, which came four hours later. By the time I got home it was usually time for my next class. In just three days, I was overworked, underslept and utterly miserable, yet I dragged on.

One morning, after a good day at school, I was especially cheerful. After I got home, I put on my uniform for work. Just when I was about to leave, I caught my reflection in the mirror. I turned around and studied this man for the first time. I saw Ram Pyara Lal from the Soda Fountain staring back at me.

That memory, that face and that uniform was too much to take. I broke down and saw tears spilling down Ram Pyara Lal's face. I could not be a waiter, anything but that. I quit my job the same day.

Next, I landed a job as a busboy at the Ambassador Hotel in D.C. The pay was okay, and the hours weren't bad. I had no complaints until they told me I couldn't eat in the dining hall. For me this was just another reminder of my status quo, and once again my past came rushing back to haunt me.

The following morning, when I heard there was an opening for a cashier in the same hotel, I jumped at the chance without considering the pay or hours. By late afternoon, I was eating in the dining hall and being served by waitresses. As a cashier I put in longer hours for a fraction of what I was earning earlier, but suddenly life seemed a lot brighter.

Then came the day when I bought my first car. It was a beauty and a bargain, a Ford Falcon for $300. The first day I drove it to the Ambassador hotel, I was so proud of my achievement that I parked it right at the entrance. Then, I walked inside to get to work. Six hours later, when I walked out again, I could not believe my eyes. My car was missing, then I raised such a din that I had to be calmed down by two guards on duty. It turned out that my car had not been stolen but towed. I went to the station, paid the fine and got my car back.

I kept switching jobs, always on the lookout for better prospects and bigger earnings. When I got tired of following orders I became a taxi driver for a while. I drove all over Washington and loved picking up Indian passengers.

My last job at an eatery was at a 24-hour Indian restaurant owned by a Pakistani. While driving around in my taxi I ended up at a quaint little building advertising the best Indian food in the locality. I went in for lunch and met Dost Mohammed, the owner. We hit it off instantly. In a matter of hours, we became closer than brothers. He even took to introducing me as his brother to his family and friends.

By the summer of 1968, I was driving my cab full time. One evening, when business was slow I decided to have a hot cup of chai with Dost Mohammed. His restaurant was located in a shady area, and I heard that business wasn't that great. When I reached there, I caught Dost Mohammed putting away his gun. When he saw me he rushed over to welcome me.

Then later, over a cup of chai and kebabs I asked him about the gun. He said it ensured his survival in this area. His job was dangerous and the gun was a necessity. Next, he asked me if I'd like to run his restaurant at night. I agreed, no questions asked, maybe because I craved the excitement, or maybe because I thought I was doing him a favor. Whichever the case, it was not the first time I had quit a job that paid well for a job that didn't.

The owner carried a gun and expected me to do the same. Shooting was a norm, he warned, and there were frequent incidents involving drunken brawls, violence and destruction of property. I had to be prepared.

My third night behind the register, a pimp dragged in his prostitute. There was something in his manner that put me on high alert. After they ordered coffee, I thought things wouldn't get out of hand, but they did. The two started arguing, and it got to the point where he started beating her senseless. I got up from behind my counter and asked him to leave the restaurant. I could tell they were both drunk, and neither of them was listening.

I walked over and asked again, threatening to call the police if he didn't leave with his girl pronto. This got the reaction I was hoping for. He got up and so did the girl, but then he picked up the coffee pot and started walking out with it. I don't know where I got the courage from, but I blocked his path and told him to put the pot back on the table.

My heart was threatening to burst, and I was cursing myself for not pulling the gun on him earlier. It was like a scene from a bad movie, eyes locked together, and tension so thick you could slice it with a knife. He put the pot down, and the next thing I knew he had a gun in my face.

My world stopped moving. I thought this was it. He told me to come outside. Hoping to salvage my friend's property, I nodded and followed him out the door.

When you are young, you throw caution to the wind. I could have stayed inside, called for help, diverted his attention, used my head, but no, I walked out with him. Thinking I don't know what, just that I was no coward. If someone challenged me, I was man enough to fight back.

Outside, he simply turned around and left. But I stood frozen to the spot for as long as it took him to drive away, then my world started to spin again.

QUESTIONS FOR REFLECTION

We have been fighting for the world, however, we achieved nothing but humiliation and misery. Would it be the same if we strive for a piece of heaven? Think about it.

MESSAGES AND MESSENGERS

*And We have already created man and know what his
soul whispers to him, and We are closer to him than his
jugular vein. (The Quran, 50:16)*

WHEN THE IMPOSSIBILITY of my situation started to sink in
and the ideology I lived by began to crumble before my
eyes, I became desperate for answers. There were not just
questions that needed explanations, but a yearning for knowledge I felt
I must possess. Something that was meant for me but had not been
sought up till now.

While He knew me inside out I had just a vague outline that defined
the perimeter of my faith. The God, who was closer than my jugular
vein was some days just a dark cloud hovering over my conscience and
other days a dazzling radiance that I yearned to grasp.

Allah does not forget. It is we who forget. He promised *rizq* and
guidance to mankind in this world from day one until the end of time,
and He has been true to His words. Today, we have both in abundance–
guidance and *rizq*.

Since the time of Adam, Allah communicated with mankind
through revelations, dreams, angels, signs and messengers. He
constantly kept in touch, reminding His creation of their pledge and
the impermanence of their world.

Adam was the first of 124,000 prophets chosen by Allah to guide man according to His dictates. Then, came Idris (Enoch), Nuh (Noah), Hud (Eber), Saleh (Shelah), Ibrahim (Abraham), Lut (Lot) and the list continued till Isa (Jesus) who was followed by the last prophet, Mohammed (PBUH). Belief in each of these Messengers of Allah and their teachings is an essential part of a Muslim's belief system.

The prophets of Allah were ordinary men blessed with extraordinary powers. Each one was especially chosen by Him for delivering the message of *Tawheed*. These prophets belonged to different races and groups and were assigned certain goals, but each goal inexorably led men towards a distinct higher purpose. While some men of Allah delivered verbal messages, others were bestowed with complete manuals which were later compiled into books.

All religions or messages that came from Allah introduced one God, warned against satan, and commanded men to do good and shun evil. When one religion was corrupted by man another religion was introduced but the gist always remained the same. It was a new name and a new messenger for a new race, until man mangled it again, and Allah introduced it again, and again, and again until hundreds and thousands of messengers later, came the final message, to the final Prophet (PBUH). Allah took it upon Himself to protect and preserve the final message, and to date, it remains unaltered and revered by Muslims all over the world. This message was the Quran, the receiving prophet was Mohammad (PBUH).

THE ROAD TO SALVATION

In Sahih Muslim, it is narrated by Abu Hurayrah that Prophet Mohammed (PBUH) said;

Allah has one hundred parts of mercy, of which He sent down one between the Jinn, mankind, animals and insects, by means of which they are compassionate and merciful to one another, and by means of which wild animals are kind to their offspring. And

Allah has kept back ninety-nine parts of mercy with which to be merciful to His slaves on the Day of Resurrection. (Muslim, 6908)

Allah loves His creation. To understand this love, one doesn't have to look far: our lives are a perfect example. However, the greatest of Allah's blessings were His messengers, appointed to guide humanity towards truth and deliver them from a life of obscurity.

Not all of us have the capacity or ability to discern right from wrong, defend ourselves against the whispering of satan or identify Allah on our own. One reason for this is our impure hearts and early indoctrination, where we are taught to critically examine everything except the doctrines of our culture, customs and tradition. We find it easier to accept and indulge beliefs surrounding Santa Claus, guardian angels, Jinns, witches and spirits but when it comes to satan, he never turns as real as Santa for some of us. We take precautions against the threats of disease, road accidents, plane crashes, muggings, betrayals, abuse and exploitation, but hardly ever against Satan and his minions.

Imagine, if mankind was abandoned by Allah, there would be three major entities on earth–Man, *Jinn* and Satan, and all would be engaged in a power struggle. Since Satan has cunning and intelligence, he would probably overpower both, *jinn* and man. Man without guidance from Allah would be directionless. What's more, he would be unaware of his own powers. Therefore, he would also be an easy target for *jinn*.

Today, man exists in a state of equilibrium; there is devastation but progress, too. Where there is cruelty due to satanic influences, there is also kindness due to Allah's mercy. Where there is *kufr*, rejection of the Divine truth, prevalent in this world, there are also countless Muslims working to spread the light of Islam.

Since man on his own was deemed incapable of finding the true path, he was sent help by Allah, in the guise of Prophets. The selection of Messengers and the revelation of books and laws are two undeniable aspects of Allah's mercy, through which mankind progressed and survived the dark ages.

An astounding fact about the Quran, the book of Allah, is that its laws are still applicable today even after centuries. There is not a single problem or issue that isn't discussed in it. It teaches man how to live, interact and deal with issues that afflict them and their societies. Moreover, it teaches man about man, his history and origin. It discusses his future, what is to come and how to prepare for it. And mercy upon mercy, Allah selected men from amongst them to show how doable His commands were.

Allah reveals:

And We have sent you (O Mohammed) not but as a mercy for the 'alameen (mankind, jinn and all that exists). (The Quran, 21:107)

The road to salvation was shown to the prophets and they were asked to guide mankind towards the same path. If it wasn't for the guidance, all of mankind would be destined to failure and doomed to hell. The world would still be shrouded in darkness, and the law of the jungle would prevail, where the powerful would devour the weak.

THE MESSAGE AND THE MESSENGER

The messenger who came to validate all previous messengers was Mohammed (PBUH). He came bearing the gift of *Tawheed,* and mercy for not just man and *jinn*, but for all of Allah's creation on Earth.

Nobody understands the chemistry of our bodies and the working of our minds, hearts and souls the way Allah does. So, if He informs man about his failings, like his ungrateful and forgetful nature, then his reaction should be to heed His words and correct himself. For that it is necessary to understand the message of the Quran, and Islam in totality.

Quran is a discourse on man, who is the main subject throughout the entire book. It discusses:

- Man and his relation to Allah, his Creator

- Man and his relation to the world
- Man and his relation to his family, friends, neighbors, foes and himself

The Quran focuses on all these relationships and the proper way of dealing with them. It tells man how to prioritize and give due respect first to his Creator, then to his family and relations and lastly to the world he lives in. The main theme calls man to accept his Lord and Master and do righteous deeds as defined by Him.

Allah revealed His last book to Mohammed (PBUH) who was sent to the world as a "giver of glad tidings" and a "warner" to all mankind.

THE MESSAGE

The Quran was a miracle of Prophet Mohammed (PBUH) it literally means "to read," and yet it was bestowed on one who could not read or write up until the time of his passing. Regardless, the message was preserved in hearts and consequently Islam retained its original purity.

The message of Allah came with some staggering characteristics. Here are some of them.

- The message is clear and understandable by all.
- It is a lifesaver for humanity, through which man can achieve success by Allah's mercy.
- It consists of chapters, each distinct, perfect, free of contradictions and well preserved.
- It holds verses which are evident signs of Allah's unity, His greatness and His remarkable power.
- It is truth, and it cannot be affected by falsehood.
- It is one of a kind and cannot be imitated.

THE FIRST REVELATION

When the first message came from Allah, Mohammed (PBUH) was close to forty and spent most of his time in profound thought and reflection. This was the year 610, when Makkah lay bleeding, and its people were no better than barbarians. Women were treated like animals, and slaves–even worse. Fratricidal warfare was the rule of the day. Mohammed (PBUH) saw cruelty, inequality, greed, arrogance and lawlessness draw his people towards the abyss of darkness. The decline of his people and the state of their affairs would disturb him. So he would seclude himself in a cave on mount Hira, a few miles away from his city. There he would spend his days and nights in deep reflection and communion with the true Lord.

On one of these nights, the Angel Gabriel appeared to tell him that Allah had chosen him as His Messenger, and that he, as His Prophet, would bring the light of Islam to the darkness that enveloped Makkah.

Gabriel was the angel of revelation. He asked Mohammad (PBUH) to "recite." Surprised, Mohammed (PBUH) replied that he was not one of those who recited. The angel then held Mohammed (PBUH) in a grip that took his breath away, and repeated, "recite." Mohammed (PBUH) gave the same reply. The angel grabbed him again, pressed him harder and ordered again, "recite;" this time Mohammed (PBUH) asked, "What shall I recite?" Gabriel took hold of him again, and when he released him, Mohammed (PBUH) had no more strength left in his body. Then the angel of revelation said:

> *Recite in and with the Name of Your Lord Who created. He created human from a clot (clinging to the wall of the womb). Read and your Lord is the All Munificent, who has taught human (to write) with the pen–taught man what he did not know. (The Quran, 96:1–5)*

This was the first revelation and the first message for Mohammed (PBUH) and his *ummah*. Allah introduced himself as the Creator, the Giver and the All Knowing.

UNDERSTANDING THE CREATOR'S COMMANDMENTS

The Quran is the word of Allah in Arabic. It contains messages and commandments which were delivered to us by Prophet Mohammed (PBUH). It is not just a positive book; it is the most influential, most widely-published and most widely-read text in the world today.

The book discusses Islam, which is voluntary submission before the will of Allah. In the Quran, Allah declares that the purpose of man's creation is worshipping Him, but he has the choice to be obedient or disobedient, and ultimately he will be answerable to Him for the choices he makes in this world.

The Quran describes Islam as a way of life. To enter Islam, one has to make a choice of accepting a lifestyle that defies the self and submits to a higher authority, that of Allah. The message it contains gives hope, and also warns man of Allah's wrath.

Man was promised guidance, and he was told to do Allah's bidding before being sent to earth. His mission was his own development. His free will needed discipline, and for that Allah made laws. To help man accept and follow the laws, Allah revealed Himself as the Creator who would not be denied.

THE QURAN IS GOOD NEWS AND BAD NEWS, BENEDICTION AND WARNING

The Quran implores man to change his ways for the better. It calls mankind towards truth and veracity. For those who believe in the Day of Judgment, it turns into hope and benediction, but for those who are lost in their worldly lives it is a warning.

The Quran touches souls who understand the meaning behind the Arabic. It is not just for recitation, it is Allah talking to man. We take pains to understand worldly languages, but when it comes to the Quran, most of us are satisfied just reading the words which hardly penetrate our senses. It is outrageous and downright wicked to say,

"Oh, we believe in Allah, we love Him and His messenger, and have the highest respect for Him!" but on the other hand, not have enough time or inclination to understand what the Creator is saying to us.

Ask yourself: Do I really believe that Allah is my Creator? Four five seconds your mind will weigh the possibility, for another three seconds it will accept it completely or reject it. In both cases, warning bells will start ringing in all your systems. If your mind accepts it, it will need to change for you to be able to face your Creator one day. If it doesn't, all the ringing will wake up your conscience and you will be guilt-stricken.

However, if the bells do not go off, then the *ummah* might be losing you to *shaytan*. This is your wake-up call! Take your life into your own hands.

There is no way a man can believe in Allah and not want to learn more about Him, not want to know what messages He has left for him, and not want to hear and understand the rewards and punishments which He has promised the believers and non-believers.

A muslim cannot be a true believer or follower of Islam, unless and until He understands the Quran and the message within it.

AS YOU SOW, SO SHALL YOU REAP

The Quran is emotional. It is peaceful and calm, but it is also outraged and wrathful. It tells stories about the future and the past. It reveals secrets that man could never have discovered on his own, without Allah's will. It describes Allah as loving and rewarding, but also as angry and punishing.

When Allah blew His *Ruh* into man; he started to feel. He lurched for food in haste and hunger. Creation of man was therefore an expression of emotion. Allah had *jinn* and angels and all the creation at His beck and call and yet Allah created man and blessed him with His *Ruh,* choices and the capacity to deny His existence. Man was later blessed with the world and then Prophets, one after another.

The Quran speaks of Allah's infinite love for man: every warning, every hope, every punishment and every reward speaks of nothing but

Allah's love. If it weren't so, and if hell was made to be the final abode of man, then there would have been no need for guidance or prophets. However, if man thinks that Allah will not test him, then he is naïve. With all His attributes, Allah is also Just. A believer and non-believer will never be rewarded equally. **What you sow, so shall you reap is the underlying message of the Quran.**

QUESTIONS FOR REFLECTION

- **Do you believe a man obedient to Allah would not want to know the teachings of Quran and Sunnah?**
- **What is the underlying message of the Quran?**
- **Does Quran only give glad tidings?**

11

READY FOR MARRIAGE UNITED STATES, INDIA, 1969–1978

And We created you in pairs. (The Quran, 78:8)

O NE EVENING, WHEN I met a Muslim boy from Bihar at the mosque, I hadn't the slightest notion what this little meet would lead up to. Now when I look back, I realize that was the time when small happenings started conniving together to lead me to a major juncture of my life.

The Bihari boy introduced himself as Haseeb, the cook. He was working at the Indian Embassy for Mr. Aqil Ahmad who was a Press Attaché. When Haseeb invited me over for dinner, I got a chance to meet Mr. Ahmad. He was a kind man and took a liking to me. Since he was from India we shared many a tale about the past and discussed our future goals. He told me about his brother Jamil Ahmad and later introduced him when he arrived from India.

Jamil was Indian and that was all the information I needed to befriend him. He was also a matchmaker of sorts. He had a niece, Ayesha, in India, and when he met Azeem, my old friend from the Washington Post, he decided that he was the perfect match, so without much ado he proposed.

Azeem was flattered and interested. He asked to see Ayesha's picture and was dumbstruck by her beauty. I knew he was a goner even before he inquired about her education, personality and background. It was a big yes, uttered in a small voice with a dignified nod of the head.

There were no wedding bells or drums at Azeem's telephone wedding, the telephone being the main mediator between the groom and the bride-to-be. There were just four people at Azeem's reception, Jamil, Khalil, me and the groom himself, Ayesha on the other hand, had a huge one in comparison, with all the Indian wedding perks.

Azeem was married in a matter of minutes, the telephone was back in its place and my friend was a bachelor no more. We decided to go out to celebrate his new status over dinner, where I couldn't help but reminiscence about *Barhai Bhaiya's* wedding. If his had been a three tier cake wedding, Azeem's wedding in comparison was the little cherry that sits on top of it.

1969 was the year I finally completed my credit requirement and graduated. Immediately after, I was called for an interview by Cummins Engineering Co., located in Columbus, Indiana. I had nothing holding me back, and since the offer was from a prestigious firm, I had no second thoughts to mull over.

When I arrived for the interview, the secretary at the desk ushered me into an office where the interview panel asked me just one question: since I was an Indian and had graduated from Howard, an all-black university, how did I think I would survive in the Midwestern conservative town where the company was located?

This was my answer: "At first, human beings hate each other. Then they find reasons to back up their hatred: some use the Indian vs. American reason; if that fails, they try the brown vs. white reason; if that does not hold, they try the Muslim vs. Christian reasoning; and if that doesn't work, they try the Catholic vs. Protestant; but if that falls short too, they try something else. They keep searching for reasons; until they find one to validate their hatred. I personally believe that hate is reciprocal. If I hate someone, then I am inviting them to hate me back. But since I am not a hateful person, on the contrary, I am kind, friendly and considerate; I believe I will make people run out of reasons to hate me."

I was offered the job on spot. I started out as an associate engineer but was soon promoted to the rank of full engineer. While working for Cummins and carving out a place for myself in Columbus, I completely lost touch with the Indian Embassy and the Indian Muslim Associations. The excitement of the new job and a new place had usurped all my energy, time and focus.

I was an easygoing person with a highly adaptive nature and took readily to my new environment. While putting away my groceries one day, I realized that I survived on two F's: food and friends. By this time, I had all the Halal food I needed, so I started searching for new friends. It didn't take me long to win over a few dozen–no Indians this time, just good ol' Americans.

After my promotion, I frequently rubbed shoulders with my new boss, Mr. Pellic. He was a New Yorker, and we saw eye to eye on most things. Thus, another relationship forged, and we kept in touch even after I left Columbus. I stayed with Cummins for a period of four years, and when I said goodbye in 1973, the company threw me a grand farewell party. Over five hundred people gathered to see me off. My name flashed on the electric board outside the venue, and I felt like a prince for the first time in America.

Till 1970 I was on a student visa, but during the summer of the same year, I received my green card, thanks to my employers at Cummins Engineering Co., who sponsored me. The green card meant I could now travel to India and back without complications. I started planning for my first trip home in six years.

Six months dawdled and dashed. Sometimes, time would sprint with me and other times, it would tire out, unable to keep up with my rampant spirit. Those days when it lingered, and I couldn't rush it, I would resign myself to fantasizing about India. I would dream about the fields of Sheikhupura. I would taste the ripened mangoes of Ramzanpur. I would smell the *baqarkhani* of Patna. I would hear laughter, and I would hear abba. I would reacquaint myself with the ghosts from my past, one face at a time, and would fall into a blissful sleep and dream some more dreams of India.

Come December, I was back on Indian turf. The very air seemed to rejuvenate my body and soul. I was home, ready to slip back into my old life, and possibly for good.

The exhilaration of being back kept me from examining things and people too closely. I was lost in my own fantastical India for quite some time; until reality came charging at me, forcing me to greet her. I took an instant dislike.

India had changed. People had changed. Without my rose-colored glasses even the culture seemed alien. Corruption seemed to have spread like an epidemic in the last six years. I couldn't get anything done without bribing one person or another. People seemed crude and impolite. What really upset me was the lack of courtesy and respect shown to elders and other human beings. This was not the India I had left behind in 1964.

I realized I was a foreigner in my own country and was lost and homesick for a place that no longer existed. I would not survive here long. I would have to go back.

Shahnaz Sultana was my youngest sister. She was just a schoolgirl when I had left for America. Although, she had been surrounded by family when *abba* had passed away, I had worried for her endlessly. In six years, Shahnaz had bloomed. She was still young, but by Indian standards, of a marriageable age. I started looking for an eligible young man to marry her to; that way she would be well taken care of, and I would be more at ease. Besides, after *abba*, it was my responsibility to see her well-settled in life.

Dr. Aslam Ansari fit the bill perfectly. He was mature, educated and came from a respectable family. Once the preliminaries were over, and the proposal was accepted, the wedding preparations began. I did not have much time. Now that I had decided to go back to America, I had to think about my job and returning on time before being fired. I sent a letter to Cummins Engineering Co, asking them for a few more days of leave.

Indian weddings are expensive, and they are expensive because they are not one day affairs like weddings in the West. They go on for weeks and sometimes even last a month. My carefully calculated wedding budget was a pittance compared to what I actually spent. By the end of Shahnaz's wedding, I had zero cash and zilch inheritance money. My only consolation was that it was all spent on a good cause; Shahnaz was happy and married to a decent guy. What more could a brother ask for?

While I had been busy arranging Shahnaz's wedding, I was approached by a number of people with marriage proposals. I was a prize catch for any marriageable Indian girl, but then again, anyone in my position would have been. I was well educated, well settled and held a green card. Besides, no parents meant no in-laws and an easy life for my Mrs.

One distant relative, who was also an old neighbor from Patna had a sixteen-year-old daughter and decided to propose to me for her. Kauser Asia Jehan might have been a budding Indian beauty but for me she was just a young girl, too young for me. However, what I didn't know at that time was that destiny had chosen her for me. No matter how many times I refused her, she was going to be my wife.

When the wedding fever died down, I decided to head back. I can't explain what it was like leaving India again; except that I had grown more in those last few days than I had in the last six years. I had fulfilled my responsibility to Shahnaz, and now I wanted to return.

India was not my home anymore. Whether America would ever be a home to me or not, I did not know. But I knew that I would spend the rest of my days there, get married and have kids there. I would keep visiting India, but it would never be a home to me again.

I was back. America felt like home now or something close to it. The first thing that greeted me was a letter from London, from a person named Mr. Maqbool Alam. It turned out that Maqbool was Kauser Asia Jehan's brother, and in his letter, he requested me the same thing again on behalf of his parents: marry Kauser Asia Jehan.

My answer was still the same: "No." She was sixteen, I was thirty-one. I hadn't grown any younger in the past three days, neither had she grown any older. This girl would never be able to cope with American ways and would have a hard time adjusting here. I hoped her parents would find someone closer to her own age and marry her off. Kauser Asia Jehan was not for me. I wrote to her brother, apologizing for not accepting his proposal and kindly explaining my reservations. Then, for a while, I forgot all about her.

Cummins was a good place to work, but I did not like the town where I lived. It was small and not a great place for a single young man like me; besides, I was starting to miss my Indian friends. So when I got an offer from the Mack Truck Company in Hagerstown, Maryland, I was more than ready to be their Project Engineer.

Three years passed. I had a steady job and a nice place, but it would get awfully lonely sometimes. That was when I started thinking about marriage and kids. I decided to visit India again to look for a suitable life partner. Often, Kauser Asia Jehan would drift into my thoughts, but I would shake my head in disbelief and send her off with a "No."

Marriage is not just a union of bodies, but of souls too. I was told that marriages took place in heaven before they took place on earth, and that Allah created us in pairs. There was someone waiting out there for me. I just had to hurry up and find her before I grew old and haggard.

It was December again, Christmas holidays in America and my chance to revisit India. I was going to find myself a wife this time. So when I reached there, I wasted no time and immediately sought help from all mediums. Then things finally started happening for me. Inquiries were made; interviews were conducted; photographs were exchanged, but my heart wouldn't settle for anyone. I thought it was my high standard that kept me from settling for less, when it came to choosing my better half. What I didn't realize was that my destiny had already paired me with Kauser Asia Jehan.

I was not looking for beauty, just a pretty face. I was not looking for riches, just a decent background. I was not looking for degrees, just a good character, a pleasing personality and, yes, a heart of gold. I was looking for sincerity; for a person who would walk into this marriage willing to make it last through good and bad times, someone who would stick by me through thick and thin and love me unconditionally.

Days flew by, and no decisions were reached. No one came close to meeting my criterion, and I left it up to destiny to chart my path. Once again, Kauser Asia Jehan was brought to my notice. Although, I had just seen a glimpse of her and had never talked to her, it seemed as if I had known her for some time now. She had been an invisible presence in my life for the past few years.

Agreeing to marry Kauser Asia Jehan was not an easy decision, nor was it a reckless one. I finally came to terms with the fact that she was the chosen one. Once I accepted that, I pledged to give her a very happy life. On January 12, 1974, Kauser Asia Jehan became my lawfully wedded wife – a gift on my birthday, presented by destiny.

I had just a few days to get acquainted with my wife, plus get her passport and visa to take her back with me. We travelled to Calcutta to sort out the paperwork and spent the most memorable time of our lives there. Right after, I had to leave for America. My wife had not received her visa till then and joined me two months later in March, in our new home, Hagerstown, Maryland.

When Kauser reached our apartment in Hagerstown, she seemed so small and dainty, and so much like a porcelain doll, that I took to calling her *Tuniya*. She was my *Tuniya*, my life partner and my companion. Just the thought of spending the rest of my days with her filled me with inexplicable joy.

However, our first day together in our apartment didn't start off on the right foot. Everything was wonderful, until she told me about the loans her family had been taking in my name. According to her perspective, it was my duty to repay the exorbitant sums. I was aghast. It did not make sense. Was this some kind of a joke? There were three reasons why this piece of information infuriated me and wounded our relationship beyond repair. First, I did not believe even for a second that it was my duty to repay the debts that had been incurred without my knowledge. Second, I was hurt that my wife did not see the injustice of it all and intractably defended her parents. Third, I was not as rich as everyone thought. I had spent a fortune on my sister's wedding, then my own. Now, when I had no savings left, I was being asked to settle debts, immediately.

Where was I in all this? Who exactly was on my side? Was I being used? These questions stayed with me for a long time. In India, in my early years, I had seen son-in-laws being revered and well-regarded. My maternal grandparents were in awe of my dad. They would offer him the best of what they had and never thought about infringing on his personal rights. My dad was a rich man. My mom's parents were poor, but they never staked a claim on his wealth.

After fuming for hours, I agreed to settle the debts only because Kauser was now my responsibility, and so was her happiness. Having no idea how I would handle my first financial crisis, I left it up to Allah to help me through. Then, just to salvage what was left of our day, I tried shrugging off the matter.

Kauser was an enigma, an impressionable young girl, delicate and petite but with the tenacity of ten horses. She was multitalented, an excellent cook, a meticulous housekeeper and a loyal daughter. She also loved to write, paint and sew. Every day that I discovered something new about her, I felt a little tug on my heart.

One day, an old friend Murad Khan and his wife Shaukat joined us for breakfast. Kauser had just been with me for a few days, but she was very welcoming and friendly towards our guests. She offered them tea and *pao roti*. At her kind offering, Shaukat burst out laughing. At the same instant, we both realized that Kauser had a lot of learning to do. *Pao roti* is just another Indian word for toast, but in my Americanized apartment it sounded so out of place and bizarre that Shaukat couldn't hold back her laughter. *Pao roti* became our little joke, and I would tease Kauser about it whenever I had toast.

To keep my wife occupied, I would take her socializing. Since I had quite a few friends living in the neighboring cities, I would plan weekend trips. Sometimes, my friends would make similar trips to our place, and Kauser would play the perfect host. Her cooking was finger-lickin' good. She would bake *sheermal*, *naan* and even my favorite *baqarkhani*. She handled parties of a few hundred with the grace of a seasoned matron.

Kauser never ceased to amaze me: a little chit of a girl, who had taken over my apartment and turned it into little India. Now she was threatening to take over my heart. She was shy but self-assured. To most people, she seemed timid, but I knew her better than most: She had a courageous spirit that would rise to the occasion. Whenever I shied away from posing for photographs with luminaries of the political world, she would push me until I relented.

My company Mac Truck closed down for the summer, and all employees were given two weeks off. I decided to take Kauser on a real vacation around the country, and show her America. First day first stop was a small island resort. After driving for an entire day, we both wanted to check into a good hotel and rest our limbs. Unfortunately, the hotel was completely booked and there were no other hotels in the vicinity. We were stuck. We couldn't go forward because of exhaustion, and we couldn't go back either. We resigned ourselves to spending the night in the car.

If that wasn't bad enough, I had a migraine attack with vomiting and all the associated symptoms. Within moments, my condition went from bad to worse. My *Tuniya* popped a Tylenol into my mouth, something she always kept in her bag for me, anticipating such moments. Then, she held me in her arms and comforted me until I fell asleep.

When I woke up refreshed in the morning, I realized that Kauser had been up all night worrying about me. That's when I fell in love with her. I loved the fact that my wife loved me, but I also felt guilty about spoiling her first day. I vowed to make the rest of our vacation something she would remember for the rest of her life.

In the remaining two weeks, we drove around the country covering over 4000 miles of American territory. We saw mountains and waterfalls and counted sunsets and colors streaking across the skies. We discovered quaint little restaurants and tried new cuisines. Eating with Kauser was one of those rare pleasures that I had never experienced before in my life.

When we returned home, I persuaded Kauser to pursue her love of painting, sewing and writing and got her admitted in a college. Each morning I would head for work, and my wife would head to school. Later in the evening, we would discuss the day and find comfort in each other's company. On weekends, we continued visiting friends and exploring America. We would take long walks together, go horseback riding and even boating.

We had good days and bad days. Kauser and I were like any other married couple. We had our share of small fights and our share of big fights, but my wife would never let me go to bed angry or hungry. Sometimes I felt she had gotten to know me even better than myself. She understood my need to be loved. I often saw her indulging me even when I was being unreasonable and difficult.

Often, after a nasty argument, I would refuse to eat and my wife would coax me and wheedle me until I did. I derived a smug satisfaction out of these little episodes. They made me believe that Kauser really loved me, that she cared enough to not let me sleep on an empty stomach. She reminded me of *Abba* and many similar episodes with him.

The fun and romantic courtship period ended all too soon for us; because I was ready for kids, and she wasn't. This was the second time I felt cheated and let down. Wasn't this my main reason for getting married? I wanted a family of my own. Why didn't Kauser see that I was thirty-four and didn't want to wait any longer? I became so fixated on my own woes, that I didn't even try to understand where my wife was coming from. She was young and probably scared of having a baby. It could have been that she wasn't ready and needed counseling or just someone who would hear her out, boost her courage and sway her mind using gentle persuasion.

We were both living in the moment. We both needed perspective. We both needed to step out of ourselves and listen to the other's point of view. That is what married life is about. But she was young, and I was hotheaded. Things seemed so complicated and out of our hands. We ended up playing malicious blame games and deeply hurting each other.

Today, when I look at married couples, I wish to tell them that the secret of a happily married life does not lie in great expectations but in a humble approach. Marriage is a tug of war. The key is to let go when the person on the other end is blinded by anger and hurt. At other times, you can pull with all your might, and hopefully the person will let you win and overlook your shortcomings. If you can give in with love and understanding, you can survive a marriage.

Kauser and I stopped talking. I would wake up early in the morning and go to work. She would busy herself with household chores. I had my friends to talk to, and she had her parents. She started writing letters home, and kept it a secret from me. A couple of times, I even saw her hiding the letters from her parents, which really pissed me off. I would never have stopped her from talking to her parents, no matter what.

When I couldn't take it anymore, I decided to take the bull by the horns and settle the matter once and for all. We couldn't live like this forever, not under the same roof. We both needed companionship, and this cold war was breaking our marriage.

I would rage in anger. The minute my anger died down, I would approach her and beg her to see the folly of her ways. I tried to make her happy, but everything I did backfired.

By this time Maryland was home to many Muslim families from around the world. The population had grown exponentially since 1964. Kauser started mingling with the Indian families and making new friends. Although, the Indian population was not huge in Maryland, there was an Indian Association to represent them. This organization was on the verge of going defunct, when I took charge of it, and I rejuvenated it by introducing social, cultural and educational activities.

Running the association kept me busy. I got involved in other people's lives and problems and forgot about my own for a while. Despite being the only Muslim in the organization, I distributed work without biases and did everything that I could to bring a little joy into their lives. One day, members of the association, wanting to repay me for my efforts, suggested that the association celebrate Muslims festivals, as well. I readily accepted.

Very soon, the organization grew to twice its size and became twice as active. Now, we were celebrating Hindu and Muslim festivals and having a whale of a time. My popularity grew with the growth of the

Indian Association and by the time I left Hagerstown, I held a very respectable position in the Indian community.

In March 1979, I accepted a job with Perkins Engines Co. in Detroit, Michigan, as their chief engineer. Perkins was a British firm, and I was asked to take charge of their entire North American operation. It was an irresistible offer. However, after starting work with the firm I realized that I had taken charge of a sinking ship. The main company had accumulated large losses, and I ended up cutting down expenditure and justifying my staff. I stuck with Perkins for two years and left it for Chrysler Corporation. This was another bad decision, and I left again after just nine months and joined the U.S. Army Tank Automotive Command (TACOM) in Warren, Michigan.

While my professional life kept on developing and moving forward, my personal life seemed stagnant. If anything, it was going from bad to worse. Kauser confessed that she didn't want children because she wouldn't be able to raise them without her mother. I told her I'd take care of her every step of the way, but she wasn't convinced. Later, I discovered a few letters from her mother, and I understood a lot more about my wife.

Kauser and her family had been living a hard life. Her mother had instilled the belief in her and her siblings that they would have to look out for one another and help each other get comfortably settled in their lives. My wife was simply living up to her mom's expectations, not realizing that in the process, she was setting a match to her own home.

I was not against helping her family, but Kauser had mixed up her priorities. As her husband, I was doing my best to lend my support to her and her loved ones, but she seldom seamed grateful or willing to support me in my decisions. When her brother Maqbool Alam wrote to me, asking me to sponsor him, I did not think twice. Very soon he joined us in Hagerstown, but by that time, I was leaving for Detroit. *Barhai bhaiya* also decided to join us at the same time, with his son Abu Zaffar. We got our guests comfortably settled in our home in Hagerstown and flew back and forth over weekends.

What is meant to be, will be. I wish I had understood that sooner. Kauser was pregnant soon after, but we had drifted apart in those few weeks. She decided not to tell me. She needed a friend and would go out often. One of her friends insisted that she share the news with the dad to be. When I heard the news, there was no end to my joy.

I started lavishing Kauser with all the love and care that I could. I would take her shopping and make sure she was eating well. My wife grew lovelier every day. With each passing day, my excitement mounted. I couldn't wait to hold my baby in my arms, not caring if it was a girl or a boy. I just wanted a child of my own, and finally it seemed my wish would be granted.

Kauser and I selected a site in Novi, Michigan, to build our home. By the time we were ready to move in it was December 1979. *Barhai bhaiya* had returned to India but had left Zaffar with me. He wanted me to get him enrolled at a good college, and I opted for Schoolcraft Community College, Northville. Every morning, I would drop him off to college and pick him up in the evening on my way back from work.

A few months before the birth, the doctors told us that we were having a boy. That's when I started dreaming. Sometimes, I would be in the delivery room, waiting and waiting until I heard the first cries of a newborn. I would rush to hold him in my arms and give *azan* in his ear. Sometimes, I would see him older, going with me to parks and riding my shoulders. Some other times, even old enough to go to school and I would be helping him with his assignments and projects. I also saw him as a teenager with hardly any time for his old man. There were nights when I would dream about him turning into a handsome young man, graduating and finally getting married. And then, there were nights when I would see his children, my grandchildren, surrounding their old grandpa, and I would smile in my sleep.

On the 12th of July 1980, at Annapolis Hospital, Wayne, Michigan, I heard the first cries of my son. I rushed, as if in a dream, to hold him in my arms, and gave *azan* in his ear. We named him Bin Yamin.

I was a dad, the happiest dad, and I just didn't know how to thank my wife. If I could have, I would have plucked the brightest star from the sky for her. That's how I felt that day. Instead, I bought her a beautiful pink pearl necklace, as a token of my love and appreciation.

I was in love again, this time with my little Bin Yamin. He was the center of my world. After I returned from work, I would spend most of my time cuddling and pampering him. I would hold his little hands and feet in my hands and marvel at their perfection. Kauser and I would go out often and never return without buying something for our little baby, it was clear that our focus had shifted from our needs to that of our little one.

Bin Yamin was a healthy boy and loved the outdoors. On one of his birthdays, I surprised him by building a play area in our backyard. I worked for long hours in the heat, digging holes and making sure that Bin Yamin was asleep or out with his mom while I worked. I installed a swing, a slide and parallel bars. The joy on his face when he saw the brand new play area was priceless.

Two years later, Yusuf, our second child, came into this world on the 28th of February 1982. It was time again to celebrate, to dream and to redo the baby room. My relationship with Kauser was undergoing enormous changes at this time. The entrance of Bin Yamin and Yusuf in our lives took a lot out of us both. With all the sleepless nights, hormonal changes and lack of communication, we ended up arguing on a lot of petty matters. As our children grew, our philosophies about life changed and developed with them.

When Yusuf was just a few months old, Kauser decided to take both the kids to visit their grandparents. The trip lasted for eight months. In that time, I missed my family terribly. It seemed that Kauser had left me in darkness deliberately and taken the light from my life. As misunderstandings grew between us, so did irreconcilable differences.

After Yusuf's first birthday, Kauser returned back. Tagging along with our two children was Tunni, Kauser's younger sister. They were followed by my in-laws, Kauser's brother and parents. Very soon, we were also housing Kauser's elder sister and her family.

I sponsored all of Kauser's family, and all of them stayed with us for quite some time. My eldest brother in law was already living close by, and he helped out with his parents from time to time. When Kauser's sister and her husband, who was a practicing doctor in England, were returning home, they invited Kauser and my kids to go live with them for an indefinite period. I realized at that point that our relationship problems were out in the open and people were intervening in my personal life. I also realized that Kauser was being heavily influenced by her family.

No two relationships are the same. Nobody could have understood the dynamics of our married life better than us. When Kauser looked to her family for support, she gave her side of the story. I don't blame her. She was young and probably at her wits end. She needed direction, and her family gave her one.

She chose to leave me again and go to England with her sister.

LESSON LEARNED:

By now I learned the most important lesson - Don't ignore the advice God gave in the Quran: Be aware of the Devil, he is your enemy and he will destroy you whenever he gets a chance. He will destroy you, your family and maybe even your community. So declare Jihad against him and get rid of him.

I learned, if I am under the Devil's grip I become blind. I don't see I am falling in a trap, and every decision I make tends to be wrong.

12

PILLARS OF ISLAM

You shall have your religion, and I shall have my religion. (The Quran, 109:6)

I HAD MY RELIGION but my problem lay in not understanding it. I kept up my nightly vigils, trying to grasp as much as I could. I would meet Imams and listen to scholars. Ask questions and search for answers. I would engage anyone who was willing to talk about Islam, Muslims and their digression from it. Every wisp of knowledge I collected thereby helped me put together this manual on Islam, but more importantly it helped me see my religion in a completely new light.

Today Muslim societies are buckling under outside pressures and lateral forces because their foundations are sloppy and fail to support the edifice of Islam. It is also because we have no idea what we are building on. We do count the five pillars on our fingers, and yet our buildings are shabby, dilapidated structures which present a warped and distorted picture of our religion.

Across the world, pillars are deemed the most important elements of a building, offering not just compressive support, but also structural. The five mandatory pillars of Islam were meant to serve the same purpose. While Muslim children grow up hearing and reading about the five fundamental pillars that hold up the entire edifice of Muslim belief, somehow the significance is lost in translation.

If Islam is a building, then its continued existence depends upon the strength of the five pillars; Shahadah, Salah, Zakat, Saum and Hajj

UNDERSTANDING *SHAHADAH*

Shahadah is declaring there is no god except Allah, and Mohammed (PBUH) is His Messenger. When a man recites *shahadah* he is considered and accepted as a Muslim.

How a person recites *shahadah* is very important. Does he recite it by the movement of his lips, or does his faith go deeper, spiritually connecting his heart and soul to Allah?

Shahadah is considered the foundation of Islam for a reason. When a person recites it with his heart and soul, he makes a commitment to follow the commandments of Allah, and the teachings of His Messenger Mohammed (PBUH). Moreover, his personality, character and actions reflect this commitment for the rest of his life. What Muslims must realize is that Allah does not give much weight to reciting *shahadah* unless the declaration shines through in the person's actions.

In Surah Al-Hujurat, verse 14, Allah asks Mohammed (PBUH) to correct the bedouins when they say, "We believe." They do not believe yet declares Allah but they have only submitted themselves. They will be believers only when faith enters their hearts. **One is not *Mumin* until his heart connects with Allah and his belief reflects in his character.**

UNDERSTANDING *SALAH*

Salah is a prayer that a believer is duty-bound to perform five times a day. Allah decreed *salah* on mankind, who accepted Him as the owner of the heavens, Earth and the Day of Judgment. During *salah*, Allah's servants stand before Him and ask for His guidance.

Salah with its precise and repetitive movements may seem like a ritual performance to a non-believer but there is more to it than meets the eye. Allah does not accept any religious performance unless it is performed spiritually with heartfelt commitment and concentration. During *salah* men stand and pray before Allah. When they bow down for *ruku* and put their foreheads down on the ground for *sajda*, they accept His greatness. This gesture is an acceptance of Allah's ownership of every creature, the universe, and the Day of Judgment.

However, **when man indulges his *nafs* and devilish desires even after performing *salah* then his offering is reduced to a mere ritual with no spirituality, and loses its true purpose.**

UNDERSTANDING *ZAKAT*

Zakat is one of the five pillars of Islam and another opportunity to spiritually connect with Allah.

When Muslims give *zakat* their hearts fill with love for Allah and His people. They try to give more to win the pleasure of Allah and to ease the suffering of the poor. However, those people who consider *zakat* just another obligation, and do not see it as a way of connecting with Allah through his people do not gain much. Their hearts do not bleed for their less fortunate Muslim brothers, and they are not motivated to lessen their burdens.

Sometimes man is so taken by his own needs that he sees little else. He strives to fulfill his greed, ego and lust for more. It is *zakat* that puts a check on such infatuations and pushes man to understand the needs of others.

For pleasure seekers, the obligation of *zakat* is a burden which forces them to share their wealth. Some men go to great extent to avoid giving *zakat*. These men forget that *zakat* is as much for their benefit as for their brothers. Consequently, they spend every penny of their savings on their *nafs* and provide silly excuses to their guilty conscience. They tell themselves that Allah made religion easy, that Allah is very loving and caring, and will forgive their sins and shortcomings, and last but not the least, 'I can do only as much as Allah gave me *taufeeq* or ability to do', and so on.

UNDERSTANDING *SAUM*/FASTING

Man's body and soul both need nutrition to survive. Since the body comes from earth, so does its nutrition. But since the soul comes from heaven its nutrition also comes from there, through remembrance of Allah. Like a body can't survive for long without food and sustenance, a soul can't survive without *zikr* or remembrance of Allah either.

Fasting is a way of nourishing the body and the soul. It provides an opportunity to the believers to strengthen their ties with Allah.

Fasting was ordained on Muslims in the month of Ramadan by Allah so the souls may be nourished and strengthened. If fasting is not practiced, the soul weakens and becomes vulnerable to outside influences.

UNDERSTANDING *HAJJ*

Hajj is essentially following the practice of Abraham (PBUH), who holds a special status in the court of Allah for his remarkable strength of belief and astounding sacrifice—so much that it was turned into one of the fundamental pillars of Islam.

Muslims all over the world who are financially sound, and able are commanded to perform *hajj* and revive their *iman*, plus their connection with Allah, once in their lifetime. This is achieved through remembering the sacrifice of Abraham and re-enacting his deed. When Muslims perform *hajj* and sacrifice animals, they are not just performing a ritual but also reviving their *iman*.

The sacrifice that Abraham, his wife and son made for the love of Allah helps Muslim pilgrims understand what true *iman* is. It is only a similar *iman* that would earn them a place in heaven among Allah's favorite people.

Allah loves those who are willing to sacrifice their most precious possessions for Him. While preparing for Hajj when Muslims try to sacrifice their wealth and comfort for the sake of Allah, the devil tries to mislead them. Only those with strong *iman* can resist him, identify him and rebuff him like Abraham (PBUH) did.

Through *hajj*, Muslims are taught a lesson in spirituality, but only those who look beyond the ritualistic performance have a chance of forging a true connection with Allah.

SIGNIFICANCE OF PILLARS

The five pillars mentioned above denote the basic moral, ethical and corporeal requirements of Islam and also the barest minimum. An entire structure is yet to be constructed on the support lent by these pillars. The design, quality and construction of the pillars, together play a major role in determining the height, structure and longevity of the building that will rest upon them. If the pillars are strong and sturdy, the building of Islam will stand tall. But if the very foundations are faulty, the building will collapse sooner or later. Similarly, if the pillars are designed to resist harmful forces the building will endure for life.

Increasingly, the five pillars of Islam are being considered the be all and end all of Islam. As long as they are looked upon as building blocks of Islam, that statement holds true; however, the minute they take the shape of mere rituals devoid of morality, the statement becomes false. Unfortunately, very few Muslims today understand this basic concept of building upon the five pillars.

Examining the state of the five mandatory pillars is a good way to gauge a person's Islamic standing or his quality of belief. Poorly built, wobbly pillars, or those that have the right appearance but lack the substance within, clearly indicate that one needs a better understanding of the foundations, and also needs to learn the proper techniques of building them. **This can only be achieved if a person is willing to understand the morality behind each pillar and is ready to reexamine his faith.**

RE-EXAMINING FAITH

The Islam we practice today is a mere caricature of what the Prophet Mohammed (PBUH) taught to the believers. Most of the *ummah* has completely deviated from his (PBUH) teachings and are living a life of apathetic ignorance and in some cases willful and stubborn defiance.

When it comes to our faith, we Muslims are hopeless idealists. Here is a little reality check for all of us: *shahadah* is the first foundation or pillar; ask yourself how strong is your *shahadah*? Go back to the chapter on *tawheed* and be your own judge. *Salah* is the second pillar. Ask yourself if your *salah* is strong enough to build a structure upon? Probably not. There are also the pillars of *saum, zakat* and *hajj*. Together, we believe, perhaps they might support a building. But for how long? If the foundation is weak, the first winds of adversity will make the building come toppling down like a house of cards–and that'll be the end of our so called religiosity.

In actuality, life of a Muslim is an endless struggle for perfection in all acts that are good and true. Hence, if a man is seeking to construct a life around Islam and has no clue about its foundations, then the entire structure would be at fault and pose a risk not just to himself and also to those around him.

TOTAL OBEDIENCE IN ISLAM

Islam is a religion that mandates and demands a way of life which is in total obedience to Allah's laws, as ordained in the Quran and in the teachings of Prophet Mohammed (PBUH).

Total obedience is not just ritualistic, but also spiritual. Since each individual has the spirit of Allah within him, but is also partly matter, he aspires to fulfill his spiritual calling and aspirations while fighting the limitations of his physical self. It is the matter of man or the physical body that is inclined to disobedience, whereas the spiritual self tries to lure it back to the path of the righteous.

Spiritual obedience is the *nafs* accepting, without a shadow of doubt, that Allah is the Absolute.

Spiritual submission is:

- Acknowledging His absolute perfection, Lordship and sovereignty
- Recognizing Him as the true Creator and Sustainer of the universe
- Recognizing Allah and His Divine qualities of absolute perfection, absolute knowledge, absolute power, absolute justice and absolute mercy
- Accepting Him and Him alone as the true source of life and energy, and as the Creator of Heaven and Hell
- Believing and recognizing Him as being close and nearer to man than his jugular vein

WORSHIPPING ALLAH

worship: *the adoration, devotion and respect given to a deity.*

Worship is a word synonymous to great devotion, excessive love, respect and religious adoration, and all the services that are offered to express the same. To treat an entity as divine and show respect by engaging in prayers and acts of devotion is also called worship.

Although, people accept that worship is to respect someone greatly, excessively and unquestioningly, in popular culture most hardly understand it. Worship is a word which, in modern terminology, depicts religious congregations, mass prayers, fasting, hajj and all those actions which give a clear-cut picture of an individual submitting to a higher authority and frequently denying himself by going against the norm.

For instance, if one takes a leave from friends at a social gathering to offer *salah*–that is worship. If one takes a break from shopping to look for a place to pray – that is worship. If one is circumambulating the Kaaba, that is worship. Worship is something that immediately marks the believer as a doer of an action.

Today, worshippers are treated like oddities and queer fish. In polite societies, people call them "religiously inclined," and in not so polite societies, they are called religious fundamentalists.

The truth is, rituals and services performed as means of gaining Allah's pleasure are only a small aspect of worship. A believer's entire life can be an act of ceaseless worship, but that is only possible if the thought behind the action is not buried under the weight of physical obedience.

In reality, there are basically two types of beliefs:

1. *Wahdaniyat* or monotheism, no god except Allah.
2. Everything else that goes against Allah's *wahdaniyat*.

Wahdaniyat is much more than belief in God's Oneness. When man accepts Allah as God, he also accepts His divine attributes, His Messengers, His commands and His powers of creation, sustainment and retribution. However, this belief, which is declared with *shahadah*, becomes null when man shuns responsibility for his actions, is disobedient to Allah, neglects his duties and commits sins without the fear of Allah crossing his heart.

In the same way, establishing the mandatory pillars of Islam i.e., performing *salah*, giving *zakat* and fasting, while simultaneously being a slave to one's *nafs* and running after base desires expels one from the first category of belief. *Shahadah* is not just lip service. It is spiritual subjugation in the true sense.

If *shahadah* means accepting Allah as Lord and Master, it automatically turns *shaytan* into an enemy. Claiming to believe in Allah while letting one's actions prove otherwise, is siding with *shaytan*, who dared to challenge Allah. Not stopping to think before committing sins, not turning away from vices, and not hating the attributes of the devil are not the traits of true believers.

Establishing the pillars does not automatically turn one into a believer. **Worship does not mean just doing good, it also means recoiling from** *shirk* **and waging** *jihad* **against the evils of hatred, avarice, pride, materialism, conceit, bigotry, intolerance, racial discrimination, and everything immoral and forbidden by the Lord. Worship is not just doing good, it is also for abstaining from un-Islamic acts.**

PILLARS AND MORALITY TRAINING

Salah is performed five times a day, but is hardly related to morality a single time out of those five. Morality training is a concept seldom attached to *salah* when in fact, in its entirety, it is training our morals to consciously and lovingly submit before the will of Allah.

Salah is standing before Allah, aware of our humble origins and status, and is a constant reminder to guard against evil. Purifying before *salah* is an act that promotes cleanliness and hygiene. The act of *salah* itself is to keep five daily checks on the believer. *Salah* is a daily visit to the court, where a believer not only reports for duty, but renews his oath and puts forth his requests. He accepts his shortcomings and asks for exoneration and more chances.

Every single time a true believer presents himself before his Creator, he knows where he has faltered and vows to not make the same mistakes again. The five daily prayers, therefore, prevent him from shameful acts and cruel deeds and keep the thought of Allah fresh in his mind.

Salah is worship, when man bows before Allah, and prayer when man speaks to Him. Our dilemma is, we talk to the Highest Authority every day, five times a day, without an appointment. Yet if a non-believer asks us what we talk to Allah about, we would be put to shame. We say the words we only just understand. We talk of heaven and hell with a face and a heart that is empty of emotion, we yap and yap and yap and we comprehend nothing. Are we so naïve as to think that Allah would count *salah* offered without heart? Or that Allah would turn to us and watch us make a spectacle of ourselves?

In the Quran it says;

Prayer restrains from shameful and unjust deeds, and remembrance of Allah is the greatest (thing in life) without doubt. And Allah knows the (deeds) that ye do. (The Quran, 29:45)

At another place, in a tradition reported by Al Bazzar, who was an eminent and learned scholar, it is said that **Allah accepts prayers from those who:**

- Humble themselves before His glory;
- Do not oppress any of His creatures;
- Spend the night in repenting their immoral and wrongful acts;
- Spend the day in His remembrance;
- Are kind and merciful to the destitute, wayfarers and widows; and
- Are compassionate to those who are injured and suffering.

This is the morality behind *salah*.

Another pillar of Islam is *zakat*, which is taking out a share from one's savings to give to the needy. The idea behind *zakat* is not the same as taxation. The former is a religious, moral duty; whereas, the latter is an imposition by the state.

Zakat must foster love, compassion and mutual concern towards the less fortunate members of the Islamic society. It is not just taking out a percentage every year from the excess wealth and distributing it to the poor. It is developing the qualities of generosity and humility through giving.

Zakat also cuts at the root of greed, and purifies the heart that gives, from selfishness, and the heart that receives, from envy and hatred for those more fortunate. Therefore, like *salah*, *zakat* also has a deeper spiritual significance along with its outward economic objectives.

Fasting is another ritualistic pillar, which on the surface, looks like an act of refraining oneself from eating and drinking from dawn till sunset. This is not the aim of fasting. Starving oneself is not the goal. Fasting means to stop oneself–not just from food and drink. but from bad deeds and anything and everything that displeases Allah. It fosters self-restraint in a believer.

Fasting is a way of encouraging inward reflection and outward expression. Sleeping all day long because one is fasting, not offering the daily *salah*, or spending the day in front of the TV or listening to songs to kill time till it's time to break the fast, is making a mockery of fasting.

In the Quran, it says:

Fasting is prescribed for you as it was prescribed for those before you, that ye may (learn) self-restraint. (The Quran, 2:18)

If a person who is fasting does not keep his anger, emotions and desires in check, then the purpose of fasting is lost. One must realize that for the pillar of *saum* to be strong, it is essential to learn both spiritual and physical self-restraint. If another person is a victim of our verbal or physical abuse, then simply starving the body for half a day means nothing to Allah.

Finally, comes *hajj*, the last pillar of Islam and the most demanding. This pillar is a test of faith. It is also meant to test the strength of the pillars discussed earlier. After *shahadah*, when man declared his belief in Allah and his Prophets, came the decree of *salah*, which was not just submission before Allah, but also a training to live one's life according to Allah's dictates. *Salah* was followed by *saum* and *zakat*, which were both aimed at perfecting the qualities of a true believer and purifying them from sin. Lastly came the commandment for *hajj*, which today is considered simply travelling to the holy land of Makkah, putting on specified clothing and performing the rights prescribed by the Quran and Prophet Mohammed (PBUH). Where is the morality in that? *Hajj* is not entirely about sacrificing one's comfort and money in the way of Allah, but the entire journey itself is a test for the believers. Travelling to a place with a million others, bearing the heat and living in close quarters with strangers, suffering the discomfort of a long journey, and yet not letting it get the best of you, is the morality behind *hajj*. **Being patient, kind and generous, and putting all those moral lessons into action that one has learned from *shahadah*, *salah*, *saum* and *zakat*, is the real test of *hajj*.**

MORALITY AND WORSHIP

A careful study of all the pillars of Islam and the acts of worship makes it evident that although the pillars may appear to be pure acts of devotion the connection between them and morality is undeniable.

In Islam, worship and personal behavior must be consistent and aligned with each other. The Quran does not make a distinction between belief and actions; one must always support the other. In the light of Islam, if an individual does not practice the morality preached by Islam in his day to day life, it is a clear proof of his weak faith, regardless of his actions or claims. **The faith of a true believer is visible in his actions.** He understands that not even mountains of worship will make up for lack of morality.

According to a hadith in Muslim, Prophet Mohammed (PBUH) asked his companions once:

"Do you know who is truly bankrupt?"

The companions replied that probably someone who has no money or property. To this the Prophet (PBUH) said:

"No, the one who is really bankrupt is the one who comes on the Day of Judgment with impressive things in his record like prayers, charity and all that; and he cursed and swore at such and such a person; made false accusations against such and such person; when he usurped unjustly the property of such and such a person;

killed such and such person; and beat such and such person. All this person's acts of credit will be taken and given by way of retribution to those whom he wronged; until all the deeds that should have helped him get into Paradise are exhausted. And when there are still people who have been wronged by him who did not get their rights, God will take from their evil deeds and add them to his own till he is thrown into the fire." (Sahih Muslim, 2581 book 32, hadith 6251)

We as Muslims must understand the wisdom of Islam and stop deluding ourselves into thinking that we would earn Paradise by our good deeds alone; that passing on a certain message of the Quran or from the Prophet Mohammed (PBUH) would add to our good deeds, regardless if we follow it ourselves or not; that giving charity would count, regardless of our cruel behavior to those inferior to us in status and wealth; that constructing a mosque would make up for missed *salah*.

Moral character and good actions can never take the place of faith, but **faith is nothing if it does not change the person for the better.**

Worship is not mere ritual. Along with *salah, saum, zakat* and *hajj*, there are still plenty of ways to worship the Lord. In fact, all actions and activities have the potential to turn into acts of worship in the presence of two conditions:

1. Pure intention behind the action, and

2. When the action is performed within the limits prescribed by Allah.

In view of the above argument, a person's entire life can turn into a potential act of worship, including his sleeping and waking up, work and earning, marrying and raising a family, relationships, shopping and even recreation. At a point in the Quran, Allah says:

I have only created jinn and men, that they may serve Me. (The Quran, 51:56)

This does not mean that men and *jinn* were created to pray all the time, but that simply living one's life according to Islam and Allah's dictates is a service to the Lord and falls under worship.

Another remarkable aspect of Islamic faith is its cohesion with knowledge. Islam does not object to or restrain the process of thought, nor does it oppose knowledge. **The act of learning is synonymous to the act of worship, provided that it fulfills the conditions of:**

- purity of thought, and
- the prescribed limits of Allah.

Even the first verse or command that was received by the Prophet Mohammed (PBUH) was, "*Iqra*," meaning read, recite, proclaim. The pen is also mentioned in the Quran as a tool that aids learning. Further study of the Quran and the life of the Prophet (PBUH) give substantial proofs of Islam's affinity towards learning and acquiring knowledge.

It says in the Quran,

Those who truly fear Allah, among His Servants, are given knowledge. (The Quran, 35:28)

The verse implies that people with the right kind of knowledge and attitude towards learning, people who are sincere and receptive, and people who are objective have a better understanding of Allah and His powers. These are the very people who are given knowledge and are widely favored over the ignorant.

At another place in the Quran it says:

And when ye are told to rise up, rise up, Allah will raise to (suitable) ranks (and degrees), those of you who believe and who have been granted (mystic) Knowledge. (The Quran, 58:11)

All those genres of knowledge that bring a man closer to recognizing Allah, and help him better execute His commands as His vicegerent, are means to move forward in Islam and higher in the ranks of the pious. Moreover, there are several sayings of the Prophet Mohammed (PBUH) emphasizing the need for gaining the right kind of knowledge. He (PBUH) even said;

Seeking knowledge is mandatory on every Muslim. (al-Tirmidhi, 74)

Therefore, Islam makes gaining knowledge, studying and learning not a privilege, a pastime or a diversion from the duties of faith, but a duty itself. It is said that even the angels spread their wings for those who seek knowledge.

Islam brings together morality, the thirst for knowledge and worship into a single sphere. If these basics are understood by Muslims, Muslim societies would become the most civilized societies of the world.

THE RIGHT KNOWLEDGE

What is the right knowledge? For Muslims, the key rule is that the pleasure of Allah is the ultimate good and the only thing worth living for. The goal, therefore, is to pass through the test and tribulations of this worldly life with honor and flying colors.

All acts that are geared to earn the pleasure of the Almighty are considered good; whereas, all acts that earn Allah's wrath are bad. Knowledge that advances man's thinking regarding the ultimate good is the right knowledge.

The fundamental sources of right knowledge are the Quran and other Divine revelations. This, however, does not mean that Divine revelations are the only sources of knowledge. There are other springs of knowledge, as well, but Divine revelations are the ultimate sources–specifically the Quran, which has precedence over all.

Allah made man His deputy, and in doing so, made the earth subservient to man. To be able to derive and gain the best from the world, man was given thirst for knowledge. Knowledge was made positive. The first man, Adam, was made to learn the names of things. He was given the power to identify and label. His progeny followed in his tracks.

KNOWLEDGE REGARDING THE PILLARS

To achieve the goals of Islam, knowledge regarding the fundamental pillars is crucial. **The chief objective behind the pillars of Islam and the morality they advocate is developing individuals with Islamic characters and nurturing personalities with a sense of direction and clarity of vision.**

The pillars foster responsibility and a sense of accountability in believers. They also aim at developing individuals who stay away from evil and believe in the power of truth and goodness. Such individuals are not self-serving but self-effacing and charitable.

The pillars, thus established according to the teachings of Prophet Mohammed (PBUH), set the foundations for a prosperous Islamic society.

Muslims, who believe in the declaration of faith, or *shahadah*, consciously submit while offering salah, and commit to Allah's dictates, are the ones who understand the significance of the pillars of Islam. These are the very people who fight off temptations because they fear Allah. Moreover, it is their love and understanding of their mission that keeps them on the right path, and eventually will be their ticket to heaven.

FAITH AND MORALITY

Prophet Mohammed (PBUH) said:

I was sent in order to perfect moral quality, to bring perfection, completeness and comprehensiveness into the highest and most noble moral qualities that have been preached by all the Prophets. (Musnad Ahmad, 8595)

Modern societies today have started to segregate faith and moral conduct. Religion is something that is not allowed to mix with daily routine and events; there is a time for faith, and a time for living one's life. In such cases, Islam ends up taking the backseat, and life becomes a pool of desires at which one sits all day, fishing and waiting to catch the biggest desire. This is not Islam. **Islam is a lifestyle. Either you adopt it, or you don't.** There are no middle grounds, and there are no excuses.

The source of true knowledge, Allah, proclaims in the Quran;

Verily never will Allah change the condition of a people, until they change it themselves (with their own souls). (The Quran, 13:11)

Building institutions, funding charities, bringing about reforms are all modern methods of instigating change in societies; but unless individuals at the highest and lowest echelons of society change their hearts and their ways, and commit to Allah, no change can endure.

Quran is replete with examples of civilizations that perished despite resources and wealth because their people were ungrateful to Allah and morally corrupt.

The Prophet (PBUH) said;

Among the believers those who are most complete in belief are the best in behavior. (Al-Tirmidhi, 1162)

Islam is a dignified religion and it demands dignity of character in its followers. The Prophet Mohammed (PBUH) was a living example of the character excellence that must be the foremost personality trait of all Muslims. **They should be known for their generosity of spirit, humbleness and morally strong characters.**

Muslims who are corrupt, prone to cheating and lying, and who indulge in all kinds of sin, without considering the faith to which they belong, are playing with fires of hell. Islam is not forced upon people. It is an invitation to accept the veracity behind the creation of man. If one commits to Islam, then acts as if nothing has changed for him, woe unto him. Today, this lack of character has caused Muslims to lose face all over the world.

The Prophet (PBUH) also said that the closest to him on the Day of Judgment will be the best among his *ummah* in manners and morals. In Islam, faith and behavior are two sides of the same coin. Whenever Allah addresses faith in the Quran, He also discusses virtuous deeds.

If Muslims were true to their belief, they would be exhibiting Islamic character in their day to day lives and would not be suffering their present fate. Today there is conflict not just between Muslims and non-Muslims, but also between Muslims and Muslims on the basis of nationality, community, politics, social and business affairs and even Islam itself. The sad truth is that most Muslims talk the talk, but don't walk the walk.

Faith is hard work, and only true faith breeds morality, which is a daily struggle. Talking about faith and morality, the Prophet Mohammed (PBUH) said:

Faith is not something that comes by wishful thinking but is something that is entrenched in the heart and is confirmed by deeds.

Muslims worldwide are holding fast to the book of Allah, but unless they understand and execute the commands of their Lord the way they were meant to, they are no better than mules carrying loads on their backs.

LESSON LEARNED:

The difference between a believer and a non-believer lies in character and behavior.

QUESTIONS FOR REFLECTION

- What are the Pillars of Islam?
- Why do we call them Pillars?
- Can we have strong Islamic Faith if it is built on weak Pillars?
- Are we Mumin if our hearts are not connected with Allah and our belief does not reflect in our character?
- Would our Salah be acceptable if we obey our Nafs and get indulged in Devilish desires?
- Is Zakat an obligation or an opportunity to gain Allah's favors? How does Zakat gain Allah's favor?
- How do Fasting and Zikr Allah keep our soul alive?
- What do we learn by performing Hajj?
- Do we believe that five pillars denote the basic moral, ethical and corporeal requirements of Islam?
- Does Islam mandate a way of life that is in total obedience to Allah?
- What is total obedience, spiritual obedience and spiritual submission?
- What is Wahdaniyat and what do we have to do to change our ritualistic Ebadah into worship?
- What do we have to do to change our current Muslim Nations to the most civilized nations of the world?
- What are right knowledge, good deeds and bad deeds?
- What is the chief objective behind the Pillars of Islam?
- What happened to the civilizations who were ungrateful to Allah and morally corrupt?
- Who would be close to our Prophet (pbuh) on the Day of Judgment?

13

FALLING APART
NOVI, UNITED STATES
1979–1987

Verily, with every hardship comes ease (The Quran, 94:6)
Life consists of two days, one for you and one against you. So when
it's for you, don't be proud or reckless, and when it's against you, be
patient, for both days are test for you. (Hazrat Ali (AS))

USBANDS AND WIVES disagree over all sorts of things, from day
one through the rest of their lives. The topics of contention
range from food to kids, from in-laws to money matters, but
no matter how serious things get, if both of them are bent upon making
the marriage work, it eventually does.

Mine didn't.

My personal life was quickly transitioning into public domain. I
felt like a pariah in my own house. Every day, when I returned from
work, I stepped into a house filled with unwanted guests. My walking
in would put a hasty stop to conversations and moods would change
automatically. Such episodes invariably put me in a bad temper and led
to arguments with Kauser.

Hungry and tired after work, I looked forward to cozy evenings
with my family, but we seldom got a chance to indulge each other.
Kauser was a fantastic host, and sometimes in her zeal for being the
perfect hostess, she would end up ignoring me. I remember that was
the time when we started to drift apart.

With each passing day, it got harder for me to live with our house guests. They had overstayed their welcome, and I wanted them gone for good. I wanted my house back and peace restored, but instead of communicating my need for privacy to my wife, I ended up picking fights with her.

As misunderstandings grew between us, so did the distance. Kauser was the single most important person in my life. I wish I could have conveyed that to her, but whenever I confronted her, I saw accusation in her eyes. I wondered if she saw hurt in mine.

I could not believe that everything we had achieved in our relationship was being ripped to shreds by a bunch of people occupying our living room. The unwanted guests in my house, my upset wife, and the simple business of not being understood, despite trying, stirred my anger to alarming degrees. Sometimes I verbally lashed out at my wife, provoking her. At other times, I silently pleaded with her to make me see, to make me understand and to tell me that she cared.

One day, when I told her I couldn't take the commotion anymore, she brought up divorce. I was shell-shocked. My little Indian wife was talking divorce; something that carried a huge stigma in her motherland. During this time, she was pregnant with our third child, and I could not understand her actions. Was she ready to give up without a fight, without even trying to make it work for the sake of our kids?

I realize today, that she must have struggled too, and possibly so much more than I did, but I just couldn't see it then.

I tried to go back and understand where I had gone wrong, but I couldn't. Kauser's lack of concern for my needs was excusable; she had plenty on her plate. I should have been more considerate and supportive in those tough times, but I was fighting my own demons.

When our arguments turned into blame games, and my anger started scaling new heights, my wife felt compelled to seek outside help. She approached her family, my friends, members of the community, social workers and Muslim community leaders, anyone and everyone whom she believed would have the smallest chance of helping me. But instead of resolving our issues, her cry for help aggravated things even more.

I was as desperate to restore peace between us as Kauser was, but I was a victim of false pride and paranoia. It was my fault that Kauser saw me as a monster who wanted to cut off her family ties, and it was my fault that I saw her as a disloyal and ungrateful wife. The sad, tragic truth was that I needed help. If I had succeeded in taming my demons, our children wouldn't have had to suffer, and things might have fallen back into place again. But some things are just not meant to be.

When random people started approaching me trying to hammer sense into my head, and others started looking at me as if I had anger management issues, I withdrew more into myself. Nobody in this period tried to find the root of the problem, or even asked me what I wanted or what was pushing me over the edge.

Soon my friends and acquaintances started giving me relationship advice, but when they started telling me how to take care of my family, I erupted like a volcano–tactlessly substantiating all the stories doing rounds about me.

During this period, I lost many friends. My real story was buried somewhere beneath a pile of fiction. I was working day and night to support my lifestyle. When I returned home, I wanted it all: a life that was peaceful, an environment that was to my liking, a wife who was attentive and supportive, and kids who loved me half as much as I loved them. Instead, my home was whipping up a storm inside me. Lack of communication with my wife was driving me up the wall, and being attacked by every Tom, Dick and Harry was wreaking havoc on my nerves.

All the negativity surrounding me turned me negative. I grew obnoxious and unapproachable. I would fly off the handle at the slightest provocation and get into heated arguments with people who were closest to me. Forgiving others became next to impossible for me. I would recount conversations and fume over them for hours. I resented all who tried to help. I could see the transition in me, but I was just a helpless bystander.

I started hating myself and the pain that wouldn't go away. Most of all, I hated my inability to protect my kids. Kauser was pregnant. I wish I could have taken better care of her, like I had promised, but some lessons in life are learned the hard way. My problems had robbed me of all good sense.

During this time, a community social worker decided to approach me. When she saw the pain seeping out of my eyes, she advised me to get a divorce. She offered to help by calling a meeting of all the community members who would work out a practical financial arrangement between Kauser and me, but Kauser for her own reasons would hear nothing of it.

In my darkest hour a light shone through, and Mariem was born on June 24, 1986. Although at that time I had no idea about the kind of life that I would give my baby girl, her presence in my life gave me new strength. I had always loved children, and now I had three that I loved to bits.

When husbands and wives become parents, the center of gravity changes for them. They must acquire light and warmth to nourish the new lives they bring into this world. There is no room for ego, selfishness or individualism. Often, when they refuse to embrace their new identities, they set themselves up for loss. I became selfish for a while, and that selfishness scarred me for life. I allowed others to sway my judgment and decide the fate of my kids. In doing so, I wronged my children.

After Mariem, I felt as if I was lacking in things like the simple art of expressing love. I loved Kauser, yet failed to win her heart. I loved my sons Bin Yamin and Yusuf, but failed to create a strong bond with them. I wish they could tell it was love when I did things for them: when I took them to picnics, movies and games; or when I took them to school and soccer practice; or when I helped them with their projects, encouraged their interests and made myself available. These were the only ways I knew how to love.

A few months after Mariem's birth, I returned from work and walked into an empty house. My wife had left me. My kids were gone. Lying face down on the table was a court notice. Kauser had filed for divorce and left for Canada.

After a week, my wife returned with the kids. She did not discuss her actions or the notice by the court. At that point, I decided to get a lawyer.

During the day, my wife and I would haggle in court. At night, we would return to the same house and lie under the same roof. On those nights, sleep would shirk me like everybody else, and my mind would run like a racehorse, weighing a hundred and one possibilities, doubts and fears. I was afraid to dream on those nights and was terrified of losing what I had.

I had a life that revolved around my work and my home. Since our move to Novi, I hadn't had the time or the inclination to socialize or to commit to cultural organizations. I did not have a support group or even family members on whom I could depend on for help in those tough times. My kids were young and needed constant supervision. If the court found out that I lived alone and worked all day, they would withhold custody. But then again, if by some miracle I did get custody of my kids, what would I do? How would I take care of them and manage my job at the same time? Would I be able to provide them with the care and love they deserved? These questions would keep me up till the wee hours of morning, and then it would be time to drag myself out of bed and face the world again.

My nights were cruel, and days were leaden. Consequently, I started to lose control over reality. I started to think that Kauser and her family would use my children against me and would not rest until they pinched the last penny out of me. I had a notion that they were out to destroy me. I grew fearful for my kids and for their future. These preposterous ideas made me sick. I would cry often; sometimes tears would run down my face and catch me unaware.

A few close friends who witnessed my steady deterioration persuaded me to get out of the house and enlist with some social and cultural organizations. If it hadn't been for their timely intervention, I would have lost my sanity.

For the next few months I concentrated on matters outside my personal life. I established committees and whiled away my time organizing and running social and cultural clubs, holding meetings and delivering speeches. Each day, I deliberately worked my mind and body to a pulp, so that when I dropped in bed at night, I was dead to the world, and the world was dead to me.

LESSON LEARNED:

- Life is a lesson, provided one can read it.
- Most important lesson of life: If YOU can't resolve your marital problems, nobody can.
- Remember Allah's reminder in the Quran: The Devil is your enemy, if you don't watch him, he will destroy you.

Purification
of the Heart

On the Day of Judgment, no one is safe, save the one who returns to God with a pure heart. (The Quran, 26:88-89)

B IT BY BIT, light started to enter the darkened chambers of my heart. Things and words that made little sense up till a few years ago, shone with a brilliance that was hard to ignore. I started to find answers and feel connected. Finally, I was on a path and a long road lay ahead of me. I could see turnings and for the first time in my life I knew where they would lead me.

—⟋⟋⟍—

To err is human; to forgive, Divine. Man will continue to err as long as he strives, he will continue to strive for as long as he lives, and he will continue to live for as long as his heart beats inside his body.

All men strive relentlessly, some for power, some for peace, some for big significant changes and others for little, inconsequential ones. While the brain takes most of the credit for man's biggest achievements, it is the heart that pulls man out of his darkest moments and gives him strength to pull through. The part that the human heart plays in the life of man is that of a king. A king that not only uplifts, leads, and motivates, but a king who has the power to destroy it all if he so wills it. A dark king will lead his subjects astray whereas a good king will lead them to salvation.

HOW DID THE PURE HEART TURN BLACK?

Adam was sent to earth with a pure heart, his was the repenting heart. When the first child was born, he came with a pure heart as well. No man on this earth was born a sinner. Each came like the one before him, with a heart as pure as gold. With time however, Satanic influences succeeded in tarnishing the heart; hence, the first murder was committed on earth. Cain, son of Adam, killed his brother Abel in cold blood, out of jealousy and hatred.

With the passing of years, the hearts of men turned more vicious and vindictive than ever before because the world they arrived in had become a product of greed and envy, a hub of anger and unchecked desires, a place which was more of a home to Satan, than to man himself.

Today, the world may be called modern, but it cannot be called civilized. **When Islam came to Makkah, the world was much the same. Killing was a norm. The rich and powerful committed heinous crimes against the poor and weak.** Even the rule of the jungle seemed humane in comparison: animals killed out of hunger, not out of insatiable greed or unrestrained power struggles.

For a civilized world, men must learn to control their desires and tame their hearts. The massive deposits of filth and grime that mar the hearts must be chiseled away to restore it to its original purity. This is not a one-day job but a lifelong process.

NATURE OF MAN

History divulges the true nature of man. Man is not an angel because he is prone to making mistakes, he is also a rational creature, who likes to think and deduce. Some men are fools; others are self-indulgent and selfish. Most think that *seeing is believing*. Others blindly trust every Tom, Dick and Harry.

The verdict is: **man is a complicated creature. He functions on three different levels, the heart, the brain and the soul,** and it is not always easy to make all three see eye to eye. So how does one bring man to submit or change his ways for the good of Allah's creation? We look at history again, and it tells us that **man responds to the potent modulators of reward and punishment.** For some men the threat of punishment works and for others the enticement of rewards.

Allah created angels with reason but no desire. He created animals with desire, but no reasoning. **Man was given both; reason and desires. When man's reason is stronger than his desires, he sheds sins and moves towards purity, becoming more like an angel but when his desires are stronger than his reasoning, he strives for self-satisfaction and becomes more like an animal. For man to succeed in this world, it is necessary for him to achieve a perfect balance between desires and reasoning.**

Man is similar to other creatures of Allah in some ways, but also different in so many more ways. He has the same Creator, but while rest of Allah's creation submits to His greatness without question, man questions. Man repents, makes mistakes and repents again, and that is the only attribute of man that singles him out from everything else Allah created. Remember, Satan made a mistake and what made his mistake unforgivable was his insolence; while Adam, a man was pardoned because he repented with a pure heart.

UNCONTROLLED DESIRES: THE ROOT CAUSE OF ALL EVIL

Allah, the All Knowing, created man to see if he would acknowledge His Lordship using reason, and struggle against his very nature in order to stay true to his Lord and Master. **Angels, the creatures of reason, feared that men would fail to control their desires and cause bloodshed and destruction on earth.**

The fear expressed by the angels was justified. Man, essentially, is a keeper of insatiable desires, and desires have the power to sway the strongest of men. **Once a slave to desires, man resorts to cheating, lying, and unethical and immoral ways to achieve satisfaction.**

Furthermore, the fulfillment of base desires plants seeds of greed, arrogance and apathy in the heart; the plant bears fruits of hate, jealousy and resentment, which ultimately cause irrevocable damage to the heart.

A pure heart desires the love of Allah and a place in heaven, while a damaged heart desires the world. When man starts listening to the vile demands of his tainted heart, it lines up more and more demands until man is so caught up in them he can't see beyond them. He spends his life running after satisfaction, which remains just out of his reach. While he pushes to achieve one worldly goal after another, he strews the seeds of desire and keeps harvesting the same fruits. The result is more greed, more jealousy, more hatred, more arrogance, more anger and more lust for the world. This vicious cycle continues until it destroys everything in its path.

DESIRES ARE DECEPTIVE...

Desires when connected to man and the world, are deceptive. On the surface, it might look like man is trying to please Allah by doing good deeds, but if his heart carries the seeds of ego, arrogance and pride or if he feels superior to the rest of humanity because of a few good deeds, then he is similar to Iblis. He, too, was one of the angels, until his pride turned him first into Iblis—he who is despaired, and later to *Shaytan,* the Deceiver.

Once a believer decides to live for Allah, his ego takes a backseat, but the struggle does not end there. *Shaytan* comes after him with the biggest force, not wearing horns, but dressed as his heart's most intense desire. That is why it is crucial for a true believer to stay vigilant throughout his stay.

...BUT INTRINSIC DESIRES ARE NOT ALL BAD

Desires seem to be the root cause of all vices. However, everything that comes from Allah is good.

When a baby is born, it desires food; as it grows older the desires multiply and diversify that is when parents start controlling desires they deem superfluous. If the baby is allowed to grow unchecked along with his desires, very soon the child will become a man with the desire to own the world. Such a man would not hesitate to destroy any opposition that comes in his path. He would harbor the belief that deriving satisfaction from the world is his right, so if he wants the world, it should be his. The aftermath of such uncontrolled desires is chaos.

Allah would reward those who control their desires for His sake. Blind pursuit of one's own satisfaction leads to utter pandemonium in the world, and whatsmore it blackens the heart. When man has been distinguished as the best of Allah's creation, then is he not obliged to prove himself worthy of such an honor?

It is true that desires have the potential to lead man astray, but they weren't bestowed on men as punishment. Desires and strive are yin and yang: Two halves that complete each other to support life. On the surface, they may seem like stimuli for vices, but they achieve a much bigger objective.

DESIRES SERVE A BIGGER PURPOSE

Allah is Kind, Merciful and especially Merciful. He appointed man his viceroy and conferred on him the highest status, plus the potential to conquer the world. A good example are the Muslim caliphs, who despite being raised in underdeveloped regions with very little education, ended up conquering half the world. They ruled not just the largest empire the world had seen, but simultaneously controlled some of the most important centers of civilization, all due to their desire to excel.

To be able to fulfill the duties of a viceroy, it is essential for man to have the desire to serve Allah, because without the driving force of desire, nothing is achievable. Moreover, man does not just need desire for reaching the highest goals, he needs it to hold his position once he's at the top.

Since, Allah knows who among mankind would use their physical and mental capabilities to excel, He bestows power and sustenance accordingly. Nevertheless, Allah requires His viceroys to control their desires and not lose themselves in the ritz and glitz of the world.

Man, as viceroy of the Lord, must understand that blessings are to be shared with the less fortunate, and that **Islam puts more stress on serving than on being served**. For a just and a peaceful world, desires and their derivatives must be kept under check. When Muslims embraced these dictates of Allah, they became masters but when they started seeking self-gratification, they lost their status and became slaves.

DESIRES ARE A PREREQUISITE FOR GOOD AND BAD

The creation of desire was a necessity, it was to be a stimulus for man's progress, and man's very survival depended upon it. However, "Did desire have to be a prerequisite for evil?" questions man. Why did God have to create evil? Why did God create Satan? Wasn't He aware of what he would do?

The answer is simple: Allah is good, and everything that comes from Him is good and just. Allah also knows ahead of time. Satan was not created for evil, but for the repentance that Adam and Eve did.

Adam and Eve recognized the wrong in what they did and were sorry for it. Not just that, they promised to change their ways. So what appeared to be an act of shame and disdain, on the part of Adam and Even was, in hindsight, a crucial lesson taught to them and the rest of mankind about Iblis.

The sins of Adam and Eve were washed away because of their repentance. Iblis was doomed, however–which, again, is a reminder to the sons and daughters of Adam about the consequences of stubborn defiance to Allah.

Evil is the product of unbridled desires. These erupt from impure hearts and are fueled by greed for more and more. **The very wish to fill our lives to the brim with everything that we desire puts a curse on our hearts, and the world becomes a place of eternal toil, where satisfaction is just within our reach but unfortunately never ever, completely, and solely ours.**

Misusing the powers bestowed on us by Allah might earn us temporary relief, short-lived happiness and success in this world, but such actions invoke the wrath of Allah. Sooner or later, the evil behind the actions catches up, and the bubble pops.

DESIRES ARE PART OF THE TEST

It is a well proven fact that even if the body is healthy, the mind alive and the stomach full, the entire world of man can crash because of an empty heart.

The world was created by Allah to teach and test man. While the messages and messengers from Allah were sent to prepare man for his test, desires were sent to test him. Therefore, it is not surprising that **the messengers tried to teach man to: gain control over their desires, get rid of greed, hatred and all vices, purify their hearts, share fortunes with the less fortunate, promote, economic and social equality and live in harmony with love, peace and justice in the world.**

Sadly, instead of learning these lessons and readily incorporating them into their lives, men mocked, humiliated, tortured and killed most prophets who came bearing these messages.

OF HEART AND BRAIN
WHAT MAKES PEOPLE OBEDIENT OR DISOBEDIENT TO GOD?

The human body is a miracle of creation. All its components work around the clock, and the mind is no exception. Its main function is to process the information it receives, analyze it, take a decision and delegate commands to the rest of the body. Interestingly, this entire process takes an unbelievably short time, since the brain takes an immediate decision. However, there are times when we take hours, months and even years to complete an action. This happens because the mind does not consider the action critical or urgent, and therefore refrains from commanding the body to execute it.

In such cases when the mind receives instructions to do something by internal desire or external request, regardless of it being ethical or unethical, religious or nonreligious, **the brain assesses the value of the action with regard to the individual. The calculative mind takes a decision to execute, depending entirely on the possible reward or positive outcome of the action.** If the action appears to be profitable, then the brain is eager to complete it successfully but if not, then the command is ignored altogether. When the brain fails to convince itself of the profitability of the action but still sends out orders for its execution, then the action is performed half-heartedly, and that, too, only when the body's comfort is not compromised.

Secular actions and religious actions are evaluated differently by the brain. If the heart is pure, religious actions are performed immediately by the brain, without excuses or delay, but if the heart is not entirely submissive to the Lord, then the possible benefits of the action are weighed by the brain. Ultimately, all the secular actions that appear profitable are performed without delay.

Consequently, whenever we hear a commandment of Allah in the Quran or through the teachings of the Prophet Mohammed (PBUH) our mind instantly decides whether to perform the action or not. This decision is based on an individual's value system. The action to be performed is pelted against the following:

- the degree of *iman*, the intensity with which the belief is practiced by the individual
- limits of his comfort zone; and
- possible interference with his other, worldly desires.

A PURE HEART IS NECESSARY FOR DIVINE KNOWLEDGE

Our Lord, and send among them a Messenger from themselves who will recite to them your verses and teach them the book of wisdom and purify them. Indeed, you are the Exalted in Might, the Wise. (The Quran, 2:129)

We have sent among you a Messenger from yourselves reciting to you Our verses and purifying you and teaching you the Book and wisdom and teaching you that which you did not know. (The Quran, 2:151)

The above lines are keys to understanding the core message of the Quran. These are also the gist of the teachings of Prophet Mohammed (PBUH), and weapons against the Devil and all tribulations present in the world today.

These reveal that Messengers were essentially sent to purify men from vices, to teach them wisdom and do away with their ignorance. Allah wanted His creation purified and cleansed from sins while they lived on earth; perhaps because a heart infected with vices and afflicted with sinful desires can't recognize or retain divine love or knowledge.

Humans are born pure and innocent. **Since man is born with goodness, all the good deeds man does are a part of his inborn nature. The test of man is to retain that goodness and strive to protect it from the Devil and the sinful world. The mercy which Allah would bestow on His creatures on the Day of Judgment would ultimately depend upon the magnitude of these efforts.**

Our Prophet Mohammed (PBUH) had the purest of hearts. He retained his inborn piety; therefore, his heart was receptive to divine knowledge. His mission was to purify the hearts of his followers, and he practiced the same, even before he received the first revelation.

Going back to the first verse, which speaks of Abraham (PBUH) praying to his Lord and Master. While laying the bricks of the Kaaba with his son Ismail (PBUH), Abraham (PBUH) asks for the following gifts in this order:

- a. A messenger from among his clan,
- b. Who would recite the word of Allah,
- c. Who would teach his people wisdom from the book, and
- d. Who would purify them.

Abraham (PBUH) prayed for guidance and Allah, the Merciful granted him his wishes, but looking at the second verse, we realize that Allah, the All Knowing, changed the order of the gifts. In the preceding line from the Holy Quran, 2:150, Allah, the Benevolent, asks the believers not to fear their prosecutors, but to fear Him alone, because only then will Allah complete his favor upon man and bless them with true and eternal guidance. Then, Allah reminds us how He sent:

- a. A Messenger from among Abraham's clan–Mohammed (PBUH);
- b. Who recited the word of Allah;
- c. Purified man;
- d. Taught the book, and wisdom, and that of which man was ignorant.

Allah speaks of purification before He allows any understanding, wisdom and insight to seep inside the followers of Mohammed (PBUH). Abraham (PBUH) asked for all that he thought would benefit his people. Allah, the Merciful, granted him not just his wishes, but also the scheme for achieving guidance. **The verse clearly indicates that purification of the heart must come first, before light can take the place of darkness.**

Every letter of the Quran has a message for the seeker of true knowledge. However, the incredible continuity and wisdom in the synchronization of each word and sentence is not evident to everyone. Only a true believer, who is driven to understand the words of his Master can grasp some of the underlying wisdom behind the divine words.

A person who is willing to dive into the depths of the unsullied waters of the Quran with a pure heart, has a better chance of succeeding in finding answers to questions that baffle mankind, as opposed to someone who simply prays and waits for divine guidance, without endeavoring to seek or purify his heart.

Allah, by changing the sequence of Abraham's *dua*, while answering it, not only affirms His status as *Al Alim*, the All Knowing, but also as *Al Lateef*, the Most Affectionate and Knower of Subtleties. Allah puts "purify" before "teach," because He knows that no lesson can be learned by the bearer of an impure heart. **A heart full of vices and devilish desires, a heart ruled by the *nafs*, would never submit.**

Teaching wisdom and knowledge of the Quran to owners of such hearts would be a worthless exercise, because nothing would penetrate a blackened heart. To be able to derive wisdom, it is necessary to have the desire to seek truth, and that is only possible if the heart is alive with love for Allah.

Through love, comes familiarity. Through familiarity, comes realization. Through understanding and realization, come the etiquettes of love. **It is love that humbles man before the Lord. It is understanding that turns man submissive. Together, love and realization nurture *iman*, the practice of one's faith.**

A heart that is not receptive to the word of Allah needs to be cleansed. **An impure heart weighed down with desires will never be obedient to Allah.** Today, Quran is being studied by a majority of Muslims, who hardly understand the message behind the words. And those who do understand the message are impervious to it, because their hearts are corroded, hard and blinded by layers of worldly desires.

When man refuses to acknowledge the word of Allah, He seals their hearts, and no matter what the scholars and prayer leaders, or imams, teach, the light of *iman* doesn't penetrate such hearts.

The world acknowledges truth; even evil acknowledges good. If it did not, good would lose its own character. The character of the Prophet Mohammed (PBUH) made him shine, even before he received the seal of prophethood. He was known and acknowledged as *Al Sadiq* and *Al Amin*, the truthful and the trustworthy, by the people of Makkah. Today, although there are more Muslims in every corner of the world than ever before, they are not recognized by such traits.

We all understand that Islam is a way of life, but have failed to adopt it. It is no wonder that we haven't achieved any substantial results, despite the efforts of imams and scholars over the past several centuries. We know more about Islam than some previous generations; we are debunking myths, researching and writing papers on the life our Prophet (PBUH), but we are not celebrated, known or even recognized for the traits that are the hallmarks of Islam. We have failed Islam, and we have failed our Prophet (PBUH).

The evident dearth of dignity in Muslims is a cause of shame; the deplorable condition of the *ummah*, where one brother is out to get another, where the enemy is not just outside the bond of Islam, but within, discredits us as Muslims. Moreover, the utter lack of love, compassion, tolerance, trust, modesty, respect, morality, courage, fear of Allah and accountability is a cause for alarm. We are losing our identity as Muslims, because we are allowing our hearts to turn impure.

Today, Muslims are suffering in Tunisia, Lebanon, Egypt, Bosnia, Chechnya, Burma, Syria, Iran, Iraq, Palestine, Afghanistan, Pakistan, India, Kashmir, Bangladesh, China, Kenya, Mali, Sudan, Somalia and Nigeria. Some of us raise voices; some raise banners; some reach out to help; and some question Allah. Why are Muslims all over the world enduring such a ghastly fate? Weren't we Muslims promised honor in this world and hereafter?

Ask yourself why our scholars and those who give our sermons are failing to answer this question? Are they afraid to investigate its causes, or are they indifferent to the plight of the Muslims?

CAUSES OF THE MUSLIM DOWNFALL

It is reported that Ibrahim ibn Adham, a ninth century Sufi of Khorasan, was once passing through the market of Basrah when people gathered around him and asked:

"Oh Abu Ishaq [Ibrahim ibn Adham], Allah, the Exalted, says in His book, 'Call on me. I will answer your prayers.' We have been calling on him for a long time, but He does not answer our prayers."

Ibrahim replied, *"O people of Basrah, your hearts have died in respect to ten things:*

1. *You know Allah, but you do not give Him His rights;*
2. *You have read Allah's book, but you do not act by it;*
3. *You claim to love Allah's Messenger, yet you abandon his Sunnah;*
4. *You claim to be enemies to Shaytan, but you conform to his ways;*
5. *You say you love Paradise, yet you do not work for it;*
6. *You say you fear the Fire, yet you put yourself close to it by sinning;*
7. *You say death is true, but you do not prepare for it;*
8. *You busy yourselves with the faults of others and disregard your own;*
9. *You consume the favors of your Lord, but are not grateful for them; and*
10. *You bury your dead, but take no lesson from them."*

Islam was the reason behind the glory of the Arabs, and it was their losing touch with its basic message that caused their downfall. The modern Muslims are no different. They have forgotten the core message of Islam and are engaged in blind imitation of hackneyed customs and conventions. **Consequently, their ritualistic worship, lacking in moral fiber and devotion, fails to cleanse their heart.**

One must understand that rituals were made to strengthen man's conviction and to help him stay on the right path. Islamic rituals like *salah, saum, zakat,* and *hajj* all focus on cleansing the heart and keeping it pure. However, if one fails to truly connect to Allah, while performing these rituals, then cleansing of the heart is not possible.

A true and pure heart neither hates nor harms; neither has it any cause for alarm nor fear. In the Holy Quran, Allah says:

Behold! Verily on the friends of God there is no fear, nor shall they grieve. (The Quran, 10:62)

A sincere Muslim is a practicing Muslim. He not only offers *salah,* **but is conscious of Allah at all times.** This might sound implausible to those who haven't found their connection yet, but that is how it normally is. Those who have been in love might find it easier to understand what it's like to be connected to someone at all times, despite the lack of physical presence. When connections are genuine, they live forever—overcoming time, situation and distance. They can be ignored, walked away from or buried, but never cut off completely. Similarly, when a pure heart connects with Allah, it stays connected 24/7 and for a lifetime.

PURE HEARTS EARN ALLAH'S FAVOR

For believers who constantly guard themselves against sin and desires of the *nafs,* **Allah sends great news.**

It says in the Quran:

Those who believe and (constantly) guard against evil;
For them are glad tidings,
In the life of the present
And in the Hereafter;
No change can there be
In the words of God.
This is indeed

The supreme felicity.
(The Quran, 10:63-64)

Accepting Islam is not as simple as reciting the *shahadah*; that is just the doorway to it. Once a person enters the door of Islam, he must decide to live the rest of his life according to the dictates of Allah.

Islam means to strive for perfection with a true and sincere heart and ultimately, it is our strive that is measured and not the distance covered. Although, we are different from one another, living in different environments with different possessions, we each have the same heart, holding the same potential. It is up to us to protect its purity and to strive for success.

When the Quraish of Makkah offered Prophet Mohammed (PBUH) the desires of the common man: promising him power, women, wealth and kingship, if only he would stop preaching morality, the Oneness of God and inviting people to the fold of Islam. The Prophet replied:

Allah the Almighty has sent me as His Messenger to you. I have to convey His Message. In case you accept my teachings, you will be crowned with success in both the worlds; if you reject them, I shall be waiting for the Decision of Allah the Almighty. (Page 112, The History of Islam, Volume One, by Akbar Shah Najeebabadi and Revised by Safi-ur-Rahman Mubarakpuri)

Although Allah assured the believers of success in both worlds, Muslims today are victims of malicious propaganda; calculated, goal-oriented smear campaigns; humiliation; degradation; hate and war crimes worldwide.

Instead of looking outside for causes, the shortest way to an answer is looking inside you own heart. **Are we really a true believers?** It's not an easy question. Look at your life, your job, your relationship, and someone you answer to—your boss perhaps. How much are you putting inside all these relationships? Are you working as hard for your connection with Allah? Isn't He your real boss? Do you take out time to read the memo He has sent to you? Do you make efforts to deliver on the promises and deadlines that He has assigned to you? Or have you conveniently forgotten about Him?

You are showing up for work, but not working; completing tasks, but not getting results. This is the kind of employees most of us are when it comes to Islam, when it comes to Allah. In our worldly lives, however, we know very well that if we carry the same attitude to work and put up a similar performance, we wouldn't last three days.

PURITY OF HEART INVITES *IMAN*

The word of Allah, the promise of His Prophet (PBUH), stand true, for those who guard their purity and *iman*.

In Holy Quran, 2:151, Allah uses the word "purify" after "recite Our Revelations to you." What Allah is saying is that purification of the heart is not a condition for reciting the Quran, the recitation is an outward form of worship. Those who read the words of Allah will need to purify themselves before they can gain any wisdom or benefits from the Quran.

The same verse also reveals that Mohammed (PBUH) was sent to earth to deliver the message of Allah and to teach the Quran, and its wisdom. He (PBUH) was blessed with the best of character. He (PBUH) could cleanse the hearts of the believers, teach them to tame their desires, control their *nafs*, and build dignified characters.

A glass that is already filled with water loses its capacity to hold more, unless it is emptied and refilled again. Just as nothing can be poured into a glass full of water, no virtues can be poured into a heart that is full of vices. One has to let one thing go, in order to let the other in. This process of cleansing the *nafs,* or getting rid of vices one after another, not just makes room for purity, *taqwa* and *iman* inside the heart; it welcomes these holy attributes.

For a person who is struggling with *iman*, who tries to please Allah but fails to change his ways out of habit, ignorance, indolence or love for the world, *iman* is but a fleeting thing.

It is narrated under the authority of Abu Huraira that Prophet Mohammed (PBUH) said:

Initiate good deeds, as there will be ordeals like the blackness of night approaching: where a man is a believer in the morning and an infidel at night, and where a man is a believer at night and becomes an infidel in the morning, disclaiming his religion with a priceless matter of dunya. (Sahih Muslim)

LOVE ENTERS WHEN HATE LEAVES THE HEART

The heart can't be purified unless one learns to love, understand and forgive. One must realize that love can only enter the heart if hate is kicked out. **If a person is hoping to nurture qualities of compassion, kindness, generosity and humbleness, the first step is to eliminate hate, discontent, envy, resentment, grudges, ego and hurt.** One has to let go and forgive, for the sake of Allah, to make one's heart lighter and lighter until it can soar way above the worldly tribulations, and bask in the glory of the Lord. Once the heart feels love for its Creator, it readily incorporates goodness, and thinks twice before erring.

Love is a powerful tool. A heart pulsating with love has a tremendous capacity for:

- **Sacrifice.** Recall the sacrifice of Abraham (PBUH) and the miracle of Mariam (PBUH)
- **Tolerance.** Recall the tolerance of Mohammed (PBUH) after the incident of Taif
- **Fairness.** Recall the fairness of Nuh (PBUH) when he left behind his wife and son
- **Justice.** Recall the justice of Omar Ibn al Khattab.

These were some mortals who stood out because of their love for

Allah, which manifested in their actions. The stories of Prophets tell us no man can be just and unjust, kind and cruel, tolerant and intolerant, selfless and selfish at the same time. Similarly, a heart that belongs to Allah cannot be seduced by the attractions of the world.

RECOGNIZING THREATS TO THE HEART

Sins, if not slammed, can easily and rapidly become a part of our personalities and characters. Once they stick, the immoral acts turn from mere infections into life threatening diseases that are almost impossible to cure. An enormous effort and Allah's mercy is needed to cure the incurable.

Some people are led to believe that *salah*, *saum* and *hajj* wash away sins. This statement holds true, but if a person takes time out for *salah* so he can go back to sinning, or fasts so he can wash away his previous sins and start fresh without actually changing his corrupt ways, or performs *hajj* with similar intentions, he is just looking for temporary solutions to his recurring problem. Instead of cleansing his heart and changing his ways for the better, he is simply deluding himself into thinking that everything is well and that he is a good Muslim.

If a heart listens to the pleas of the Devil, the *nafs* and the world, then it is doomed. A believer must declare *jihad* against the *nafs* and the Devil in order to purify his heart. It is also crucial to get rid of all vices before he returns to Allah.

The devil does not come wearing a nametag; he comes in the form of our desires. He comes dressed as wealth, prestige and love for the world. Sometimes, he dresses up as a man's rationale. He is clever and knows more than man, so he uses all his vile tricks to deter a believing man from his true goals. The devil seeps into the hearts like smoke seeps into homes, even after the windows and doors have been shut. You seldom see the smoke, but you can always smell it. Unfortunately, you can't see or smell the Devil.

Bit by bit, slowly and steadily, the Devil overcomes one resistance after another. He lulls, and he coaxes. Then he waits. He never gives up, until finally a wall crumbles in a moment of weakness, and he wins his first round. The next round is tougher. If man doesn't recognize or lament his sin, the Devil wins again. The third is the toughest round for the Devil and the easiest for man. The Devil has to wait and to silently implore man not to repent before Allah. Man simply has to bow his head and beg Allah for mercy. If man wins, he is blessed. If he loses, the Devil carves a little niche for himself inside the heart. Next, the Devil begins to convert man. He transfers his prized qualities into man, until one day, he loses his dignity and the favor of Allah.

The Devil is man's biggest threat and his hatred for man can be witnessed in his relentless scheming against him. When man proves himself unworthy of his God-given status, the Devil dances in joy as he drives his point home. He told Allah that man wasn't worthy of the honor He bestowed on him, and these wins satisfy his pride more than anything else.

Man proves himself a fickle creature when he allows the Devil to lead him a merry dance. When we defy Allah and violate His laws, we are actually rebelling against the Almighty, the Creator of the Universe. This bravado emerges from a false sense of self: from pride and the audacity which the Devil plants inside us.

LACK OF FEAR HARDENS THE HEART

Can any man willingly face the wrath of a pride of lions? Can any man living in America, break the laws of the country and not fear prosecution? Can any man blindly walk into the Grand Canyon? These are not absurdities, we commit these stunts every day.

Allah is so much Greater, so much more powerful and His punishment is so much more worthy of being feared. This *khawf* should cause a rapid movement of the heart which results from a fear of punishment. We should also have *khashiya*, a profound humility before Allah, and *rahba*, the instinct that warns us in the presence of danger. But, alas, man has gone blind and his heart has hardened.

Only a hardened and blind heart refuses to obey the Creator. A

man who does not experience *wajal*, trembling of the heart upon remembering the power and punishment of Allah; or *haybah*, awe and fear that comes from witnessing the Supreme power; is far, far, far from Allah. The minimum that a believer must hold is *khawf* for Allah, and that would be enough to stop him from polluting his heart by lusting after the world and committing immoral and unethical social crimes.

IMPURE HEARTS AND EMPTY SUPPLICATIONS

A man who submits to the Devil, loses his innocence and purity. The Devil speaks through his tongue, and he finds excuses and reasons to justify his actions. He sees no wrong and sadly, hears no truth. Allah then closes his heart, and the man becomes deaf, dumb and blind to the decrees of Islam.

Allah is Well Aware that falling into the traps set by the Devil will affect our degree of *iman* and would subsequently affect our actions, to the point where they will become mere acts devoid of belief. When this happens, all good deeds lose their significance, since they are not performed for earning the pleasure of Allah, but for self-glorification.

Displays of piety and exhibitions of *iman* remind one of the hypocrites of Medina who, when in the company of true believers, would publicize their *iman*, but when in the company of non-believers would automatically change sides. The times may have changed, but the people have not. Today, Muslims might not be sitting with the disbelievers and plotting against Islam but somehow they are just the same. Most have planted their feet in two boats, each going the opposite way.

Confusion arises when man's heart is not sure about what he wants. When there are unresolved conflicts–such as when man prays five times a day, yet does not carry his *iman* with him all the time–the heart clouds over.

LOSING THE HEART TO THE DEVIL

Deeds which are performed without the heart mean nothing to Allah. **When a man loses his heart to the Devil he loses the weight of his good deeds.**

Once the Devil takes over a man's heart, the man not only commits sins but fails to recognize them as such. In other words, the bad deeds do not look bad. Furthermore, the perpetrator defends his sinful acts vehemently. Occasionally, when he concedes to the sin, he believes that Allah would forgive him because He is Compassionate, Merciful and Forgiving.

However, these are mere delusions to get rid of guilt. No doubt, **Allah is Merciful, but He is also Just. He would never allow men to make a mockery of His verses, or to take His words lightly.**

Most Muslims do not want to spend the time or energy figuring out the secret of creation, unless, of course, they have been jolted awake by a tragedy or an unexpected turn of events, which left them feeling utterly helpless. Most refuse to pick up the Book of Allah for the simple reason of understanding His message. The result is *salah* devoid of meaning, *dua* empty of emotion, and a life which revolves around the self, not the Giver.

Every day, Muslims stand in front of their Lord five times and repeat the following words;

In the name of Allah, the Entirely Merciful, the Especially Merciful
All praise is due to Allah, Lord of the worlds,
The Entirely Merciful, the Especially Merciful,
Sovereign of the Day of Recompense.
It is You we worship and You we ask for help.
(The Quran, 1:1-6)

They supplicate in front of Allah, telling Him that they believe in recompense, in the Day of Judgment, in His Benevolence and in

His Greatness. They declare Him their only Savior and Helper, but when they finish with *salah*, they have the audacity to live their lives according to their own whims and wishes. They put themselves before their own Master. What kinds of servants are these?

They beg Allah to guide them towards the path of the righteous and to steer them away from the path of the doomed. They ask Allah not to make them among those who flare His wrath, yet the minute they roll up the prayer mat, they indulge in everything that would ignite it.

Then, a couple of hours later, they return to their Master, make the same declaration of faith, and ask for the same things again. Five minutes later, they make a mockery of their words all over again.

Do they even realize what they are doing? They are provoking Allah's wrath and ridiculing themselves. It is no wonder that Allah asks again and again in the Quran:

Do they not think? (The Quran, 30:8)

And

Will they not then consider the Quran? Or are there locks on their hearts? (The Quran, 47:24)

What kind of a heart would do what we do with our Lord? Only a cruel and a darkened heart and a heart that fails to see.

Allah calls such men the worst in His Sight:

Truly, the worst of creatures, in the sight of Allah, are the deaf, the dumb, those who do not use their reason/think. (The Quran, 8:22)

ARROGANT IGNORANCE AND BLIND OPTIMISM

A majority of us believe and desperately hope that Allah will overlook our every fault and reward us for our hypocrisy. We go on hating His creatures on the basis of race, religion, economy, education, color, beliefs and anything that doesn't agree with us, and after all that we expect Allah to shower us with love.

We are all on a fool's errand, attempting something that has a zero chance of success, while believing that God will indulge our idiosyncrasies, when we have done absolutely nothing to deserve His mercy.

Allah is marvelous, capable of anything and everything, but if Allah is great in His mercy, He is also great in His justice and great in His wrath. Why do we simply ignore these attributes of Allah? **Maybe because we are arrogant in our ignorance and blind in our optimism, and if we change, our carefully constructed world would collapse on our heads.**

DISPARITY BETWEEN BELIEF AND PERFORMANCE

Our religious understanding and our religious performance simply do not complement each other. Although Islamic teachers and scholars have existed in all ages after the time of the Prophet Mohammed (PBUH), the spirit of Islam has been dying little by little. The remainder left today is not enough to pull together the *ummah*. Nor is it strong enough to push back the enemies who are daily committing atrocities against Islam and the believers.

Islam had a humble beginning with a handful of followers whose strength of belief and *iman* escalated their numbers into the thousands within a short time. Today, we are millions, but our *Iman* and our belief in Allah is nothing compared to the *iman* of the companions of the Prophet (PBUH). Their *iman* led them to conquer and rule the world with dignity. Our *iman* hasn't the strength to liberate us from the clutches of our *nafs*, let alone conquer the world.

Today, so called religious leaders, scholars and teachers have

written truckloads of books on their philosophies of religion, delivered lectures and conducted talks, blatantly conclude that God will forgive all sins if man simply:

- Accepts the founder of each religion as a savior;
- Attends religious congregations in synagogues, churches, temples, mosques, etc.; and
- Performs rituals.

These are flagrant lies, which should be obvious to the believers who understand the Quran. Such scholars must realize that they would be answerable to Allah for their misguided and erroneous ways.

In the following verse, Allah talks of people who speak half-truths and divulge only that which benefits them. For people who keep truth from the believers for even small worldly gains, Allah will dole out harsh punishments.

Surely, those who conceal what Allah has sent down of the book (the Quran), and purchase therewith a small gain (worldly things), they do not eat into their bellies but fire. Allah will neither speak to them on the day of Resurrection, nor will He purify them, and for them will be a painful punishment. (The Quran, 2:174)

PURIFICATION IN THE WORLD AND HEREAFTER

Diving a little deeper into the Quran, in 2:125 Allah asks Abraham (PBUH) and his son to purify the Kaaba, the house of Allah, for those who walk around it, for those who stay in it and for those who bow down and pray there. Here Allah uses the word "purification" for cleaning the Kaaba from all sinful acts.

The heart can be looked upon as the house of Allah, as well; because, it is the heart that holds love for Allah. One must remember that **love for Allah can only stay alive in a person's heart if it is pure and free from vices. Purification of the heart means freeing the heart from lower desires and refraining from sinful acts.**

In 2:174 of the Quran, Allah says that He would not purify sinners who hide the words of Allah or mold them to suit their own purposes. **This indirectly tells us that Allah would be purifying people on the Day of Judgment. It is safe to assume that He would purify those with whom He is pleased, which again implies that man would need to be purified before entering heaven.**

So Allah is asking man to purify his heart while he resides on earth, but He understands that man cannot be completely pure and free from sin, unless He, Himself, does the purification. Therefore, on the Day of Resurrection, Allah will purify men by washing away all their sins, but one must not forget that such mercy will only be bestowed on those who guard their hearts in this world and keep them pure for the love of Allah.

A sin remains a sin no matter how much one rationalizes it. Some of us commit them intentionally; others unintentionally out of ignorance, carelessness, and uncontrolled desires. If a man steals to feed his family, then one might justify his actions, but let Allah be the final Judge, since He knows best. Similarly, if a man commits a sin out of sheer stupidity, thinking Allah is forgiving, and thus would forgive his transgressions, too; or that since he is a follower of the Prophet Mohammed (PBUH), he can commit any sin; then he is provoking Allah's wrath upon himself.

Man was made better than other creatures of Allah, but he is not perfect. He is attracted to a life of ease and comfort, because Allah put this in his makeup. When man journeys through this world, he accumulates sins and good deeds, based on how he handles his attraction to this world. When believers reach the court of Allah, none is perfect, and none is untouched by sin. Therefore, Allah purifies his true believers, showering them with His mercy so that they may enter Paradise.

As long as a believer keeps struggling to protect his *iman* and guard his virtue, his sins will not weigh heavy. The minute he lets down his guard, his desires and attraction to the world will overpower him and push him towards committing sins.

Life was not meant to be easy; Allah promised that man would be tested on earth. Sometimes we lose our patience and hope during these trials and tribulations. When this happens, we end up failing the tests and blackening our hearts. Exercising patience and keeping faith in Allah are two ways to pass through tests. Remember, man will commit sins again and again, knowingly and unknowingly, but we will be judged by our intentions and by our efforts to keep our hearts pure.

A person with a pure heart and pure intention can falter and slip, but he always repents and returns to Allah, the Merciful, and that is all that Allah asks: *sincere effort made by a pure heart and repentance that comes from a pure heart.* The deciding factor is always the heart and its purity.

In the Quran, Allah tells us that Mohammed (PBUH) was sent to purify us. Plus, He says purification is a must before entering into Paradise. The stress on purification, from time to time and in different verses in the Quran, is a recurring reminder to gain an understanding of what "purification of the self" really means. This understanding can only come through understanding Allah's Book and the teachings of His Messengers, and by realizing that our health, happiness and success in this world and the hereafter depend upon our efforts to understand and incorporate these into our lives.

Prophet Mohammed (PBUH) said that only those believers will be successful, who turn to Allah with pure hearts. **He described the attributes of a pure heart in the following words:**

He has been successful:

- *Whose heart Allah has made sincere towards faith,*
- *Whose heart He has made free from unbelief,*
- *His tongue truthful,*
- *His soul calm,*
- *His nature straight,*

- *Whose ears He has made attentive and*
- *Eyes, observant."*

The ear is a funnel and the eye is a repository for what the heart learns. He is successful whose heart is made retentive. (Tirmidhi)

PURIFICATION IS ESSENTIAL FOR *IMAN*

Understanding purification of the heart is critical for acquiring *iman*. Consider purity a pillar on which rests your *iman*. **Without a pure heart, iman cannot be acquired, realized or completed.**

In Holy Quran, 49:14, Allah corrects the Bedouins when they say, "We believe," saying:

You have not (yet) believed. But say instead, 'we have submitted' for faith has not yet entered your hearts. (The Quran, 49:14)

Iman is the faith that emerges through one's actions, yet it is not synonymous to submission. Submission has its rewards, but the development of *iman* is what Allah demands from the followers of Islam. In the next verse Allah explains who a true believer is;

The believers are the only ones who have believed in Allah and His Messenger, and then doubt not, but strive with their properties and their lives in the cause of Allah. It is those who are the truthful. (The Quran, 49:15)

A true believer loves Allah, and love for Allah can only enter the heart if it is free from vices. It is love for the Lord that cultivates *iman* and increases knowledge. The more a believer learns and understands, the more he fears Allah, and the more he commits himself to Him.

For a true believer, part of worship is to constrain the *nafs* and steer clear of sins. He knows that his good deeds won't count, unless he stops himself from committing sins. He endeavors to purify himself, every day and every moment of his life. He tries to protect his *iman*, and to nurture it by doing deeds that please Allah.

CHARACTER REFLECTS THE STATE OF THE HEART

Our religious performance and our characters together can be evaluated to gauge the various degrees of *iman*. *Iman*, along with Allah's mercy, will be the breaking point on the Day of Judgment. Whether Allah would favor us or not will depend upon whether we favored Him or not, not just by performing religious rites and services but also striving within our hearts, characters and day to day business.

If we behave like true believers and develop characters which are in sync with our religious practices, then the love and respect for Allah and His Prophets would shine through. However, if we behave like true believers, perform the religious obligations of *salah, zakat, saum* and *hajj* **but for some reason, our characters do not reflect our love and fear of Allah, then it means that our belief has not changed the condition of our hearts. We are not believers then, but pretenders.**

A character that reflects the Devil's attributes, portrays the person literally as the Devil's advocate. If one harbors hatred in his heart, he invites friction, conflict, jealousy, envy, false pride, ego, arrogance, cruelty and biases into his life, his family, friends, local community and eventually, the *ummah*.

A heart that begets such evils can never gain the approval of Allah. Allah has given man choice, but Allah has also given him a heart, a brain, guidance, and the Book. With so much help and support, if man still refuses to see the truth and runs after temporary delights, while forsaking his eternity; Allah is not to blame.

We may claim that we love Allah, and we may proclaim that we have *iman,* but as long as we create *fitna* among Allah's creation by falling into sin and hypocrisy; confusing truth with falsehood and misguidance; creating differences among people and causing lack of agreement; persecuting others; blocking and turning people away from truth–and these without thinking twice and without changing our ways for the better, then we have no right to stake a claim on His mercy.

Hate is intense dislike but it does not stop there. It evokes anger, hostility and animosity. These feelings change the dynamics of human beings, making them unhappy, displeased and discontent. Furthermore, these feelings reflect in their actions. Our dilemma is that we do not understand the enormity of this little sentiment which has the power to sweep away not just our happiness but our *iman* with it. Every single time you are rude to someone, angry at someone and just about to lash out, remind yourself who you are. You are the follower of Mohammed (PBUH), the man who won over his worst enemies with his words, deeds and sentiments. He responded with kindness and generosity and left behind a legacy of unconditional love for his followers.

STAYING PURE IN A WORLD FULL OF FITNA

Man has moments of weakness. It is not always possible to defend oneself against the attacks of Satan. Plus, the world is a place littered with temptations, each one more appealing and tantalizing than the other. How can one stay pure and free of vices in such a world?

No one said it was going to be easy. Having said that, we still have it easier than the companions of the Prophet Mohammed (PBUH). Allah knows the challenging tasks He has set before us and offers more than a just reward for those who succeed, in the form of heaven.

A heart open to vices is a heart open to the devil. Even if a person rids his heart of all vices but leaves one out, like hate, ego or greed, that one vice would hinder his heart's progression towards purity. Furthermore, it would dupe the man into perceiving his big sins as minor and inconsequential, while his small virtuous deeds would seem like hefty and significant contributions to his *iman* and hereafter.

Deliberately allowing a single vice to dwell in the heart is similar to closing all doors to the Devil but leaving a window open for him to climb in. If you are thinking the Devil would miss the window, you are mistaken. **He waits for these little openings, and once he is inside the heart, he takes over the thought process, judgment, and understanding and keeps on conquering little bits of man, until he owns him completely.**

When man loses himself to the Devil, he turns into his crony. Slowly and steadily, Satan hardens the hearts of men, eliminating fear of Allah and replacing it with love for worldly pleasures. He whispers half-truths into the hearts of men, until they can't tell the difference between right and wrong. **He tells them that Allah is Kind, which is true. He says Allah's love for man surpasses the love of seventy mothers, which is also true. He convinces him that man is weak, which is another truth. Then he says that the Prophet will rescue all believers: This is *partially* true! When man falls for this piece of reasoning, then engages in actions that offend Allah and His Messenger, he stumbles and relinquishes control to the Devil.**

The Devil makes man believe that whether he fails or passes the tests of Allah, he is still going to be forgiven, in any case, and would eventually reside in heaven. What he keeps to himself is that those who do not try to mend their ways will get a taste of hell, as well.

We have acquired a cavalier attitude towards everything that should put us on high alert, like the punishment of hellfire, the wrath of Allah, the trials of the grave, avoiding *haram* and *shirk*. On the other hand, we have become obsessed with the material and transient provisions of the world, like our houses, families, wealth, prestige, popularity, technology and appearances.

Prophet Mohammed (PBUH) revealed the source of such thoughtlessness, pointing at the heart:

Indeed, there is a piece of flesh in the body. When that stays right, the whole body stays right; when that goes astray, the whole body goes astray! Listen carefully, that is the qalb (the heart). (Bukhari)

The *qalb* is not just the organ that pumps blood inside the body; it is also the instrument that is blessed with the ability to perceive divine power. It is also the seat of love and hate. Whoever Allah wishes to guide, He opens their hearts to love, *iman* and knowledge.

The straight path is narrow and fraught with difficulties. It is especially easy to deviate from such a path and flounder in the 360-degree space around it. Today, it is not just Muslims who have lost their way, but most of mankind. We have forgotten our values and lost our purity to this world and to Satan. Most of what we were taught has been forgotten. What is left is a mere carcass in the form of tedious and meaningless rituals, which do nothing to purify our hearts and reinforce our beliefs.

Rituals were exercises meant to develop devotion, sincerity, piety, fear of Allah, and love for mankind. They were not meant to be the ultimate requirement but it was the obedience of Allah sought from rituals by men of character, purity and dignity.

Unfortunately, the institutions that were meant to set man straight, ended up derailing him. Our organized Islamic bodies turned into *fitna* that divided the *ummah* in the name of Islam, on the basis of minor differences. Mole hills were turned into mountains by religious scholars, speakers and prayer leaders, and Muslims dispersed like pearls from a broken necklace.

Those who should have set examples, set about name-calling, humiliating and defaming their equals, allowing their own supporters to think it was permissible and acceptable to hold such negative emotions for their Muslim brothers. Instead of propagating love and way of the Prophet Mohammed (PBUH), the so-called preachers of Islam set about preaching their own dogmas, using all their energy to publicize their sub-standard stance of Islam. In doing so, they did more harm than good.

When a person walks into Islam, he walks in completely. He accepts everything, because he is not given options to choose from. It is all or nothing. Either you are in or out. There is no middle ground. Substandard Islam is not Islam at all; it is a watered down version of the original. **What we are following these days is a hodgepodge of our own desires and dictates of our *nafs*. We have only labeled it "Islam."**

The shift from spirituality to rituals, materialism and self-satisfaction has made our hearts bitter, indifferent and selfish, and turned our religion into an accessory to be used for effect.

The way to protect your heart from the *fitna* that engulfs the world today is through constant zikr. The remembrance of Allah lights a tiny flame inside the heart, and its glow has the power to consume all the darkness that resides there.

A heart that decides to keep the fire alive starts the process of purification; it gets rid of vices and submits to the Lord. The struggle does not end there. The heart wages constant *jihad* against the *nafs* and all the devilish desires. This process brings it closer to Allah, His mercy and possible deliverance on the Day of Resurrection.

When the forces of the West conquered Muslim colonies, they imposed their own governments, value systems, laws and way of life on the Muslim populations, slowly marginalizing Islam. Consequently, Muslims deviated from its basic reality.

The mission of the Prophet (PBUH) was:

- To establish the Kingdom of Allah on Earth;
- To deliver the message of one and only one God, who is the owner of whole universe and of Day of Judgment;
- To teach us to cleanse our hearts and declare *Jihad* against the Devil, and to strive to transform our devilish characteristics into angelic characteristics.
- To develop dignity in our characters;
- To establish love, peace and justice within ourselves and in our societies, nationally and internationally;
- To be obedient to Allah and to submit to Him like true slaves.

Today, if we ask a Muslim his mission, his goals would hardly match those of the Prophet (PBUH).

ADOPTING A NEW LIFESTYLE

Cleansing the heart of corruption and immoral habits that have become second nature to it is a huge task. It is next to impossible to rid oneself of the diseases of the heart completely. Purification is not a one-day job. It is a continuous process which has to be adopted for life, with conscious choices made for a new, different and a healthier lifestyle. You cannot clean your heart just once and expect it to stay pure forever.

The heart has the power to comprehend, to reflect and to reason, but it is only a healthy and a pure heart that is capable of understanding. **Here are a few qualities of a true heart:**

- It pushes man towards Allah, and it repents;
- It doesn't grow tired of worshipping or remembering Allah;
- It feels pain when it sins;
- It finds peace and satisfaction in worship;
- It does not waste time;
- It is more concerned with its good deeds being accepted and performed correctly, than with the deed itself;
- It offers *salah* and feels free of worries.

Above all, a pure heart always prays for guidance.

Our Lord, let not our hearts deviate after You have guided us and grant us from Yourself mercy. Indeed, You are the Bestower. (The Quran, 3:8)

QUESTIONS FOR REFLECTION

- What are the three levels on which man functions?

- Why is the man created with both reason and desires?

- How does man behave when his desires are stronger than his reasoning?

- Why did Angels fear that man would be violent?

- When man obeys his desires, what changes take place in his character?

- Does obeying desires change the condition of man's heart?

- What changes take place in the heart when it is connected with the world and how they affect man's character?

- What kind of heart is required to love Allah?

- Would Allah reward those who control their desires for His sake, or reward those who obey their desires?

- What made the rightly guided Caliphs excel despite being raised in underdeveloped regions with no or very little education.

- What made Muslims the masters who achieved success in every field, and what made them lose?

- What did Mohammad (saw) teach us?

- What did Allah ask mankind to do to prove they are the best of His creation?

- Brain assesses the value of the action and takes a decision to execute depending upon_____.

- What is the decision to act according to the Quran and Sunnah pelted against?

- What is Allah telling us in the verses, Quran, 2:129 and 2:151?

- All the good deeds done by man are part of his inborn nature, then what is the test?

- Can a man with an impure heart be obedient to Allah?

- When is it that the light of Iman does not penetrate the hearts?

- What are the causes of Muslims' downfall?

- Can mere ritualistic worship that lacks moral fiber cleanse man's heart?

- What great news does Allah send in Quran, 10:63-64?

- When we are on the spiritual journey, would our striving have weight or the distance we cover?

- Are we true believers? What makes us true believers?

- What do we have to do to nurture qualities of compassion, kindness, generosity, and humbleness?

- Can a hardened and blind heart obey the Creator? What makes our hearts hardened and blind?

- When does Allah close a man's heart, so that he becomes deaf, dumb and blind?

- What happens to man when Devil overpowers his heart?

- We recite surah Fateha in every salah, and then we have the audacity to live our lives according to our own whims and wishes, is it not hypocrisy? Are we not provoking Allah?

- What make us arrogant, ignorant and blind optimist?

- Do our religious understanding and our religious performance complement each other?

- A handful of followers of Islam conquered and ruled the world with dignity, but today, despite being over a billion our Iman and our belief in Allah does not even provide us a dignified life, let alone make us conquer the world. Why?

- What are the differences between the teachings of Quran and Sunnah, and the teachings of our current religious leaders, scholars and teachers?

- Do we think that one of the reasons why our Iman and belief in Allah is not as effective because we have deviated from the teachings of Quran and Sunnah and are following the teachings of our religious leaders and scholars?

- What is Allah warning us of in Quran, 2:174?

- What does purification of heart mean? And what do we have to do to qualify for Allah's Mercy on the Day of Judgment?

- What are the attributes of a pure heart?

- Can Iman enter into an impure heart?

- What is Allah saying about Iman in Quran, 49:14-15?

- If our characters do not reflect our love and fear of Allah, then are we believers or pretenders?

- Can we protect ourselves from Devil if our hearts are open to vices?

- How does Devil deceive us and harden our hearts?

- What are the qualities of a true heart?

- What was the mission of our Prophet (pbuh)?

15

TEARS
NOVI, UNITED STATES,
1988 - 1996

Wherever water flows, life flourishes;
Wherever tears fall, Divine mercy is shown.
(The Masnavi, Book 1, 817-820)

"W*HEN GOD WISHES to help, He lets us weep—but tears for His sake bring happiness.*" I don't quite remember where I heard these words, but it felt as if someone had gently encased my heart in a grapheme sheath, pain became bearable and my axis realigned.

At first, the change was hardly discernible by others, yet I felt myself slowly and steadily slipping into a new existence. I had been rapidly evolving and morphing during the last couple of years, largely due to domestic issues and my inability to cope with growing stress. All of these rapid transitions came to a screeching stop, and the wheels painstakingly started to turn the other way.

When my focal point shifted, I realized I had two choices: I could either let this pain destroy me, or I could let it eat away my veneer until my true self emerged, the self I hardly knew. So, instead of fighting the pain off, I quietly let it engulf me.

Disappointment in the men of God pushed me to seek out God Himself. I started studying the Quran. Initially, I was seeking answers for my plight. I was looking to blame someone, anyone, so I could find my peace. I discovered that man was just an instrument of Allah's will. The problem was not between me and man, but between me and Allah.

According to the book of Prophetic traditions, when man suffers pain and hardships, it is for one of three reasons:

1. He has disobeyed Allah, is being punished;
2. He has disobeyed Allah, and Allah wants him to repent, so that He will forgive him;
3. And for some men, Allah has designated a lofty status in the afterlife, and when in Allah's court, the status of a man exceeds beyond his actions then Allah sends trials, and tests him through his family, wealth and health. These trials are to stimulate man and to hasten him towards his goals. (Musnad Ahmad, 22337-22338)

The third reason left me dazed for weeks. I would go back to it again and again, countless times a day, and ponder over my existence.

Here I was, drowning in my own sorrows; while Allah was helping me out. Suddenly, all my woes and anguish became meaningful. I was still asking the same question though: "Why me?" Earlier, I couldn't understand why Allah chose to hurt me this way. Now I couldn't fathom why Allah chose to love me this way.

My family problems had gotten the best of me. I was struggling to maintain my self-confidence. When I had come to Detroit as a Chief Engineer of a big international corporation, Perkins Engines Company, I had believed in myself. Now I felt shaky and indecisive. When an economic recession made jobs with private companies insecure, I decided to move to a federal government job.

My Masters in Management helped me land a position with Tank Automotive Command (TACOM) in the United States Army. After several years of hard labor, I was promoted to Senior Project Engineer in the Saudi Arabia Management Office (SAMO) in Foreign Military Sales (FMS). As Production Engineering Manager I was placed in charge of all engineering activities for the development and fielding of two world class, state of the art and unrivaled tanks, the KSA M1A2 and the KSA M1A2S. This was a huge achievement for me. I felt driven to excel once again. While I ran the American office, Mohammed Doweesh, an Arab engineer, supervised the Saudi Sword Project Management Office (SPMO), which was headed by Prince Khalid bin Bandar bin King Abdul Aziz. Since I was responsible for overseeing the development of their tanks, I often met the Prince and escorted him around the country.

While at work, I was on the up and up. At home, I had a hard time getting my act together. It was then that I decided to visit the Kaaba for the optional pilgrimage, or *umrah*.

In December 1988, I laid my eyes on the Holy Kaaba for the very first time. I was surrounded by millions of pilgrims, but while standing before the Kaaba, it was just me and my Lord. I was a child again, not a man who must carry his burdens without complaints. I grasped the *kiswa*, the covering of the Holy Kaaba, like a child would clutch his mother's dress, and cried my heart out. There was no point telling Him about my life; He already knew everything. I unburdened my soul. and when I was ready to leave, He bequeathed me faith.

My next stop was India. The last time I was there, I had been a foreigner not just to the people, but also to my faith. This time, I tried making amends for my earlier transgressions. I visited mosques and strove to strengthen my ties with Allah.

When I returned home, I was rejuvenated. I was calmer, more content and ready to take on whatever life was planning to throw at me next. I did not know it would be another miracle. I was still reeling from the one in Makkah.

I heard that Kauser was ready to take matters to the next level. She called a meeting, where we both sat down with our lawyers, and decided to close the case for good. My lawyers had given me no false hopes, and I was ready to accept all terms and conditions just to put an end to it all. However, when we started the discussion, Kauser's attorney revealed that the deciding judge would consider sixteen points before awarding custody, and most of those points were in my favor. Hearing his words made me change my mind. I told him I would fight for my kids till my last breath, spend the last penny of my earnings if I had to, and sell the house if it came to that, but I would not back down, until I got my kids. The guy was taken aback. After the meeting he convinced Kauser to drop the case.

Our family was together again. Kauser threw herself into her chores and studies. First she joined Oakland Community College for her diploma and then Eastern Michigan University to procure a Bachelor's Degree in physical therapy.

In June 1994, I took another trip to Makkah to perform *hajj*, an experience of a lifetime. Like a non-Muslim can never feel the euphoria experienced by a *hajji*, a Muslim who hasn't performed *hajj* can never appreciate its powerful catharsis. My trips to Makkah were changing me in more ways than I thought possible.

In October 1994, I had to go to Los Angeles, California to fulfill an academic requirement of my job. I was away from my home and kids for a month. Distance had never been my friend. When I returned home Kauser announced that she had plans to spend Christmas holidays in Atlanta, Georgia. Later, however, she changed her mind.

Time flew and my wife and I built higher walls around ourselves to keep out pain. My little Mariem was eight years by then, not quite so little anymore. Yusuf was twelve and Bin Yamin was fourteen, both smart beyond their years. My marriage, however, was going on twenty and in shambles. Our case had been presented in a divorce court and after the hearing I went to live with my sister Shahnaz in Ann Arbor while Kauser and my kids continued to live in Novi.

Although living our separate lives, my wife and I were still bound tightly together. Some of our friends talked us into settling our dispute out of court. Thus, a meeting with Imam Muneer was arranged, and we met again in Troy mosque.

On our way to the mosque I asked the kids if they wanted to live with me or their mom. My children especially Mariem were being tugged and yanked by opposing forces. For them Mom or Dad was not a choice at all, and whichever side they chose would ultimately result in immeasurable loss for them. My only consolation at the time was that I was offering them what I could, a say in where they wanted to live and with whom.

When we met Imam Muneer, I told him that I wanted the children to live with me but that I would honor their wishes if they preferred to live with their Mom. Muneer conducted separate talk sessions with all of us and finally announced that the children would live with their mother. I was stunned. Too shocked to say anything except to nod my head, and afraid to meet my children's eyes, lest they see the pain in them, I walked out to my car. After I composed myself, I returned to the mosque to collect the kids.

Children are highly intuitive. They are also highly protective of their parents; although, it is not their job. If my kids had a real choice, I knew they would have preferred their parents to live together. The *imam* understood this better than any of us, and in order to keep the family together, he took a decision that did not sit well with me at all.

One day when Yusuf came to visit me in Ann Arbor, he told me that his Mom was planning to take all of them to Atlanta. After a few weeks, I talked to Yusuf again, and when he convinced me that he really wanted to come live with me, I rented a two-bedroom apartment in Novi. Then, one morning I borrowed a truck, called up the police and asked them to escort me to Kauser's house to pick up Yusuf.

The police officers who turned up at my place refused to help me, since I did not have custody papers. After I explained my plights to them, and my son's wish to live with me, they agreed reluctantly. At Kauser's, we found Yusuf waiting at the front door with his luggage. Despite that, the officers informed Kauser that she had the right to refuse me and to stop Yusuf from leaving the house. I braced myself for another showdown, but Kauser surprised me. She told the officer she would not, could not, stop Yusuf from leaving with his Dad, if that was what he truly wanted.

Yusuf and I returned to our brand new home. I learned how to cook for him. In the beginning, when I served him dinner, I tried to catch his unguarded reactions. My child never once complained.

A few weeks went by, and Bin Yamin moved in with us, too.

Mariem came over on the weekends. On those days, when I had all of them to myself, I felt like I had squeezed the entire world into my tiny apartment. I wondered if a part of me still believed that things would miraculously fall back into place, and we would welcome good times one more time. But when I heard about Atlanta from the kids again, suddenly things became crystal clear. I had to accept it was over. I had to accept that Kauser was trying to move on and start a new life. I had to accept that we couldn't move in circles our whole lives. We had to stop and decide wisely for the sake of our kids and for our own lives.

On August 24, 1996, our divorce was finalized, and we were awarded joint custody of our children. I cried that day for the loss of our marriage, for the years of love, heartache and misunderstandings, and for finally closing a painful chapter of my life.

If marriage is life, divorce is death. Twenty-two years ago I felt like the happiest man on earth when I married Kauser Asia Jehan, and twenty-two years later, that man died. Divorce is also rebirth. And as hard as it was to believe, on the morning of August 24, 1996, I knew that one day I would look back again on my marriage with Kauser and not feel like a million pieces.

My life has taught me a lot, I discovered that man is just an instrument of Allah's will. Furthermore, I learned that suffering, pain and hardships are not Allah's punishment. Rather, they are warnings and reminders to help us correct our actions.

MISCONCEPTIONS ABOUT ISLAM

Islam is simple. People are impossible.

I WAS APPALLED AT what I had conveniently accepted as my religion. I had believed everything I was told about Islam from just about anyone, as long as they called themselves Muslims. My only excuse was ignorance and apathy to a certain extent. However, my study of the Quran helped clear out many false impressions and mistaken beliefs.

FALSE IMPRESSIONS AND MISTAKEN BELIEFS

Man has always been afraid of the unknown. Today, Muslim hatred is mostly due to the same fear factor. While misconceptions harbored by non-Muslims about Islam are understandable, the ones harbored by Muslims are not just mind-boggling but completely inexcusable.

A majority of Muslims believe that they understand Islam, follow the fundamental laws and uphold the pillars, but they are ignorant of what the word "Islam" actually means. They are so wrapped up in their worldly lives, that they seldom stop to think and reflect upon their identities and the purpose of their lives. Meaningless repetitions and even fervently uttered declarations regarding their faith make them Muslims in their own eyes. Although these very common, yet momentary, outbursts fail to change the lives of such Muslims, they have an effect on the listeners, who inevitably make judgments based on the utterances and actions of these individuals. If the words support the actions, the listener passes a good judgment. If not, then instead of blaming just the doer of the action, the listener inexorably condemns not just the perpetrator, but also Islam and the entire Muslim community. The two main reasons behind such hasty rulings are ignorance and the negative propaganda that is being systematically spread against Islam and its followers.

Many Muslims unknowingly commit breaches against Allah every day, due to actions which appall and defame true Muslims and Islam. By not validating their religious proclamations and statements with appropriate demeanors, and by improper conduct, ignorant Muslims do more harm than they realize.

Muslims forget they are blessed. They were not just provided with guidance, but with a messenger who relayed the message of their Creator. Today, if they deliberately choose to forget the honor they were given, if they choose not to recognize their own designation and fail to probe into the reality of their faith, then the fault lies with them and no one else. To set the world straight, regarding Islam, it is crucial that we set our own people straight first. To set our own people straight, it is necessary to start with ourselves.

UNDERSTANDING ISLAM IN TRUTH

Islam is the religion of all Muslims. For many it means belief in:

- Allah, the one and only God;
- The Last Prophet Mohammed (PBUH), plus all other Prophets of Allah;
- The Quran, the holy scriptures and all other holy books;
- The angels of Allah;
- The Day of Judgment; and
- Life after death.

Some Muslims, who have a better understanding, would add following the dictates of the Quran, to the description of Islam.

Look up Islam in an English dictionary, and it would give the following definition: "A monotheistic religion based on the word of God as revealed to Mohammed (PBUH) during the 7th century." The same source, Encarta Dictionary, also describes Islam as, "Muslim people and their culture." Surprisingly, that is exactly what most Muslims would state if asked to define Islam.

WHAT IS ISLAM?

What is Islam if not what has been stated above? In order to understand Islam, it is essential to find its root meaning.

Islam is an Arabic word, and Arabic is not just another language. It is the language that was chosen to relay the divine message. The more one studies it, the more one understands. The word "Islam" existed even before the Quran was sent to Earth. Back then, the word was used to describe an action, a quality, a condition of self-surrendering or making peace. The word Islam was an abstract noun or a verb, but not a title with religious connotations. When the Quran chose Islam to represent the faith of Muslims, it revealed that every atom in the universe willingly or unwillingly surrendered to the greatness of Allah, i.e., was already in Islam.

ISLAM MEANS SUBMISSION
TO THE WILL OF THE TRUE LORD

When one proclaims to be a follower of Islam and a Muslim, one must remember the meaning behind the word Islam: surrendering your will to Allah. Being a Muslim is that state of surrender. The minute you put your will before that of your Allah, you step out of the circle of Islam. It is as simple as that, either you are a Muslim and in Islam–or you are a hypocrite.

And Allah will surely make evident those who believe, and He will surely make evident the hypocrite. (The Quran, 29:11)

For a Muslim, being in Islam is a perpetual state of striving. Putting Allah's will before yours is not easy, but it is essential, if you are to be in Islam. So what do you do? Do you walk away, ignoring the impending doom, or do you search for a way to make that submission easy? **The only thing that makes surrendering your will easy, is recognizing Allah. Find and recognize the true Lord and your body and soul will submit of their own accord.** Since being in Islam is a natural state for every atom in the universe, a part of us adheres to the same pattern. However, it is man's free will that complicates matters. **Once a person conquers his will and relinquishes it to Allah, he is completely in Islam.** Pay heed, when Allah says:

Do they seek other than the system of God, when all things in the Heavens and the earth, willingly or unwillingly, have surrendered to Him, and to Him they will be returned? (The Quran, 3:83)

Islam isn't the title of a clan. For those who enter Islam, the Quran says:

Surely those who believe, and those who are Jews and the Nazarenes, (followers of Jesus of Nazareth) and the Sabians, whoever believes in God and the Last Day and does good, they shall have their reward from their Lord, and there is no fear upon them, nor shall they grieve. (The Quran, 2:26)

THE REALITY BEHIND SUFFERING OF NATIONS

The Quran is a benediction for those who fear Allah. Some people question the validity of the above verse by posing questions regarding the suffering of Muslims and their dire conditions in places like Burma, Syria, Kashmir, and more. While some of us believe that Muslim suffering is a test of *iman*, others are hard put for an answer. The truth is, pain and anguish are not always a test from Allah; sometimes they come as punishment.

Allah has bound the Earth and its inhabitants by moral and physical laws. When these laws are broken repeatedly, man suffers the consequences.

Allah says in the Quran:

If they treat thy (mission) as false, so did the People before them (treat their Prophets): The People of Noah, and Ad and Thamud, those of Abraham and Lut, and the Companions of the Madyan people, and Moses was rejected (in the same way). But I granted respite to the unbelievers, and (only) after that did I punish them—but how (terrible) was My rejection (of them)! How many populations have We destroyed, which were given to wrong-doing! They tumbled down on their roofs. And how many wells are lying idle and neglected, and castles lofty and well-built? (The Quran, 22:42-45)

Allah also says:

So each We seized for his sin, and among them were those upon whom We sent a storm of stones, and among them were those who were seized by the blast [from the sky], and among them were those whom We caused the earth to swallow, and among them were those whom We drowned. And Allah would not have wronged them, but it was they who wronged themselves. (The Quran, 29:40)

The verse proves that suffering of entire nations is a sign of Allah's wrath. When men continually violate Allah's laws and exceed the limits set by Him, complete nations are wiped out by natural calamities or by ruthless tyrants.

BREAKING THE LAWS OF ALLAH

Muslims are being killed and humiliated all over the world, because they have rejected the teachings of Islam. By changing the Islam that was taught by the Prophet (PBUH) into something more to their liking, they have ignited Allah's wrath. Today, the Quran is still the same, but how people interpret and follow it, if at all, is not the same.

While the Quran and *Sunnah*–the way of the Holy Prophet Mohammed (PBUH)–have taught Muslims to do good, to shun evil and to fear Allah alone, Muslims nowadays have stopped struggling to meet these standards. The life of ease has not just deterred them from putting strict checks on themselves, but has vanquished the fear of Allah from their hearts.

Even Islamic orators and scholars focus more on Allah's mercy and love, and little on His wrath and retribution, which has further worsened the situation. Most have chosen the verses of the Quran that suit and sooth and have skimmed over lines that fill the hearts with dread and apprehension.

People have unwisely chosen the comforts of this world over the rewards of the afterlife and are consequently denied both, just as Allah has promised. Whether men who have met the rejection of Allah on Earth will find acceptance in the hereafter, or rejection again waiting for them, only Allah knows, but one must understand that Allah won't be too pleased with lawbreakers, wrongdoers and sinners.

For those who make a mockery of Allah's words, the Quran says:

On the Day, the punishment will cover them from above them, and from below their feet and it is said, 'Taste [the result of] what you used to do.' (The Quran, 29:55)

The verse above is a warning for those who say they believe but disobey Allah on a daily basis.

Indeed, we will bring down on the people of this city punishment from the sky, because they have been defiantly disobedient. And We have certainly left of it a sign, as clear evidence for people who use reason. (The Quran, 29:34-35)

Suffering and pain is also a way of turning man towards Allah. While for some nations it is punishment, for others it is a warning. For individuals, it is a test of faith and of commitment to their brothers in need. When faced by the wrath of Allah, we must check whether we have broken any laws. If so, we must repent and commit to living more responsibly. Whether test or punishment, only true repentance can save man from a bitter end.

THE REALITY BEHIND THE PEOPLE OF PARADISE

The biggest misconception that many Muslims find refuge in is their theory regarding the people of paradise. They believe that heaven is guaranteed to them because they are Muslims and not idol worshippers. They see themselves as the people of Paradise from the onset or later on, after they have endured a little punishment in hell. To them it only matters that eventually they will reside in heaven, regardless of what they did on earth.

The truth is that a few good deeds and a lifetime of immoderation are not the attributes of the people of Paradise. One may not be prostrating before stone idols, while doing what little good that one can, **but unless one refrains from sins and cleanses one's heart, expecting Paradise is ludicrous.**

THE REALITY BEHIND
'GOOD DEEDS WASHING AWAY BAD DEEDS'

Most men failed to understand God's plan, the secret behind creation and their role in the universe. They understood little, and from what little they grasped, they ascertained that they were the best of Allah's creation. Although, this was true, the fact went to their heads and fed their egos. When the ego asked for more, men started measuring themselves up against other humans, and more often than not, judged themselves better and superior: sometimes on the basis of color, race and language, and other times on the basis of morality and religion.

Today, very few Muslims seem doubtful about their final abode. For most, a castle in heaven is a foregone conclusion. It's almost like it has been promised to them, no matter what they do. While some Muslims assign an enormous value to good deeds, they hardly ascribe any negative value to bad deeds. Many believe that they have earned heaven, because they do a lot of good. What they seem to forget is that righteousness does not just imply "good" actions but also staying away from sin. Good is controlling the *nafs* and its voracious appetite for more and more. Good is aspiring for a character that resembles that of Mohammed (PBUH), and it is not just apparent dignity, but the hidden purity of the heart.

However, since they see "good" as just outward actions, they do not count their sins. Moreover, when they commit sins they think to counter them with a good act so as to nullify the deed. Consequently, while their good deeds pile up so do their sins.

Muslims must understand that an action knowingly committed in defiance of Allah's will, will not be easily forgiven. For example, a Muslim man, returning from work, stops at a bar for drinks, while being aware that it forbidden in his religion. He feels guilty, but does not refrain. When he leaves, he hands a $50 bill to a homeless man. Immediately, the guilt leaves him, and he deludes himself into thinking that he has erased his sin.

If only it was that easy. We, Muslims, are in a serious relationship with Allah. Playing games will not help our cause. **Pick up the Quran and the books of *hadith* and read. There isn't one such episode, where it says you can do that. A good deed may have the power to wipe out sins, but not when we turn it into some kind of a trade.**

Man is responsible for his actions, the good and the bad. He will be taken into account for both. Whoever believes that good deeds are his ticket to heaven must rethink the entire possibility. Unless man does good and refrains from bad, like he has been asked to, the prospects of residing in heaven will disappear altogether.

PURSUING BIGGER DEEDS FOR BIGGER REWARDS

Muslims who have become obsessed with good deeds have also decided to play it smart. According to them, since they need lots of good deeds to eradicate their sins, they have started to focus more on deeds that have the potential for bigger and continuous rewards, for example; converting people to Islam, building mosques, distributing the Quran, etc. All these acts would encourage others towards good, and they would get a share in their rewards, which would obviously keep piling up.

Although, there is absolutely nothing wrong with any of the three acts mentioned above, **it's when people fail to change themselves but invite others to embrace that change; when people do not offer prayers, but want to help finance a mosque; when people do not read the Quran, but pass it on hoping that it would be read and understood, and all for the sole purpose of cashing in on the rewards, there is something wrong with it.** It is tragic to witness mature and intelligent Muslim men and women transform into naïve and ignorant fools, when it comes to Allah and the Day of Judgment.

THE REALITY BEHIND RITUALISTIC WORSHIP

A common example of ritualistic worship is *salah*. Some less common ones are *saum, zakat* and *hajj*. Another widespread misconception about worship is that it is simply the physical movement of body parts, whether it is the head bowed low in prostration, whether the hands folded or raised before Allah or whether the tongue praising the Lord. In the case of *zakat* and *saum*, worship becomes adhering to the formulas of worship, like not eating for a specific period of time and paying a specific amount every year.

Most Muslims regard the pillars the end all and be all of Islam, because they have been taught to value these rituals of worship more than any other dictate. The basic purpose of necessitating these rituals for all Muslims was to bring them closer to Islam and Allah and also to help develop appropriate Muslim characters. A person who is not a very good Muslim, but offers prayers, might one day change his ways and understand Islam a bit more. Ritualistic worship is to keep man tied to his religion, so he would keep returning and submitting to the Lord. People who think that offering *salah* and paying *zakat* is all the worship that Allah desires from them are mistaken.

Salah, saum, zakat and hajj carry the power to change man. The body's submission is supposed to encourage the submission of the nafs. This is the true purpose of all worship.

Thousands of prophets came bearing the messages of Allah. While some focused on rituals, others talked about purifying the heart, improving relationships, handling businesses, developing dignity of character and taking care of Allah's creation. If Allah wanted man to worship Him, and if rituals were the only form of worship, then there was no need to emphasize anything else.

If man was left to his own devices, he would perform rituals and go back to serving his desires. Satan would make sure of it. So to keep man and his lust for more in check, Allah commanded and warned man to control his devilish desires and to exercise his virtue. To motivate man, Allah appointed him His viceroy and promised heaven and hell as just rewards.

Heaven is not for worshippers who focus on rituals and do not clean their hearts of greed, ego, pride and hatred. People who bow before Allah five times a day, but are arrogant, unforgiving and pitiless towards Allah's creation, are not gaining anything from *salah*. Remember, *salah* or any other ritual of worship, alone, will not suffice, if the goodness of each ritual does not enter the heart and change man for the better.

Today, most Islamic teachers are advising Muslims to resurrect the five pillars of Islam and perform good deeds but they are not telling them to clean their hearts of greed. This is like teaching people what good is, but not the path that leads to it. Although it is true that the soul of Islam is preserved in rituals, Muslims can only benefit from them, if they submit their souls to Allah along with their bodies. **When the *nafs* is insatiable and hungers after the world, the good deeds performed serve as food for the ego and satisfaction for the *nafs*.** These good deeds glorify the self and not the Lord, and lose their worth in the eyes of Allah.

THE REALITY BEHIND 'REWARD AND PUNISHMENT'

Like the Quraish of Makkah, the tribe that opposed the Prophet Mohammed (PBUH), Muslims today have become followers of their ancestors, believing what their parents or grandparents believed and not what is actually taught by the Quran and Sunnah. If the parents are knowledgeable Muslims, their children end up on the right path; however, if the parents are ignorant and followers of their own ancestors, then they end up making the same mistakes as their parents. This blind devotion does not help anyone.

Allah asks man to think. The more man learns the truth the closer he gets to Allah, but if man keeps on repeating and establishing customs that have nothing to do with Islam and expecting to be rewarded, then he is trying to fish the moon out of the ditch.

One example is celebrating the birth of Mohammed (PBUH) and expecting to be rewarded. We all know, that Mohammed (PBUH) did not celebrate birthdays, neither did his wives, nor his closest companions, not even, after his (PBUH) death. We can celebrate Mohammed (PBUH) by adopting his ways but we choose to adopt a practice, which belongs to non-Muslims to celebrate our Muslim savior.

Another thing to reflect upon is our greed. When we pray, we pray for bigger and better, for Jannah in the world and hereafter. We pray because we want to be rewarded, we are enticed by promises of heaven, and that is all we end up seeing. Instead of thanking our Benefactor wholeheartedly, we just dream about living in heaven one day.

Every little good we do, we expect to be rewarded, forgetting that even doing good deeds is a blessing from Allah, and it is His right to reward us or not. **Only deeds that are pure and performed for the sake of Allah alone are accepted and rewarded. Allah is the true Judge of our intentions. When man believes it is his right to be rewarded for whatever he deems good then it is a sign of arrogance and the deed is lost.**

While some do not commit sins intentionally, neither do they consciously make an effort to stay away from them, curb their desires or exert self-control. Reward and punishment are also steps to encourage men to learn more about their Creator. Only a true Muslim understands that he must ask and work for Allah's pleasure, and all would be his.

Muslims, men and women, may dream about heaven, but they never deliberate over accounts of hell or promises of punishment. The truth is, hell is as real as heaven. Sins and wrongdoings will be penalized. When we do good, we expect to be rewarded but when we commit sins, we depend upon Allah's mercy to save us from punishment.

Allah constantly reminds men of His just nature, of hell that has been created for transgressors, and terrible punishment. **If we dwell upon the wonders of Paradise, while conveniently ignoring the horrors of hell, then it is just a matter of time before we will be forced to see the folly of our ways.**

THE REALITY BEHIND
ALLAH'S LOVE AND MAN'S REPENTANCE

All human beings belong to Allah, their relationship being similar to that of a mother and a child; albeit, Allah being the greatest, His love is also great and incomparable, surpassing that of seventy mothers. We owe our breaths, our heartbeats and every second of our lives to Him alone. Since Allah is always there and His love forever vigilant, man has started to entertain the notion that he would never be thrown into hell.

All men are Allah's creation, and, regardless of their beliefs, understanding and practices, are equal in His eyes. However, those who have received guidance believe that since they recognize Allah, say the *shahadah* and accept Mohammed (PBUH) as the last prophet, they have earned the right to enter heaven despite their sins.

The truth is that Allah gives a chance to everyone, whether Muslim or non-Muslim, to turn towards Him. Humoring oneself by believing bits and pieces of facts, especially those that agree with us, while ignoring those that make us uncomfortable, is living in a state of denial.

Muslims who depend upon Allah's great love and see it as a one-way ticket to heaven are entertaining false beliefs. Haven't they heard about Allah's wrath and His justice? It is Allah's love that frequently forgives us and gives us truckloads of chances. It is the same love that sustains us, despite our disobedience and ungrateful tongues. Muslims who have an unshakable belief in Allah's love must recognize His other attributes as well. Allah is Kind and Merciful, but Allah is also *Al Hakam* (the Impartial Judge), *Al Muntaqim* (the Retaliator) and *Al Qahhaar* (the All Prevailing One).

The teachers of Islam are doing a great disservice by teaching material that takes the fear of Allah away from the hearts of the Muslims. **Yes, Allah is the Great Forgiver, but He is also *Al Mudhil*, the Abaser, the Humiliator and the Destroyer. He will forgive us only if He wills it, but there is also a possibility that He may decide to summon us for a reckoning. What then?**

REPENTANCE BEFORE THE EVER ACCEPTOR OF REPENTANCE (AT TAWWAAB) AND THE ALL OBSERVING WITNESS (ASH SHAHEED)

When Iblis said to Allah that he would misguide His creation on earth, Allah replied that He would keep forgiving man as long as he turned to Him in repentance. A huge misconception that was derived from these words was that **Allah will forgive everything as long as man repented. Wrong; Allah will not forgive those who sin, while deliberately planning their repentance ahead of time.**

Muslims, who think that they can do whatever they please and indulge in as many wrongdoings as they can, as long as they return to Allah at the end of the day and ask for forgiveness, must remember that Allah is All-Knowing. He knows what lies in the depths of the heart. Allah is also the All Observing Witness. Then are we so naïve as to think that we can deceive Him?

True repentance will be accepted, and true repentance means a guilt-torn heart and a stubborn resolve to not commit the same sin again. Man may stumble again, but the next repentance will be even more uncomfortable and the heart heavier, still, with shame and remorse. It is the love of Allah that will accept the second, third and fourth repentance of the same sin and more, in a row, but only so long as Allah sees the repenting heart.

And Allah will certainly know those who are true from those who are false. (The Quran, 29:3)

PROPHET MOHAMMED'S (PBUH) RESCUE

A few would go to any length to support or justify their wrong acts. Won't the Last Prophet (PBUH) plead with Allah until He lets all of his *Ummah* enter the doors of paradise? Since they think this makes life easy for them, they refuse to hear any other part of Islam. People who are not sincere in their devotion to Allah make light of their sins by telling themselves that Prophet Mohammed's (PBUH) plea will be enough to get them by, so they can do what they like.

Prophet Mohammed (PBUH) came bearing not just glad tidings but also warnings from Allah. We accepted what our hearts desired, the rewards, and ignored the forewarnings of Allah's wrath. No matter what one chooses to believe, the people who struggle their entire lives to please Allah will never be on the same footing as those who live only to please themselves.

Prophet Mohammed's (PBUH) intercession may eventually rescue all of his people from hell, but some of us have the impudence to think that hell will be bearable, that it will be okay as long as we end up in heaven. We make light of the fires of hell, the same fires that have been burning since the beginning of time. We ignore the fact that Hell was built for *kuffar*, the rejecters of faith, hypocrites and sinners as well. The existence of hell justifies the existence of heaven. If the best of us would reside in heaven, where will the worst of us go? May Allah have mercy on us and forgive our ignorance.

Although we stubbornly hold on to the promises of our Prophet Mohammed (PBUH), we never once consider his teachings which preceded them. Would we then take the entire message in vain? Is that not an extreme offense to the one from whom we want intercession?

Muslims were invited to subjugate their own wills, to bow down before Allah's commands, knowing the rewards for their efforts would come later. However, the hasty and forgetful creature that man is, he deviated from the actual message, abandoned the Prophet's mission and lurched for the cake.

A thorough evaluation of our current religious beliefs and a comparison with Prophet Mohammed's (PBUH) teachings will show us exactly where we stand. If we are his true followers, we have a right to hold on to his promises; otherwise we don't.

THE MISSION OF MOHAMMED (PBUH)

Prophet Mohammed (PBUH) came not just to deliver the message of Allah but also to implement those commands and establish Islamic laws. His mission was:

- To eliminate social injustice and inequity,
- To liberate the poor and suffering,
- To establish a regime based on peace and justice,
- To reform the social and cultural structure according to the laws of Allah

Mohammed (PBUH)'s teachings wiped out all differences of race, color and clan, and an individual's status was recognized based on his love and sacrifice for Allah and His creation. He delivered the message that Allah values only those people who raise their status by caring and sharing their wealth with others, eliminating the suffering of weak and poor, and also those who have a high degree of love for Allah and His Messenger (PBUH). People who raise their worldly status by stockpiling their wealth and making others suffer have forgotten the teachings of Mohammed (PBUH).

Under Islamic rule, Muslims were expected to develop their abilities and to perform their best, because they had the perfect teacher and model in the guise of Mohammed (PBUH). If only the Muslims had made the mission of Mohammed (PBUH) their own they would have excelled in the world and would have been the most prosperous nation of the world today. Unfortunately, most of us have either given up or forgotten what his (PBUH) mission was and yet we doggedly hang on to his promises. **The promises of Mohammed (PBUH) were for those who would keep believing in his cause and fighting for it throughout their lives–not for slackers.**

THE REALITY BEHIND
ALLAH'S ADDRESS: THE QURAN

The Quran is Allah's address to us. He is talking to all men and women, not just scholars, *imams* or teachers of Islam. Instead of going to scholars for every little issue, man should start reading the Quran on his own and discover what Allah has to say. This is critical to understanding Islam, plus it is mandatory for all believers.

Muslims who do not speak Arabic, wrongly believe that understanding the Quran is secondary to its recitation. When one does not understand a language but mimics the sounds and words, especially of the divine Book, then one acquires the barest minimum from it, almost nothing. Consider an example: memorize an entire book of science in a foreign tongue, not understanding a single word. Then sit for a test. What expectations do you have? Do you seriously believe that you will understand a single question, much less be able to answer one? It is a foregone conclusion that you would fail badly. Now, let's replace the science book with the Quran and ask the same question again. Do you think you will pass?

If we do not know what we are saying and refuse to take Allah's word seriously, how can we expect Allah to take us seriously? During the time when alcohol was not made *haram*, Muslims were prohibited to offer *salah* while under the influence of wine. The reason given was that they wouldn't understand what they were saying. Today, the problem of alcohol isn't what keeps us from understanding our *salah*, but our ignorance and laziness.

When Allah, the creator of the Universe, heaven and hell, has something to say to us, then it is our duty to try to understand what He is saying. Increasingly, people, especially the new generation, have started to argue that the Quran came centuries ago, and that the times and circumstances just aren't the same anymore. Wrong. If only they would sit with the Quran and read it with understanding, they would discover that every word and verse is as relevant today as it was in the time of the Prophet Mohammed (PBUH). Those who make these claims without reading and understanding the Quran, must remember that **the people who found excuses to avoid Allah's commands while claiming to be believers, were called hypocrites.** The Quran is for all times, and that is just one of the miracles of Allah's book.

OPTING TO STAY IN THE DARK

Another misconception entertained by Muslims is that man won't be questioned for unawareness or for a lack of knowledge. So to avoid punishment for not following the dictates of Allah, some Muslims simply prefer to stay in the dark, arguing that as long as they stay ignorant of the laws, Allah won't question them. Again, this is just Satan duping man's reason.

You have the book, the Quran. All the commands are right there. Open the book and read; procrastination is no excuse.

The Quran bears truth, and that is what gives it a timeless quality. The truth it holds is the same that was revealed in previous scriptures to Abraham, Moses, Jesus and so many more. However, the Quran is the final divine revelation to mankind. Together with Muslims, it urges people of other monotheistic faiths to return to their original teachings and reject all man-made additions and alterations.

The Quran is objective, and a method chosen by Allah to educate minds and the change human attitude towards life. It aims to strip away the inessential and transitory, reveal the true nature of man and the world, and bring about a revolution inside man himself, because after all is said and done, the external material civilization is the expression of the internal spiritual condition of man himself.

The Quran is not just a reminder of the promises our souls made to Allah, but also a reminder of beginnings and endings, of friends and enemies, and of rewards and punishments. In certain places, the text reminds us of universal truths that are present within us and around us; it is no wonder that Allah calls it a Reminder.

The Quran is also a discourse on man and a manual for life. It discusses man, his heart and soul, his creation, purpose and history; his spirituality, psyche and his overall ways. It is also a guide to living a better life–a life that is infused with the principles of justice, truth and kindness. It teaches man how to realize his true potential, individually and collectively, while choosing the right path.

The Quran should be read with an open mind, not to refute and contradict, but simply to consider, weigh and ponder over its truth. Those who do that see the light and revert to Islam. Then they read it again and again and again, and as long as they seek truth, the Quran keeps revealing it.

LEARNING IS A PAINFUL EXERCISE

Learning is making an effort to open your mind and exploring new territory. It is also finding the strength to accept the truth and incorporate it into one's life. After a certain age, it becomes a painful exercise because it calls for change. Most of us neither welcome change after adolescence, nor are we fans of textbooks and exams. On the other hand, we love doing things we are comfortable with and showing off our acquired skills, like beating someone in a chess game.

Since time does not always remain the same, and early learning moulds characters and develops habits, Muslims must be taught to understand the Quran in the earliest stages of their lives. **If we are taught to recognize and obey Allah from the onset, if we are trained to perform the rituals and behave like true Muslims as children, there is a 90% chance that we will pick up the Quran for guidance more often and perform our duties as Muslims with ease and sincerity, even in the later stages of our lives.**

MEMORIZING THE QURAN

Muslims also believe that those who memorize the Quran will be saved from hellfire, because they have the words of Allah preserved in their hearts. This is true, but one must understand that the actual *hadith* goes as follows:

Hazrat Ali relates that Prophet Mohammed (PBUH) said:

Whoever recites the Quran, memorizes it, accepts its halal (lawful things) as halal and haram (forbidden things) as haram (i.e. his beliefs in these matters are correct), Allah, the Exalted, will enter him to Paradise and accept his intercession on behalf of ten such persons of his family upon whom entry into Hell has become incumbent (i.e. Allah will forgive them because of his intercession). (Tirmidhi, Fadail Al-Quran, 13; Ibn Majah, Muqaddima, 17.)

It is not just memorization that would earn a *hafiz*, or guardian of the Quran, freedom from hell, but also acting upon its dictates. Only people with weak *iman* look for easy ways to get out of their commitment with Allah. One must remember that Allah can easily wipe the Quran from the hearts, if He is not satisfied with our endeavors and level of obedience.

THE REALITY BEHIND "*HADITH* AND *SUNNAH*"

(*Hadiths* are the sayings of and narratives about the Prophet (PBUH). The *Sunnah* comprises his complete lifestyle and actions. Under this topic, however, *Sunnah* and hadith would be used in the widest sense, encompassing all attitudes, actions and sayings of Prophet Mohammed (PBUH))

The Quran is an instructional manual on matters pertaining to morality and faith. While it divulges the reality of man, prophethood, the Judgment Day, heaven and hell, the rituals of worship and man's relationship with Allah and His creation, it also lays down divine laws. The Quran was intended to be for all men. To make it easier to understand and accept, Allah sent the last Prophet (PBUH) to set an example for the rest, providing man not just a how-to guide, but also an instructor in form of Mohammed (PBUH).

The life of Mohammed (PBUH) was an illustration of the Quran. When we step into Islam, we declare two things: belief in the word of Allah and acceptance of Mohammed (PBUH) as His Apostle. From then onwards we are bound by our own oath to implicitly obey the words of Allah and those of His Prophet. Most of us rely on the Prophet's words because we understand that his was the path leading to success. However, some completely neglect the *Sunnah* and *hadith* in favor of the Quranic verses. Ignorance and lack of knowledge pushes them to compare Mohammed (PBUH) to other mortals, and due to incorrect conclusions, they lose the light and fall into darkness.

The truth is that following Mohammed's (PBUH) commands and example is following Islam, and discarding his *Sunnah* and *hadith* is discarding Islam. Mohammed (PBUH) was no ordinary man. He spoke only with the will of his Lord as Allah reveals in the Quran:

He does not speak out of his own desire. (The Quran, 53:3)

Whenever we come across *hadith* and *Sunnah* we are compelled by our faith to accept it and follow it, provided that it is authentic and fully established.

Everything that Mohammed (PBUH) said and did is of utmost importance. While some of his *hadiths* carry greater significance, and others lesser, none are unessential or disposable.

Islam provides a system that is in complete harmony with the moral and material aspect of man. The same concern was visible in the teachings of Mohammed (PBUH). He strove to find the perfect balance between the spiritual and material worlds. Today, unfortunately, most Muslims have segregated both aspects. The teachings of Mohammed (PBUH) have become purely spiritual and devotional matters which no longer play a role in the material world of Muslims societies and their everyday lives. The utter disregard of laws pertaining to *haram, halal,* businesses, relationships and morality, and the ready espousal of rituals depict a superficial spirit of Islam.

Even a cursory look at the life of Mohammed (PBUH) would be enough to set one straight. His life, teachings and mission were not just about offering prayers the right way, growing facial hair or performing rituals correctly, but they were about pursuing goodness with a pure heart. Everything else was secondary to perfecting Muslim characters and *iman.* It is easy to see why. If man perfected his *iman,* strove to purify his heart and build his character, in accordance with the teachings of the Quran and *Sunnah,* everything else would automatically fall into place.

The Quran was not what exalted Mohammed (PBUH) into an extraordinary being, it was Allah and His blessings on him that did that. He was given the qualities and character of a true leader even before he received the seal of prophethood. Therefore, he endeavored to correct the morals of his companions from the very beginning.

After the Quran was revealed to Prophet Mohammed (PBUH), he started encouraging his followers to connect their hearts, souls and bodies to Allah, to obey His will and to suppress their desires and *nafs.* Today, our dilemma is that **we have interpreted the *hadith* to suit our lifestyles. We have unconsciously eliminated spirituality from the teachings of Mohammed (PBUH) and the result is mental, physical and emotional turmoil.**

The life of a Muslim is supposed to be a conscious and voluntary cooperation between his spirit and his body. **Living according to the** ***Sunnah*** **means the teachings of the Prophet (PBUH) must be reflected in our moral, practical, social, individual and collective activities.**

IDENTIFYING TRUE *HADITH* FROM FALSIFICATIONS

The Quran can only be understood to the best advantage in the light of ***Sunnah*** **and** ***hadith*,** **conversely the understanding of** ***hadith*** **and** ***Sunnah*** **requires an understanding of the Quran.** Therefore, those who spend time in absorbing both, find explanations, applications and developments in the Quran and the life of Prophet Mohammed (PBUH), which supplement and support each other.

During the time of Banu Hashim and the Umayyads, when political discord was at its peak, many *hadiths* were fabricated and distorted to disrepute the leaders. Today, unqualified public speakers and ignorant Muslims are the propagators of incorrect and exaggerated *hadiths*. Many of these hadiths have been altered and adulterated due to human shortcomings like confusion, forgetfulness and exaggeration.

While in the past, information was not easily accessible, the internet has crushed the barriers of time and distance. Consequently, modern Muslims are more aware, but are also facing a greater risk.

Passing on unauthentic *hadiths* of the Prophet, which either have a weak source or no source at all is putting not just our own *iman* in jeopardy but also that of our Muslim brothers. The *hadiths* which are frequently shared through the internet and messaging services promise easy and big rewards for small and inconsequential deeds, like being the first one to pass on a message, or reciting certain unauthentic verses. Sometimes, the *hadith* shared negates Quranic teachings and those of Mohammed (PBUH), but the ignorant Muslims have no way of identifying true *hadith* from falsifications. Therefore, it is crucial that before accepting, implementing and passing on *hadiths*, one must check their validity and authenticity by following a simple rule: **no** ***hadith*** **should contradict the Quran. For this, however, one must have complete knowledge and understanding of the book.**

A majority of Muslims also believe that if the source of any *hadith* is Bukhari then it passes all criterion of authenticity and must not be further investigated. While this would have been true a few decades ago, it is not anymore. Due to modern modes of publications, internet, e-books, blogs, etc., a lot of information is constantly flowing back and forth. Every Tom, Dick and Harry considers himself an expert on every other topic under the sun, be it religion or something as mundane as choosing the right hat. Although, some writers many be doing extensive research on topics, one simply can't rely on the words of amateurs. The sad truth is that even the Quran which is made available to Muslims on cell phones through certain applications has been altered in places, whether deliberately or otherwise, only Allah knows.

Modern Muslims who rarely pick up the Quran and have little knowledge of the *Sunnah* are likely to commit grievous offenses against Allah and His Prophet (PBUH) if they start taking every saying at face value. We must always be on high alert in matters pertaining to Allah and Mohammed (PBUH), and use the rules given under interpreting *hadith* correctly to check the legitimacy of all *hadith* and *Sunnah*, regardless of the source mentioned.

INTERPRETING *HADITH* CORRECTLY

Interpreting *hadith* may seem like a straightforward job, but the truth is that not everyone is equipped with the right tools to fully and correctly understand the import of the Prophet's (PBUH) words. However, **four basic rules that can be applied to understand *hadith* are:**

- Use Quran as the measure of truth while interpreting *hadith*.

- Use other *hadith* for confirmation or as measure of truth–a *hadith* must not contradict any other *hadith*.

- Research into the specification and generalization, and understand the situation and context of the *hadith* before jumping to conclusions.

- A *hadith* must not contradict or defy natural laws associated with man and his *fitrah*.

While studying *hadiths*, one must understand that Quran and *Sunnah* are not trivial matters. They deserve serious thought and respect. Declaring a saying true and another false, and passing on unauthentic *hadith* or sayings of the Prophet (PBUH), can have serious consequences. Whenever doubtful of a *hadith*, look for its source and do research to clarify doubts while keeping the above mentioned rules in mind.

Like the Quran, *hadith* can also hold a deeper message which is not noticeable immediately. Often a lot is lost in translation. Although, Quran and *hadiths* are both translated in every language of the world, deep and meaningful interpretations only come from Arab scholars who know the intricacies of their language. Sometimes there is discrepancy in translations done in English and other languages which fail to convey the true meaning of the *hadith* or Quranic verse. Therefore, it is imperative to study translations of scholars who are well versed not just in Arabic but also in your native tongue. The best approach is to try to study Arabic, so that when you recite the Quran, or read a *hadith* you know exactly what is being said.

Many *hadiths* focus on building characters and spirituality, so when studying the sayings of the Prophet Mohammed (PBUH) or his *Sunnah,* absorb the apparent wisdom of the words and also seek that which lurks just behind them.

LOVE FOR ALLAH AND HIS PROPHET

The faith of Muslims is considered incomplete unless their love for Allah and his Prophet exceeds that for themselves. One day when Hazrat Omar Farooq was walking with Mohammed (PBUH), he asked Omar if he loved Allah's prophet more than he loved himself. To this Omar replied that he did not. Prophet Mohammed (PBUH) then told

Omar that his *iman* would not be perfect until his love for the Prophet of Allah(PBUH) was greater than his love for himself.

This incident reveals that whoever truly understands the blessing of Islam cannot deny the importance and worth of Mohammed (PBUH). If man has a chance to rectify his wrongs in this world, it is because of Mohammed's (PBUH) teachings. Muslims would not have known how to please Allah or earn His pleasure without the guidance provided by Mohammed (PBUH).

To love Mohammed (PBUH) is not just an admission of his valuable service but also a way to subjugate the ego. While many **Muslims believe that love resides in the heart and declare their love for Mohammed (PBUH) again and again, they must understand that unless they follow the Quran and *Sunnah*, their declaration of love is worthless.**

After contemplating the Prophet's (PBUH) question for a while Hazrat Omar Farooq returned to Mohammed (PBUH) with a new answer. He had convinced himself that his love for the Prophet Mohammed (PBUH) was far greater than that for himself, and was anxious to inform him. Mohammed (PBUH) smiled after hearing his declaration and told him that his *Iman* was now perfect.

Mohammed (PBUH) must have witnessed the *iman* of Hazrat Omar first hand; he must have seen his sacrifices, his behavior and his submission before Allah's will before concluding that his *iman* was perfect. So Muslims who believe that simply proclaiming their great love is enough to perfect their *iman* are mistaken. Since the interpretation is misleading, many refuse to put in greater efforts to prove their love and therefore their *iman* suffers. **Claiming to love the Prophet (PBUH) is easy, but proving it through deeds and actions is the difficult part.**

Loving the self is a sign of ego, which is a vice that Islam disapproves. So the commandment to love Allah and His Prophet is taking an axe to one's own ego. If man refuses to kill his ego for the love of Allah and His Prophet (PBUH), then he would fail to achieve the highest level of *iman*. True love for Allah and His Prophet (PBUH) would also lead to enmity with the devil. However, if man keeps pleasing the devil by following his ways, by running after the transitory pleasures of life and by harboring greed, hatred and pride in his heart, then he does not love Allah or the Prophet (PBUH) like he says.

To be a genuine Muslim, a follower of Islam must have a burning desire to understand the messages in the Quran and those left behind by Mohammed (PBUH), plus personal experiences of the spiritual and practical realms, encompassing the devotional and the institutional teachings of Islam.

Although, time has changed a lot in the material aspect, the spiritual and moral nature of man remain the same and so does his physical nature. He still needs to eat, sleep, marry, have relationships, work, etc.; therefore, all laws laid out for man by the Quran and *Sunnah* are still valid.

THE REALITY BEHIND "RICH MAN'S BLESSING AND POOR MAN'S TESTS"

Every soul shall have a taste of death: and we test you by making your life hard, full of evil, or by making your life good and easy. After all, to Us you return. (The Quran, 21:35)

Another misconception carried by many about the trials and tribulations of Muslims is that only the poor and suffering face the tests of faith; whereas, the reality is that a life of ease and comfort is as much a test as a life of pain and misery. Allah tests men by giving them in abundance and by taking away what was His to begin with.

When a person is closer to Allah, his level of *iman* is higher, and it becomes easy for him to recognize his tests. When the level of *iman* is high, a man's good deeds shrink in his eyes and alternately his sins magnify. Such a man, rich or poor, keeps strict checks on himself and struggles for purity of his heart. However, when a person is closer to the devil, his level of *iman* is low; therefore, he finds pride in every little good that he does. His sins look minute to him compared to his good deeds. If this person is rich, he believes that Allah is pleased with him; therefore, has showered him with blessings. If he is poor, he feels that Allah is being unfair to him and not blessing him despite his good deeds.

How man reacts to a life of luxury and a life of pain determines what he is facing. A trial and a test may turn into a punishment if man is ungrateful and full of pride.

True believers are those who are patient in times of suffering and are forever grateful in times of ease. They spend their time praying, repenting and doing good; whereas, the non-believers are full of doubts and confusion. They blame Allah for their plight and question His wisdom.

IS WEALTH A SYMBOL OF SUCCESS?

In our present world, success is measured in terms of wealth, the more wealth one has accumulated the more successful one is deemed. However, **in Allah's eye, only the most pious is the most successful.** So thinking that a person is rich and successful, because Allah has blessed him, or poor and unsuccessful because Allah is angry with him or testing him is a theory that is wide off the mark in Islam. It could be that a rich person is unsuccessful and lost in the eyes of Allah, and a poor person is successful and so much closer to his Lord.

Unfortunately, it is a common misconception that if one is successful in this world and has it all: money, power and position–it is due to Allah's pleasure. However, we must understand that materialistic gains are not indications of success or God's pleasure. **Allah is committed to taking care of us in this world,** regardless of our beliefs, performance or obedience, **and He will only judge us on the Day of Retribution.**

Another argument is that no one was created in vain. Allah will not allow any man a free passage in this world. Every mortal would be tested, as He said Himself:

Who hath created life and death that He may try you: which of you is best in conduct; and He is the Mighty, the Forgiving. (The Quran, 67:2)

When man deludes himself into thinking that some people have it easy, he must remind himself of Allah's promises. No one has it easy. Every man faces a test at some point in his life and carries a burden which only he can carry.

Be sure We shall test you with something of fear and hunger, some loss in goods, lives and the fruits (of your toil), but give glad tidings to those who patiently persevere. (The Quran, 2:155)

SIGN OF ALLAH'S FAVOR

Sickness, pain and problems are also Allah's ways of purifying us. Since we can't always tell if Allah is pleased with us or not, we can do our own little checks to find answers. **If a man is motivated to do good deeds consistently, then it is a good sign of Allah perhaps guiding him towards the path of righteousness. However, if a person keeps vacillating between good and bad then he is under the influence of the devil. Remember, a man with an impure heart and weak *iman* is an easy target for the devil. Inconsistency can be taken as a sign that is both negative and positive: negative because Allah may not be happy, and positive because one is still returning to good.**

IS ISLAM FOR THE RICH AND POWERFUL?

Islamic scholars and leaders, the *ulema* and *imams*, all teach that *iman* is the most essential element of Islamic belief. Although this statement is true, their belief that *iman* comes from knowledge, and that as Islamic knowledge increases, so does the level of *iman*, is erroneous.

The idea that more knowledge means more *iman* is fallacious because all men do not have similar access to knowledge. We all know that men would be judged on the quality and degree of their *iman*; saying that unless man has the right knowledge, his *iman* can't grow is a lot like saying that *iman* has been reserved for the rich and well to do, because a poor man would never have the same means as a rich man and therefore no chance of growing his *iman*.

Knowledge does not come easily. It requires money and time: two luxuries that only the affluent have in abundance. Since the poor neither have money nor the luxury of free time, they are denied knowledge and, consequently, the chance to elevate their *iman*. This entire concept is based on hearsay and has no validity in Islam. **The truth is that *iman* is the source of true knowledge and comes from love, purity of heart, kindness and the desire to please Allah. By practicing gratitude and graciousness, man can develop love for Allah.**

THE REALITY BEHIND "WHAT MATTERS IS WHAT IS IN THE HEART"

How many times have you heard the above statement? How many times have you uttered it yourself? While *iman* does lie in the heart and is all that matters, the statement is only valid when you understand what true *iman* is and the real meaning behind, "What matters is what is in the heart!"

Most of the times, the statement is used to rebuff well-wishers who approach us with sincere advice concerning our religion. The minute someone questions our actions with regard to our faith, we tell them it is none of their business, and what matters is what is in the heart. Are we aware all those times, that Allah sees what is in the heart? The statement might stop our parents, friends, relatives and teachers in their tracks and fill them with doubt, but can we really use that excuse to get away from the all-seeing eyes of Allah? Admit it; the statement is used to convey one message, "I am doing my best," In all sincerity, it is just a slap on the wrist, discouraging others from further intervention in our lives.

A woman who does not wear hijab and a man who does not go

for congregational prayers will both use the same excuse to cover their defiance against Allah's rules. **The truth is that true *iman* shines through a person, through their deeds and through their thought**s. *Iman* is not something to be ashamed of. Muslims should carry their oath to Allah as a badge of honor and prestige.

Today, Muslims believe that it is okay to copy and follow non-Muslims and lose their own identities while trying to be like them. These are the people who use the what-matters-is-what-is-in-the-heart excuse to get away from performing *salah*, *saum*, *zakat* and *hajj*. These are the people who indulge in *haram* with non-Muslims, and think it is okay, because, to them, their hearts are pure. For such people, it is very difficult to exhibit a strong Muslim identity, openly, because their hearts and minds are under the influence of their non-Muslim friends. These people are simply duping themselves and no one else.

"To each his own," is a dogma that would apply on the Day of Judgment; it does not apply to Islam or its followers in this world. "My *iman* is in my heart" is only legitimate when that *iman* reflects in your words and actions.

The problem is our comfort zones. Most of us are so comfortable with what we know and believe, that we do not welcome any new information, especially if it goes against our preconceived notions. People fear change and having to change. There is something within them that compels them to stay the same and hold the same belief, no matter how fallacious it is.

Accepting mistakes and faults is also a huge issue for some people. That one has been at fault not for a day or two but for one's entire life is a colossal tragedy which people simply can't bear. So they cringe and withdraw and refuse to change or rectify their wrongs. *Iman* does not reside in the hearts of such Muslims, but fear and misgivings do, and that is all that matters to them. It's sad, because **stepping out of one's comfort zone is the first step towards building *iman*.**

THE REALITY BEHIND 'BLIND CONVICTION AND UNQUESTIONING FAITH'

Muslims and non-Muslims who have little knowledge about Islam call it a religion of blind conviction and unquestioning faith. They base their theory on scriptures from the Quran which, according to them, forbid man to use his own logic and reasoning. What baloney!

Islam is the only religion which asks man to use his faculties. It gives countless examples from the past, from what is known and from what is unknown to man, to educate him about himself, his Lord, the world and the universe. Whoever questions the validity of the Quran has only to pick up facts from the book which were revealed at a time when men rode camels and had no concept of science and its wonders. **The facts came straight from the Maker and are being confirmed by science even today.**

With irrefutable evidence strewn all around us, does Allah still need to reveal Himself for us to believe in Him? Where is the test in that? He has given man books, messengers and even signs which should be enough to convince an open mind and heart of His existence. **Reading the Quran, studying the life of the Prophet (PBUH) and pondering over the mysteries of the universe persuades man to believe in a Superpower, and that is not blind conviction.**

Faith is not always unquestioning. Allah has proved His Lordship over and over again. Even Moses (PBUH) believed in Allah, but his heart wanted conviction. He asked Allah to reveal Himself, but he could not witness His light.

And when Musa (Moses) came at the time and place appointed by Us, and his Lord spoke to him, he said: 'O my Lord! Show me (Yourself), that I may look upon You.' Allah said: 'You cannot see Me, but look upon the mountain; if it stands still in its place then you shall see Me.' So when his Lord appeared to the mountain, He made it collapse to dust, and Musa (Moses) fell down unconscious. Then when he recovered his senses he said: 'Glory be to You, I turn to You in repentance, and I am the first of the believers.' (The Quran 7:143)

Weak *iman* questions for the sake of questioning. Man is not perfect; he has his flaws and weaknesses. Among these weaknesses, is doubt. **Faith questions when a man's heart is filled with doubt, but when man is seeking the truth and nothing else, then Allah blesses his heart with conviction. Guidance is bestowed on only those who are receptive to it. Close-minded people seldom receive guidance, because Allah gives what you ask for.**

Allah will protect and value a man's *iman* if he protects it and values it himself. **To develop *iman*, man needs to fulfill two basic conditions of desire and commitment.**

1. Desire: Man must desire to please Allah by doing good, shunning vice and perfecting *Iman*.

2. Commitment: Man must show commitment to Allah by frequently evaluating his *nafs*, actions, motives, etc.

Blind convictions and unquestioning faith come with understanding of the religion, Quran and *Sunnah* and are developed with time.

THE REALITY BEHIND 'TO THINK OR NOT TO THINK?'

While the Quran invites man to think and ponder over the mystery of creation and the secret behind his descent, Muslims scholars, who are stumped for answers, hush those who raise questions by discouraging them to think. The seekers of truth are told to accept the decree of Allah and not to harbor doubts.

"Don't think, just do," is what Muslim parents tell their kids. This lesson stays with them for the rest of their lives, and they start to believe that Islam discourages thinking, when the reality is exactly the opposite. Another harsh reality is that most of us go through life reading the Quran but not understanding it.

How can one reflect over something one hardly understands? If Muslim children were taught to understand the Quran, a lot of misconceptions would evaporate on their own.

We have sent down to you a book in which is your remembrance/ mentioning. Will you not, then use reason? (The Quran, 21:10)

THE BRAIN AVOIDS PAINFUL THOUGHTS

Personal strive is important to develop *iman* and fear of Allah. Unless man thinks over the reality of his existence, he cannot develop the requisite attitude towards life. Pain is disliked by both, the brain and the body; therefore, they both go to extra lengths to avoid pain. **While the body avoids painful situations the brain avoids painful thoughts which is the main reason why people are not overly enthusiastic about attending lectures on fires of hell, wrath of Allah and the punishments of the grave and hereafter.**

This behavior is not just manifested in individuals but also in collective groups. For example, when a country is caught in economic or political turmoil its citizens hang on to little shreds of hope to avoid thoughts of imminent disaster.

People in general do not like to think or talk about the dark future as long as it's avoidable. They give themselves excuses why things couldn't be all that bad and start believing in miracles. While it is okay to think about the world that way where one person cannot change the political scenario or the economy by himself, the afterlife is an entirely different ball game where only personal efforts would count and make a difference.

Avoiding thoughts of life after death or the imminent end is idiocy; not thinking about your actions will neither change the end

nor the consequences of disobedience, but thinking might push you to act and understand Allah's will.

CHANGE STARTS WITH US

Islam is a beacon that was meant to illuminate the world. Muslims were to be torch bearers, and were meant to spread the light and end the reign of ignorance. However, the light grows dim. Misconceptions, mistaken beliefs and false impressions regarding Islam harbored by Muslims end up blocking its light from reaching their own hearts, let alone the world and its inhabitants. **Muslims today, must realize that their characters, beliefs, understanding of Islam and manner of worship have some serious flaws, and identifying these problems is the first step towards rectifying them.** Unless Muslims understand the true teachings of Islam, they cannot spread its message to the people of the world, nor can they save themselves from the final accountability.

QUESTIONS FOR REFLECTION

- Why is mankind afraid of the unknown?
- Do you agree with the Encarta Dictionary definition of Islam?
- How would you explain what Islam is?
- If Islam means to be in a state of submission of our will to Allah then do you believe we are in that state? If not, what do we have to do to return to that state?
- What would make that submission or surrendering easy?
- Do you think Allah would accept anything less than surrendering our will to Him? What do you think Allah is saying in Quran 3:83?
- The suffering we Muslims are facing all over the world, is it because we are being tested or is it because we have broken

moral, physical, ethical and Islamic laws, and have provoked Allah's Wrath?

- Do you believe Islam is a business deal where we are allowed to make a deal with Allah, one good deed to buy Allah's Mercy to delete one bad deed?

- Or we can simply buy a palace in Heaven by investing our money, irrespective of whether it is Halal or Haram, to build a Masjid?

- Or we can invest our Halal/Haram money to buy copies of Quran for distribution and collect a reward as the interest of our investment?

- Or we have to make ourselves worthy of Heaven by changing ourselves, getting out of our comfort zone and going back to Him with a pure heart?

- Do you believe knowing what is good and what Allah wants us to do would lead us to Heaven if we don't know the path that leads to it?

- When we believe we deserve a reward for every little good deed we do and continue sinning without paying any attention to the commandments of Allah then what do you think we are, humble or arrogant?

- If we don't make a conscious effort to stay away from sin because we believe Allah is Merciful and Forgiving, do you think He will forgive us based on our intention behind the disobedience?

- Do you believe Allah is only Merciful and Forgiving, and not Just, Abaser, Humiliator and the Destroyer?

- There are Hadith that mention glad tidings, punishment of grave and punishment of Hell, do you believe Prophet Muhammad (pbuh) will intercede even though we entertain ourselves with his glad tidings and pay no attention to his Hadith regarding punishments of grave and Hell?

- We claim to be believers and are very busy doing everything except following Allah's commandments. Are we Muslims or Hypocrites in this case?

- Can memorizing Quran save us from Hell Fire if we don't act upon its dictates? Can Allah wipe out the Quran from our hearts, if He is not satisfied with our level of obedience?

- Islam provides a system that is in complete harmony with the moral and material aspects of man. Can we still qualify for Allah's Mercy if we break this system and live out of it? Would Hadith be considered authentic if it does not comply with this system?

- What are the basic rules that can be applied to understand Hadith?

- What is a sign of being righteous or being under the influence of Devil?

- What is a comfort zone, how does it affect change, especially preconceived notions, and can we build Iman without stepping out of our comfort zone?

- What do we have to do to build our Iman?

RISING FROM THE ASHES
NOVI, UNITED STATES,
1997–2005

You've seen my descent; now watch my rising –Rumi

HOW LONG DOES it take a man to piece together a broken heart? Just about as long as it takes him to walk into a new relationship, but then why would a man get out of one relationship, only to rush into a second one?

While most divorced men marry again, there are few who don't. Those who do marry do it because they are so attuned to the married lifestyle that returning to an empty quiet house becomes a feat in itself. Plus, a silent house invites loneliness which preys on the mind and grieves the soul.

When I married the first time, I was like a child having a first go at building a tower of blocks. I wanted it to be tall and well-built. I wanted it to be magnificent. I admired my progress, the height of my tower, its structure and my continuous efforts to make it bigger and better. Although, I made plenty of mistakes, I was too naive and too headstrong to see the error of my ways. Then, while I was still at it, the tower started to shake and suddenly it toppled. Despite trying, I couldn't save a single pillar. My efforts, my time and my love, everything that I put into the building, unexpectedly amounted to nothing.

Needless to say, I was traumatized, but as soon as I collected myself, I started to rebuild.

It was a dull, dry October day in 1996 when I moved back into my home. All my hopes of returning to normal were dashed when I saw its rundown state. The house and its misery kept reminding me of my own. To return some semblance of normality to my life, I started fixing what was broken. I threw out everything that wasn't needed, and bit by bit, the house started to perk up like a patient in recovery. Yusuf became my eager sidekick, and together we cleaned up the lawn and planted asters: pale pinks, hot pinks and purples.

The blast of color in my garden made me feel washed out, but every weekend, I would put on my most persuasive smile and sport my tough Dad attitude for the sake of my children. Inside I felt haggard and old; I felt unsure, incompetent and guilty, and the guilt made a meal out of me just as soon as my children left.

My connection with Allah was not stable during that time. I would offer my prayers, and I would offer my thanks, and then I would allow my demons to push me into a dark abyss. I would stand there terrified, unable to move forward or backward, until the sun would rise, and my limbs would automatically spring to life.

Work was work, and I would go through it like a machine, not feeling and not caring. Home was everything, but I started to hide from people. After returning from work, I would find myself in the same chair each day. I would lose hours and not remember anything of it.

By this time, Bin Yamin had graduated from high school and was planning to join the U.S. Marines. Yusuf wanted to go to the University of Michigan after his graduation. Just the thought of having to part with them was driving me crazy. I believe, under normal circumstances, I would have been okay with it, but at that point in my life, I was not prepared, in any way, to live alone.

Empty houses are triggers for self-discovery. I discovered things about myself that I hadn't known before. I realized that I was a family man—without a family. I realized that I liked being married; although,

I was freshly divorced. I realized that I was an introvert, despite being outgoing and verbose.

My friends guessed my state from the bags under my eyes and my shrinking frame before they started dropping hints about a second marriage. And although I was a sorry mess back then, I was willing to take the necessary steps to change my life for the better.

A second marriage became an option, because nothing else seemed to be working for me. I had friends and social organizations to keep me busy and happy. I was busy, but despite letting go, I was far from happy.

I started looking for a companion and that's when I met Yasmeen. She was everything I was not looking for. She was years younger than me, but the minute we met, certain things fell right into place for both of us. It was another meant-to-be and on November 11, 1999, just two months after our first meeting, we tied the knot.

Man, in his ignorance, plans not just for the day after but for years after. He plans to minimize risks, pain and disasters in the future. My second wife and I did not rush into marriage; although, by western standards it might appear so. When we sat down at the table, we behaved like two adults who had learned well from their past mistakes. We brought our apprehensions, our wisdom, our priorities and our fears to the table and discussed everything that we were passionate about: our kids and our beliefs. We met each other halfway and settled all potentially explosive matters before saying, "I do."

Yasmeen was mature and uncomplicated. She spoke her mind and believed in discussing issues rather than bottling them up for later. I appreciated that about her, convinced that we would be able to discuss things in a civil manner without bringing out the big guns. Sadly, I was mistaken. We each made one grave error: I walked into marriage again, looking for self-gratification; she walked into it with me seeking her own fulfillment. So the minute we walked in, everything started to fall apart.

I could not let my second marriage fail. I am sure Yasmeen felt the same way–cheated by fate. Nothing matched. Nothing seemed to work. Nothing seemed good enough. In a matter of days, our differences grew as big as our house. Although, in the beginning, I tried ignoring the growing chasm, a time came when it was impossible to look away.

It had started to go downhill and all too quickly. My sixth sense had warned me that a second marriage might affect my relationship with my kids, and when it started to happen, I felt torn. Yusuf withdrew into himself, and I missed major happenings in his life.

Whatever happened to marital bliss? When our problems got out of hand, Yasmeen followed in Kauser's footsteps. She approached my friends and community social workers. Every day, I dreaded going out because I expected well-wishers to approach me with the all too knowing eyes. I expected them to answer Yasmeen's call for help, but for whatever reason, no one did.

We could not sit down and talk like civilized people. Was it us or does marriage brings out the worst in some people? Everything Yasmeen and I had discussed went down the drain. When I started to have memory lapses, I took to penning my emotions. Somehow, I had come to believe that I wasn't great at communicating my feelings. I wrote letters to my wife and to my children, clarifying misunderstandings and communicating my thoughts.

When my wife ignored my letters, my anger came back with a vengeance, and so did my depression. I would be high one day, ready to take on the world and the many challenges of a married life, but the next day I would be raging like a bull, within hours, and my energy levels would come spiraling down, leaving me depressed. On those days, nothing would cheer me up.

Our arguments continued. I left the house for a week after a particularly bad day, and when I returned, Yasmeen convinced me that I had bipolar disorder and needed medical help. I was disoriented and having a tough time coping with my second marriage. I was also at a loss and ashamed of my own uselessness. Since Yasmeen was a medical technologist and knew a lot about physical and mental health, I agreed to get a checkup. She called Dr. Nabila Farooq, her sister in law, who was a psychiatrist and asked for a recommendation. Later, I got a health check at the University Psychiatric Center (UPC), Livonia. As it turned out, I did not need medical help at all.

Certain incidents reminded me so strongly of my previous marriage that I was thrown off track quite often, but Yasmeen stuck it out with me every step of the way. Our problem was that we kept inviting each other to a destination, and when both of us failed to reach there at the given time, each resented the other and saw them as a mistake. Today, I have learnt that marriage is not a destination, but a journey in itself.

Sometimes help comes in damaging forms. Sometimes the biggest help is a kind word. An old man who is on the verge of losing himself simply needs a validation of his life's struggles. He needs to hear, to see and feel love. He needs to just be allowed to spend the remaining days of his life not trying to prove who he is, but just being.

Yasmeen might have had the best of intentions, but the support I received was crippling me. I moved out of the house on July 31, 2005.

I did not abandon my wife; I simply decided to help myself. I needed time and space, and as impossible as it was to believe, I needed to find Allah. All my life, I had looked towards people for approval, for a validation of self, for help and support. Expectations had left me wounded and more alone then I had ever felt.

For a few months, I lived the life of a recluse–cut off from everything that had once mattered so much to me. Then, out of the blue, I got a call from Yasmeen and an appointment with Dr. John P. Quarton, another clinical psychologist. I decided to indulge my wife, and after a dozen sessions, I would like to say that Dr. Quarton succeeded in his endeavors. But no, it wasn't the doctor who tamed my heart and calmed my soul. It was something else, entirely.

AL ASR:
THE DECLINING DAY

(I swear) By the time. Indeed, mankind is in loss. (The Quran, 103:1–2)

WE DON'T HAVE AN ETERNITY TO REALIZE OUR DREAMS
BUT ONLY THE TIME WE HAVE HERE.

THE WORLD IS a track; time is ticking, and man is in a race against himself. Each stride forward creates a new past and a new future. While it is true that the past and the future both shape memories and mold expectations, in actuality, they are both simulations of the mind. The former spells nothing but loss and the latter an impossible destination.

Modern men and women have become enslaved by time, predominantly the past and the future. Men dwell more in these two abstractions than in the present moment. Since past and present offer ephemeral refuge, they sometimes evade their problems by revisiting and reinventing their past and other times by fantasizing about their future. In doing so, they conveniently ignore the most important determinant of their lives–the present.

In the Holy Quran, 103, Allah puts the spotlight on man, yet again forcing him to acknowledge his present life situation. A dire urgency surrounds this message from Allah, who declares man in a state of perpetual failure. Imagine a drowning man. This man hasn't the time to look back and curse his choices or to look forward and plan his tomorrow. To survive, he must concentrate on the present, which offers him just two choices: he can try to swim and live, or he can give up and perish. Since man is hardwired for survival, every instinct in him fights for life.

WHY IS MAN IN PERPETUAL LOSS?
THE DROWNING MAN

The world is similar to an ocean, its depth capable of swallowing the whole of mankind. However, not many realize its hidden dangers. In this world, one of man's biggest detriments is time, which is constantly on the run. With each breath that man takes, time is ticking away, and whether he likes it or not, or is ready for it or not, it is steadily running out on him.

All men have a higher purpose in life–not just Muslims. Additionally, all men are immersed in a sea of loss–not just Muslims. Whoever lives, must die, because time is incapable of being stopped. It can neither be turned back, nor fast forwarded. What man loses of his life in seconds or over a period of years cannot be retrieved or reclaimed, and that is the reality of man's life. Guidance has been provided, goals have been set, and whistles have been blown: any minute, any day, anyone can be called out.

People who do not seek the truth or who ignore the divine messages will ultimately sink in the abyss of darkness. When Allah calls men to reflect on the declining day, He warns them that they are losing the battle against time. The urgency surrounding this message is to propel man to act immediately. Man has promises to fulfill before he returns and time should not be taken lightly.

The drowning man will sink to the bottom of the ocean, unless he learns how to keep his head above water. For a Muslim, this means picking up the manual that would keep him from drowning and applying its principles to save his life. This manual is the Quran.

The sooner man learns and acts, the better his chances are of survival. Once a person starts to drown, it takes around 20 seconds for him to start sinking, another 30 or 90 for him to stop breathing. After the four-minute mark, he faces irrevocable damage and imminent death. For a drowning man, a matter of seconds becomes a matter of life and death. Likewise, when man renounces his faith or the purpose of his creation and embraces the worldly life, then it doesn't take him long to go under. He sinks so deep and so quickly that swimming back to the surface becomes next to impossible.

To survive, the drowning man must keep faith and thrash about his arms and legs until he succeeds in saving himself; to keep faith is to keep the struggle alive.

CERTAIN DEATH AND UNPREDICTABLE LIFE

For many, the idea of man being in perpetual loss is hard to digest. The reason is that man has become so comfortably settled in his worldly life, that anything that makes him reconsider or critique his easy lifestyle is an instant turnoff.

Life is almost as unpredictable as death, if not more. So when the question raised is, *"Why is man in perpetual loss?,"* it is for the same reason. The world is a temporary abode-cum-examination-hall, and **forgetting the true purpose of one's presence here will ultimately lead to failure.**

We are aware that life was not created in vain. **Man was created to serve Allah and to act as His vicegerent.** He came to Earth with a predetermined lifespan and a predetermined purpose. While some live long, others die young, but young or old, all have a purpose to fulfill before they come to their journey's end. Sometimes, goals are achieved, and other times the road simply ends. Nevertheless, many forget their true calling and end up losing themselves in this pretentious world. The result is that they plunge into a sea of loss. **The tragedy is that most don't even realize they are drowning and consequently fail to save themselves.**

Since Allah knew beforehand how many would sabotage their

lives in this world and the next, **He sent the Quran as a reminder. Its message is simple enough: do what you came here to do, before your time runs out.** But man, being a forgetful creature, seldom takes heed. Many live as if they have a pact with the Angel of Death that he will call before coming when they are well into old age, and only when they are just about ready to leave the world. **This ridiculous optimism robs men of their desire to change their present. They lose the urgency and grow negligent of their duties. The outcome is disheartening; precious time is lost, and men ultimately suffer the consequences.**

THE BOTTOMLESS PIT OF MAN'S DESIRES

As the day dissolves into night and disappears forever, so do men and entire nations from the face of the earth. Men throughout history chased after wealth, power, land and beautiful things. Slaves to their unchecked desires, they accumulated colossal treasures and unrivalled powers which mystified the rest of mankind. These symbols of worldly success were beyond compare and capable of conquering the whole of humanity. However, they were no match for the Angel of Death, before whom treasures became worthless and power ineffectual.

A common misconception is that Allah addresses just the believers in the Quran. The truth is that Holy Quran, 103: Al Asr, is a personal warning for each and every man. Time is running out for all of Allah's creation, not just the believers. Men come and men depart, while time stands witness to their rise and demise. In the Quran, Al Asr rings like a loud double-bell alarm, jolting man from his slumber and propelling him to act before it is too late.

It seems like Allah has placed a magnetic attraction in this world, and man is constantly pulled towards it. Irrespective of his physical and mental capabilities, he tries his utmost to achieve the best and the biggest to quench his thirst for the world. **While man's desire for money, power and carnal pleasure is limitless, his indulgences depend upon his physical and mental aptitude, which vacillate from nonentity to entirety, giving man the choice to reduce himself to dirt or to become the ruler of the world if he so wishes.**

While the world exerts a magnetic pull on all men, **heaven and hell behave like two poles of another magnet**, not just pulling but also repelling at the same time. The north pole of the magnet, or heaven, which lies above the seven skies, pulls the righteous men towards it; whereas, the south pole, or hell, which lies below the seven terrains, repels them, simultaneously pulling the sinners to its fiery belly. (*May Allah forgive our faults and save us from the chastisement of the fire. Ameen.*)

EGOTISM AND THE DESIRE TO CONTROL

Man has a ravenous desire for control. The more he conquers and controls, be it land or people, the more he rises in his own eyes and that of others. Plus, he also harbors a desire to be pleasing not just to himself, but to other men as well. The same desire that makes man want to be liked by Allah also makes him want to be admired by the rest of humanity.

Often, innocent desires grow into a huge monster called narcissism, that lives on praise and adoration alone. The more man is acclaimed, the more he desires, and to fulfill these desires, he exhibits his wealth, influence, and possessions for the benefit of his friends, relatives, neighbors and countrymen, but more importantly for his own self-gratification. His narcissism grows to the point where he craves accolades to validate his *nafs*; his ego grows in the process, and he thrives on praise.

The desire to control and the desire to be praised are at their most innocent when they are small and above suspicion, but when they grow big and egotistical, they crave the world and devour the self. Men's physical and mental prowess becomes an exhibition of self and a means to achieve more control over the world. To satisfy his growing desires and pacify his ego, man goes after the only two commodities that can help him derive self-satisfaction: money and power.

The desire for control over all, drives man to commit serious crimes. It might start small, but one tiny offense leads to a big one, which then paves the way for a bigger one, until no crime is big enough or bad enough. In today's world, man is witness to many such power struggles, not only between nations, races and sects, but also between individuals in every walk of life. The result is always the same: more contentions, bigger disruptions and a marked escalation in the crime index.

CRIME IS PUNISHMENT

Crime is punishment in itself. While many believe that punishment is an aftermath of an offense, a true believer knows that when Allah hardens the hearts of men, it is punishment; when Allah stops the eyes from appreciating the truth, the ears from acknowledging it and the tongue from propagating it, it is punishment, and when Allah makes committing sins easy, it is punishment.

Crimes are seldom rewarding in the long run. The life of a criminal punishes in two ways: physically and mentally. While stealing, molesting and killing may or may not result in physical injuries or punishments by the law of the country, it unfailingly results in emotional turmoil and robs one of peace. Plus, a guilty conscience is extremely burdensome on the heart.

Everyone is born with a pure heart. When a person commits a crime, he goes against his very nature; this offense is never forgotten or forgiven by his soul. Unless a person's heart is dead, it always guides him towards the right path, but if a person takes a different path, then the heart falls sick. The sickness can be cured by rectifying sins, but if the offender continues to defy his nature and the guidance provided by his heart, then the sickness grows, and the heart becomes diseased. A man with a sick heart can never be truly happy or at peace.

IGNORANCE–BLINDNESS OF THE SOUL

Man's biggest weakness is his ignorance, which makes him susceptible to satanic influences, ignorance concerning his purpose of descent, his Maker, the transience of life, and if not that, then lack

of knowledge and understanding of the Quran and commandments of Allah. Together, these inadequacies create a dearth of *iman* and allow the devil an easy passage into a man's heart.

Ignorance is blindness of the soul, and the blind see what they want to see. Whether man realizes it or not, ignorance is damaging. Man cannot hide in its fog for long. Facts do not disappear, if you close your eyes. Without knowledge and information man turns into a deadly animal. Consequently, he destroys everything in his wake and ultimately meets a sorry end himself.

Given all the measures that Allah took to guide mankind. He sent thousands upon thousands of divinely mandated messengers–some of whom received new codes of law, and others who followed the code of one who came before them, until eventually Mohammed (PBUH) was sent with the Quran to this world. There is no excuse left to be disobedient. Ignoring the messages and flouting the commands of Allah will result in severe punishment.

Ignoring the messages which have been preserved over hundreds of years so that men of all times may be guided by their light, is unwise. Imagine a man walking home. On his way, he sees a wide ditch in the middle of the road and a warning sign just before it. To get home, the man must cross the ditch, but he ignores the warning sign and continues to walk towards it. What do you expect will happen? There can be two possible outcomes:

1. He tries to jump and falls in, or

2. He is stranded.

Since he did not read the sign, he does not know about the detour, and therefore does not know what to do. In both cases, the man is at a loss. His ignorance or failure to read the sign will not save him from the dire consequences.

WITH GREAT POWER COMES GREATER RESPONSIBILITY

Sharing of knowledge spurred man on the road to progress. Much was achieved, and much was lost, but what man ultimately gained was better than his past. The power struggle was always there but the forces working against it were far greater, and knowledge spread far and wide. The more knowledgeable a person was, the more power he held and consequently a bigger responsibility to transfer that knowledge into the right hands. Some people gained control over others on the basis of their knowledge; some were corrupted in the process, and some simply feigned to be knowledgeable in order to gain control.

A little knowledge is a dangerous thing. Today, we have rulers who control because their coffers are filled with knowledge. They guard it well and do not allow its light to illuminate the world or even their own minds; instead, they take a little out of it to serve their own purposes, i.e., to acquire more power and wealth. Again, it is ignorance which keeps them from making the best use of their treasures and spreading the light of truth.

With great power comes great responsibility: a reason why tyrants would face severe trials. For instance, a preacher who does not follow his own teachings or a ruler who thinks he is above the law, are not doing justice to their stations. They are simply exerting power and control over others without any positive reinforcement or understanding of knowledge.

APATHY–A HEART DISEASE

Apathy is emotional emptiness, a trait that is repeatedly condemned in the Quran. Often, when the Quran gives clear cut orders, and man is too lazy, bored or indifferent to act on them, he becomes one of the worst losers.

When Allah commands man to share his blessings with the deprived, but man ignores the command and becomes indifferent to

the plight of others, then he is in trouble. Such a man feels little or nothing for his fellow humans. His main concern is his own self. Since his *iman* is weak, he depends only on himself for sustenance. He collects wealth to secure his future and to gain control. He might say he is a believer, but he is afraid to put his trust in Allah.

One must remember that a man of faith neither doubts nor hoards for tomorrow, because his belief is strong. Some people have money and worldly treasures, but despite being blessed, they lend no help, even when their wealth can save lives. Since wealth offers them security, pleasure and control over others, they value it more than life itself, and are always fearful of losing it. Lack of concern and hesitation in doing right lead to apathy. However, those who truly believe in Allah and His Messenger strive in his cause without faltering or dithering.

Apathy may initially affect a person's dealings with others, but it also quickly eats up his morals and makes him indifferent toward the laws set by Allah. For example, a Muslim is prohibited to eat *haram* food, but if he starts to think eating *haram* is not a big deal, he is a victim of apathy. A Muslim who consumes *haram* products, deliberately does not care for the decrees of his faith. The question is, if he does not care for his faith or the commands of Allah, does he still remain a Muslim?

Apathy causes people to behave in a carefree manner. Only those who believe they are answerable to no one do as they please. When another Muslim errs, be it a friend, relative or a neighbor, we are quick to notice, judge and critique. We also become instant authorities on the Quran and its teachings. However, when it comes to our own personal lives, we overlook our errors, excuse our sins and forget offences in the blink of an eye. At such times, we are more concerned about being caught in the act by others than by Allah. This is another example of apathy, when man refuses to acknowledge the distinction of Allah and puts his fellow men above Him.

There are lots of other cases in which apathy becomes a crime against faith. A heart filled with doubt and fear and a life marred with hardships are triggers of apathy and inaction. When man is uncertain and indecisive about doing the right thing, he must remember that Allah promised to test him through fear, love, deprivation and provision. Man's predicament could be a test of faith. Therefore, how he acts and reacts to it would decide his future.

Very often, people pull back, because they don't want to get involved or make things difficult for themselves. For the people who **waver and fail to choose the right side, even after declaring their** *iman*, Allah says:

> *They waver in between, neither belonging to this group, nor that group. Whomever God sends astray, you will never find a way to guide him. (The Quran, 4:143)*
> *The only people who wish to be excused are those who do not really believe in God and the Last Day. Their hearts are full of doubt, and their doubts cause them to waver. (The Quran, 9:45)*

Muslims today have become so preoccupied with worldly affairs that they have methodically spun a cocoon of apathy around them. The "I don't care" and "whatever" mantras that are practiced a dozen times a day have not just broken familial ties, but also spiritual ties with their Master. Plus, man is afraid to feel and afraid to witness or experience the desolation and misery around him. He lives for today and tomorrow and has conveniently forgotten the afterlife. Therefore, when it is time to act in the name of God, or for the betterment of his Muslim brothers and sisters, he gives excuses to himself and others, convincing himself that he is excused since he has a valid reason. Not striving in the cause of Allah due to apathetic tendencies is a serious offence in Islam. It can only be rectified if man assesses his excuses and his behavior in response to situations where he is compelled to choose between right and wrong. To maintain righteousness, strengthen *iman* and eventually attain salvation, it is necessary that man acts righteously, upholds truth and makes a sincere effort to please Allah. Plus, he must condemn evil and propagate goodness.

Only believers who wage *jihad* **against the devil and make a sincere effort to purify their hearts possess the wisdom and fortitude to choose the right side.**

Islam has no room for apathetic believers. Since a Muslim is Allah's vicegerent he must actively participate in spreading the light of Islam. Sometimes, when Muslim leaders focus on pursuing peace with non-Muslim friends and allies, they end up trading Allah's warnings and commands for the sake of worldly gains. In doing so, they forget that **real peace can only be achieved through establishing the laws of Allah.**

Apathy hurts the soul of a man's *iman*. The soul of a person weakens when he hesitates to obey Allah. In addition, the casual, uncaring and indifferent attitude of a Muslim towards Islam and other Muslims weakens the foothold of the Islamic *ummah*.

BLESSINGS, *IMAN* AND EXPECTATIONS

Allah has bestowed man with equal portions of desire and potential, but with dissimilar mental and physical abilities. What most people fail to comprehend is that Allah gives *rizq* to people in accordance with their physical and mental ability, as well. This means that people who are born with a higher level of intelligence, strength and capability have better chances of acquiring success and enjoying the luxuries of the world than those who are weak, mentally and physically. Despite that, Allah has blessed many, regardless of their physical and mental shortcomings.

—ɯ—

On the Day of Judgment, no two men will be judged on the same scale. All men will be evaluated on the basis of their possessions, inborn or acquired, and on what they bought and sold in the world. This means that the conqueror and the conquered will not be judged with the same stick, and neither would the resourceful and enlightened scholars be placed among the destitute and the deprived.

When a Muslim lacks *iman*, he expects more from Allah, but gives less. Despite God-given gifts and the blessings that surround him, man still carries an ungrateful attitude towards Allah. **Most men overvalue, overestimate and overrate themselves and believe they deserve bigger and better. They expect and desire special treatment, more attention, popularity and all their wishes to come true. When that doesn't happen, they turn bitter or indifferent.**

The sphere of man's expectations and desires grows bigger as he climbs higher on the ladder of success. More money, stronger power and a privileged status in this world become the means to fulfill his every whim and fancy. Man becomes a slave to his ambitions. The more he feeds his desires, the more they demand from him. A time comes when he considers himself better than other men, on the basis of power and wealth. Since he does not share his blessings, his heart is hardened. He follows his own moral compass, which points wherever he wants. Allah allows him reprieve for as long as He wills and then, without warning, He intervenes and justice is served.

Money, power and position strip man of his morality, if he is not careful. Since everything is easily accessible to a rich man, it is far easier for him to indulge his fancies than a man of poor means. **A life of ease and luxury lulls him towards forbidden pleasures, plus the devil plays his part in tempting him, and the man ends up hurting not just himself, but also the society he lives in. At first he loses his morals, next his *iman* and eventually his fear of Allah. His loose morals set a bad example for the people living around him.**

While greed for wealth and power infects the hearts of men, personal gifts of Allah like beauty, intelligence and talents fill it with love and pride. Consequently, man develops a desire for attention and special treatment, but since he thinks of himself as deserving and praiseworthy, he justifies them instead of reproving them. These sentiments are entertained by not just ordinary men, but also men of the book, the religious and the enlightened ones.

Today many religious scholars, even *imams,* rank themselves above ordinary men, believing that their knowledge gives them a higher status that makes them smarter and holier than others. These men of knowledge expect believers to wait for them, even when they are late for prayers. Plus, they discourage others from consulting the Quran themselves, lest they find their own answers and not need them. These two actions are confirmations of their inflated self-worth.

Similarly, men involved in social and community work, or men who have memorized the Holy Quran or performed pilgrimage to Makkah, and like actions, frequently evaluate themselves against others and rate themselves above most. Their egos swell, turning them into special beings above ordinary men, and as a result, they expect to be treated like uncrowned royalties by everyone around them.

Unfortunately, most of us are victims of our own puffed-up self-image. We deem ourselves better, in one way or another: kinder, smarter, funnier, braver, more astute, better looking and more generous than an average man on the street.

Man over-values himself, because he is guilty of undervaluing his Creator. He sees and appreciates what he has, but forgets his Benefactor. In some cases, he thinks his traits and skills are his own achievements. He overlooks a critical line of reasoning: whoever blessed him has blessed many others. This simple fact makes him just another man on the street. Another dynamic that he ignores: whoever gave him his qualities also has the power to take them away. This fact makes him a man of the moment: he has it today, but who is to say that he will have it tomorrow.

It is nothing but Allah's kindness, mercy and blessings that man has the gifts that unfortunately become the cause of his pride and self-proclaimed superiority. **A true man of faith, when blessed, becomes more thankful to Allah, more fearful of His anger, and more humble in his dealings with other men.** He understands that bigger the gifts mean bigger the trials. He realizes that Satan attacks men of God more vehemently than reprobates. These realizations keep him vigilant and steadfast on the path of the righteous. It does not mean that life becomes easy, or that the man of God does not fight battles of his own. He does, but his recognition of right and wrong and his awareness of himself helps him keep things real.

CHANGED PRIORITIES AND FAILING *IMAN*

When man changes his priorities to suit his lifestyle, his *iman* deteriorates in the process. In the times of Mohammed (PBUH), men valued the verses that held the word of Allah. With the passage of time, life became easier and man became lazy and easy going. His priorities changed. Staying on duty 24/7 became a mountain of a task; therefore, he started to look for a way out. **Very soon he became his own priority, and the commands of Allah lost their significance for him.**

The Quran, which was once placed and revered above everything, lost its rightful place. To him, the *hadith* were easier and less demanding. They did not seem to weigh him down or interfere too much with his easy lifestyle.

To the ignorant man, the Quran is the word of Allah and *hadith* are good news. While the Quran instills fear in him, the *hadith* he chooses to follow fill him with satisfaction and soothe his spirits. The fact is, ignoring reality even for a little while will not create a new one, the problem will simply grow bigger and harder to tackle. **The Quran and *hadith* must be followed in their entirety and must be studied comprehensively. Taking little morsels from an entire body of knowledge to suits one's own palate will have dire consequences.**

Life lived in this world will be accounted for in the afterlife. Following the Quran and *Sunnah* is not child's play. No shortcomings and excuses will work; struggle and efforts will be measured. **Men who prefer the ease of this world over the comforts of the next must rethink their stratagem and prioritize their lives once again.**

DOUBTS AND TEMPTATIONS

The two biggest hurdles preventing man from accepting the truth behind the Quranic verses are: doubts and temptations.

Once doubts and temptations infest the hearts and minds of men, they distort *iman* and lead people astray. While doubts are intellectual problems created by the mind and influenced by satan that keep man from accepting the truth, temptations are purely psychological problems, created by the heart and influenced by satan, that turn man into a pleasure seeker. In both instances man's *iman* is under attack, and his faculties are too weak to fight back.

Only those who:

- believe
- perform righteous deeds
- guide people towards truth, and
- encourage them to be patient

are the ones who have a chance in this life and will do well in the afterlife.

Man is self-obsessive. Unless he looks at people who are worse off than he is, he indulges in self-pity, which makes him ungrateful. Immersed in his own afflictions and self-induced misery, he forgets the next life and the bigger trials that await him.

Self-obsessed men who find it hard to look beyond their own lives ultimately fall prey to three things:

1. They forget Allah, and their belief turns to disbelief;
2. They forget the past and the lessons taught by it;
3. They forget the Quran and its messages.

When man forgets Allah, the first thing he loses is his fear of Him. He stops seeing Him in His creation and his belief clouds over. Very soon, he forgets that he owes Allah his life and is duty-bound to Him. His own problems blind him to the bigger hurdles that he must overcome to achieve salvation.

When man forgets his past and the lessons repeatedly taught by history, he risks hurting himself, over and over again. Men who suffered previously due to their actions and inactions left glowing warning signs for those who came after. Although, the signs indicate what to do and what not to do, there are people who ignore the warnings and do as they please. The result is painful punishment.

When man chooses to forget the revelations of Allah he thoughtlessly cuts off his lifeline. There is guidance in the Quran for man, so that he may not lose his path, but the unfortunate ones neither heed the guidance nor follow instructions and invariably put themselves at unnecessary risk.

WAR TO ESTABLISH PEACE AND JUSTICE

Another reason why man is at loss is his judgmental attitude towards others. When man goes beyond his call of duty to Allah and appoints himself a judge over other Muslims, proclaiming some guilty and hell-bound, while others pious and victors, he commits a breach against Allah.

A man of faith, a follower of Mohammed (PBUH) and a servant of Allah is commanded to **invite people to the right path, not a destination.** Guidance is in Allah's hands. The work of a believer is simply to spread the light.

In his arrogance, man exceeds and goes beyond what is expected of him, and in doing so, he does more harm than good. It is religious people who give birth to atheists and the ignorant Muslims who create Islamophobes.

When Muslims kill and wrongly ascribe it to their Lord, when they condemn other faiths and force people to convert, they are not following their religion, but the dictates of their own soiled hearts. A true believer understands the message of the Quran, which clearly asks Muslims not to insult the gods of others, because it becomes an invitation to non-Muslims to insult theirs.

Islam is a religion of peace, which mandates defensive war, or *jihad,* **when a believer's life or property is under threat. Even then,** *jihad* **has a clear set of rules which forbid the killing of the elderly,**

women and children, it even forbids harming trees, while at war with the enemy.

Today, there is not one country in this world that has a similar set of rules for war and not one country that would not defend its boundaries. Islam has no boundaries. The Muslim *ummah* exists on every little strip of inhabited land, and Muslims too have a right to peace and security.

Islam permits war only to eliminate injustice and unfairness, and it is not unique in this aspect. Judaism, Christianity and even the ancient religion of Buddhism teach the same thing. Unfortunately, what the followers of these faiths do is an entirely different thing.

The ignorant fools, the mute Islamic intellectuals, and the enemies of Islam have together succeeded in tarnishing the image of Islam. It is sad how not just non-believers but even believers shy away from certain verses of the Quran without trying to seek a better understanding.

Pick up a book, randomly open it to a page, read the third line from the second paragraph. Now close the book and give your opinion of it. Is the book violent, tragic, funny, boring, informative, historic or a page-turner? That is exactly how people of the world are judging Islam: if not from the cover, then from random lines taken out of context that can be twisted to mean anything.

The Quran is no ordinary book. It is deep and mysterious, because there is so much more to it than what appears on the surface. The more one seeks, the more one finds. This does not mean that the Quran cannot be understood easily by an ordinary man, but that it will give just as much as a person asks for. Look for something deeper, more precious and more rewarding, and it will reveal its treasures and will go on revealing for as long as a person continues to search.

FORSAKING GOD-MADE LAWS

Islamic laws once held precedence over man-made laws. Today, however, man has nullified them and validated his own legislations. While it is easy to pardon the ignorance and injudiciousness of the non-believers, there is no excuse good enough for the effrontery of Muslims.

Be it a secular democratic government or an authoritarian, a plutocracy or a stratocracy, Muslims in all corners of the world are bowing to the laws created by man. They find it easier to accept and obey the rules and regulations, because the fear of man's punishment condensed in their hearts is far more real and effective for them than the fear of Allah and His reckoning. Plus, they are quick to justify and defend not just the laws they follow, but also their own actions.

Man is astute in some matters and obtuse in others. He finds it easy to understand the theory of crime and punishment. He knows actions have consequences, and that rules are made to be obeyed, but as easily as he grasps the matters of the world, the matters of the afterlife elude him. He believes in what he sees but does not try to see with the eyes of his heart. While he gives man credit and leverage for everything, he seldom finds it in his heart to give the ultimate credit to Allah, who is beyond his grasp, intelligence and imagination.

Man understands the importance of laws in a society. If it weren't for laws, the carefully created human systems would crumble, and man would be thrown back centuries. Man learned to respect power, because power created laws and held them together. He also started looking towards it to relay justice, to rescue the oppressed and to punish their tormentors. Again, when a non-believer holds this attitude, it is under-standable, but when a believer does, while simultaneously committing immoral and unethical acts without fearing the punishment of Allah, then it is completely unacceptable. When a believer hurts relations, individuals, families or societies, he must realize that a Superpower watches over him constantly and keeps records of all his acts. One day, all men will have to bow before the biggest power and bear the punishment for breaking His laws. Those who like to dole out punish-ments, and those who desire punishment for others, in this world, must reflect on their inadequacies and fear the justice of Allah.

In a secular world, when man goes awry, he is sent through a process which aims at restoring his skills, self-sufficiency and balance;

this process of rehabilitation has become quite common in the modern world.

As a child grows and more years are added to his life, his desires and needs grow with him. He loses his purity due to satanic influences, and often, misconceptions lead him on the path of doom. He sees what his *nafs* wants him to see, and the delusions lead him astray. Unfortunately, although many can tell when a heart is diseased and a person is far from Allah, there are few who try to help the lost find their way back.

An off beam Muslim can only cure his ailing heart if he declares *jihad* against the devil and his *nafs*. Declaring *jihad* against the *nafs* is a lot like rehabilitation, where man is coerced to return to his pure self. The main focus is cleansing the heart and soul of impure thoughts and the body of impure acts till a believer's *iman* revives.

THE PATH OF THE *SALIHEEN*

True glory lies in total submission to the Lord and Master of the world. Sifting through history, one comes across countless examples of truth seekers who renounced the world because they found something better and more gratifying than its treasures.

Renouncing the world does not mean giving up the world, but simply its blind pursuit and its redundant ways. Man was sent to this world not to own it or disown it, but to make use of it in the most positive ways. The priority should not be the world, but the goals beyond it. The world is means to an end, not an end in itself. Renouncing it is prioritizing life, so that Allah becomes man's top priority.

When man completely surrenders to Allah, he does not mind losing his worldly possessions, because he knows that greater treasures await him in the afterlife. He wholeheartedly believes that everything belongs to Allah, so he is forever grateful and never worried about losing what wasn't his to begin with.

However, those who do not understand this ultimate truth find themselves in incredible loss. They run after all those things that worsen their plight instead of saving them from a ghastly end. **They exchange their morals for the wealth of the world and teachings of the Quran and *Sunnah* for the transient happiness of this world.**

While most flail in a sea of loss, there are those who stand a chance, and these are the *saliheen,* the righteous. The *saliheen* conduct profitable trade for the next life. These men are not afraid of losing the world, but are terrified of failing their Master and losing in the afterlife. Such men exchange wealth for the pleasure of their Lord, and use their God-given power for the betterment of their fellow men.

So, while the disbeliever sets himself up for an uncertain and violent end, the *saliheen* plan and labor for eternal success.

For success and survival, it is imperative that man follows the path of the *saliheen.* These people correct, do good and pass on sincere and valuable advice to their brethren—worrying about them as much as they worry about their own selves. When a believer does good and invites people to it, he gives proof of his devotion, and when he shows persistence and endurance in his way of life, he becomes one of the *saliheen* and a contender for heaven.

Do not ask the lord to guide your footsteps, if you are not willing to move your feet.

There are three steps for bringing about a lasting change:

1. Accepting the problem,
2. Acknowledging one's mistakes, and
3. Coming up with lasting solutions.

Unless man realizes he is drowning, there is not much he can do to save his life. He stands a chance of surviving this world and the next only if he remains connected to Islam. If he sees problems in his *iman,* morals and dealings, he must accept them and try to rectify them. Plus, he must try to boost his *iman* by enjoining truth with patience and determination. For as long as a person keeps striving for good, his heart keeps striving for a pure life.

QUESTIONS FOR REFLECTION

- Is the Quran just for believers or for the whole of mankind?
- Allah declares that man is in a state of perpetual failure unless he_____.
- What is the wisdom behind time and why did God put mankind in a race against time?
- Can we win the race against time if we forget our true purpose of life?
- Does the Quran remind us to do whatever we came here to do, before our time runs out?
- Do we fulfill what we came here to do? If not, what is stopping us?
- Are crimes rewarding in the long run, or is it a punishment in itself? If yes, then how?
- Doesn't ignorance of man's purpose of descent create a dearth of Iman and open the door for the Devil to enter into the heart?
- What is apathy and does lack of concern and hesitation in doing right lead to apathy?
- Does apathy cause people to behave in a carefree manner?
- What are some other cases in which apathy becomes a crime against faith?
- What does Allah say in Quran 4:143 and 9:45 about those who waver and fail to choose the right side even after declaring their Iman?
- Can the believers who don't wage Jihad against the Devil and don't make a sincere effort to purify their hearts possess the wisdom and fortitude to choose the right side?

- Can real peace be achieved without establishing the laws of Allah?

- Expecting more from Allah but giving less, is it a sign of lack of Iman?

- Does man overvalue himself, because he is guilty of under-valuing his Creator?

- Does changing the priorities to suit man's lifestyle deteriorate his Iman?

- Who are Saliheen? What makes them Saliheen?

19

FINDING ALLAH
NOVI, UNITED STATES
2005–2015

I once had a thousand desires, but in my one desire to know you, all else melted away. – Rumi

Question: How Does One Find Allah?

Answer: Imagine a world, and imagine yourself as the sole human walking its turf. Your entire being will automatically turn towards the only entity that has existed forever and will go on existing forever and ever: Allah, the one and only true Lord and Master of everything.

When man's world is de-cluttered, his attention invariably shifts to bigger things surrounding him, and he is encouraged to think and contemplate. Plus, for a man who finds himself isolated on earth, a lot of the unwanted fades away, like ego, pride, fallacies and pretenses. Subsequently, his focus relocates from the self, and the outer projections of his persona change into inner reflections of his soul, compelling him to question his existence and the reality of the world. The answers ultimately lead man to Allah.

—⁕—

I did not imagine myself as the last survivor on planet Earth, but for a long time I did feel like the only man on Earth. Foiled expectations had all but finished me off. My entire world had been shaken like a bag of coins

before my eyes, and I had been powerless to snatch it back. There was a time when I was rich, but homeless; I had everything, and yet, nothing at all. That was when I found Allah for the first time.

Was it I who found Allah, or did He find me? I don't know. I do know that it started with recognition. I also know that recognition of Allah is permanent and has been engraved on all human souls. With time, however, the etch collects dust and disappears from human sight. Once man rediscovers the hidden insignia on his soul, it instigates a search for his true identity and purpose on earth.

Question: What Leads Man to Allah?
Answer: a) Man's Instincts Lead Him to Allah

Man recognizes Allah instinctively. When he fails repeatedly or faces impossible trials, he understands his true clout. With his entire physical and mental prowess, man can still be reduced to a helpless creature incapable of controlling his own life. The truth is, he neither enters the world by his choice, nor leaves by it. Once he gets his facts right—one of them being that no harm or relief can reach him without his Master's will—he begins to seek out Allah.

When all else fails, man is forced to acknowledge a bigger power. Again, imagine a drowning man. Who does this man call out for help? Who does he plead with: other men, agencies, his boss, his so-called demigods? No, he calls out to just one Deity. The faceoff with death turns man into an instant monotheist.

Every cell in a drowning man's body fights for life, including his conscience and subconscious. In the desperate struggle that ensues between life and death, the insignia on his soul is exposed. Everything becomes crystal clear for a few moments. Understanding dawns, and he recognizes a force greater than all. In the crucial seconds that follow he realizes how his life has been a house of straw kept erect and well-protected by Divine intervention. In these fleeting moments, he discovers the absolute truth and recognizes just One True God—the actual One.

b) Quran and *hadith* Lead Man to Allah

Although trials and tribulations beset all men, it is utterly insane to wait for a catastrophe or a particularly tragic event, in order to recognize the Divine Force. Today, **Quran and *hadith* serve as road maps that direct men towards the righteous path, eventually leading them to Allah.** Plus, religious obligations like *salah*, *saum*, *zakat* and *hajj* are stepping stones, which not just prepare men for the journey, but also facilitate communion with the Great Lord.

Men who seek Allah with their hearts, find Him in the pages of the Quran and in the dictates of *hadith*. However, doubtful and close-minded men, those who pick up the Quran merely to refute it, and study *hadith* only to poke holes in it, will find these sources exasperatingly impenetrable.

Quran is a revelation within a revelation; a single reading is not enough to grasp its many truths. Plus, it only enlightens those who seek truth with the purity of their hearts, and only the enlightened ones are led to Allah.

c) *Salah* Leads Man to Allah

A connection can be established with Allah through establishing *salah*. When *salah* is offered consciously and with understanding, it keeps the memory of Allah alive. **Men who strive to see through their hearts look forward to *salah* five times a day and are able to recognize Allah through His greatness and their own peripheral nature.**

True servants of Allah fly over obstacles and impediments, not letting anything slow down their progress or destroy their relationship with their Creator. However, those who offer *salah* but refuse to see with their hearts are blinded by Allah and fail to recognize His signs.

Allah proclaims in the Quran:

Lo! I, only I, am Allah. There is no god save Me. So serve Me, and establish worship for My remembrance. (The Quran, 20:14)

In the above verse, Allah beckons men to remember Him through *salah*. If a man desires to recognize Allah, he must purge his heart of all sins and fill it with goodness; only then would his heart gain the power to recognize Allah.

If a man's *salah* is sincere, his link with Allah becomes strong, but if *salah* lacks *iman* and sincere devotion to Allah, then it is a deception that fails to rejuvenate the heart and lift its many veils.

d) Fasting Leads Man to Allah

Fasting is another path that leads towards Allah. Again, during fasting, the unnecessary excesses recede, and man is given a chance to gain communion with his Master. The unfulfilled needs of his body wake up his spiritual self and drive him to seek out his true Lord. There are people who celebrate the arrival of Ramadan and mourn its departure; these are the people who know that during the month of Ramadan, they will be closer to Allah, and they relish the thought of attaining a proximity that was not possible before.

During Ramadan, these men spend a better part of their day conversing with their Lord through the recitation of the Quran. Again, **sincerity in devotion wakes up their hearts and allows them to see, hear and understand the Divine messages**

My heart woke up in Ramadan, and I found Allah in the wee hours of the night in its lingering darkness. I would leave my warm bed to stand before His greatness and shrivel in my coat of humility and disgrace. I had sinned knowingly and unknowingly. I had caused pain to myself and others, and all I would seek those nights would be His love and forgiveness.

I delighted in rising for the special night prayer, salah al-Layl, while the world slept; maybe because I found what I sought: comfort in standing in Qiyam and peace in my humble offerings. Those were the nights when

I felt the veils drawn away from my heart. Come morning and I would be full of positive energy.

I had found my purpose. I existed to serve Him, and the way to serve Him was through serving His people. My miserable heart that lay in a million pieces felt whole again. I can't explain how dramatically things changed for me, how quickly I shrugged off my bitterness, and how easy He made it for me to forgive. But despite all that, my past still weighed me down some days. There were instances when sadness consumed me and threw me back years. Although such episodes were few and fleeting, they threatened my iman. This was also the time when I had started conversing with Allah. It may sound crazy, but it was better and easier to confide in Him than in anyone else. If I was tired, I would tell Him; if I was in pain, I would complain to Him; if I needed something, I would ask Him.

One evening, when my iman felt as fragile as the dying asters in my garden, and every cell in my body screamed in protest against the burdens of this life, my heart spoke to me: It reminded me of the greatness of my Lord. It went on repeating "Allah u Akbar (Allah is Great); your Master is so much bigger than your problems," until my woes disintegrated to nothing, and the darkness receded.

From then onwards, whenever I felt depressed or disheartened about something, my brain automatically conjured up a bar graph comparing my problems to the greatness of my Lord. Then, if I didn't break down and cry, I laughed at my silliness. I had absolutely nothing to worry about.

My center shifted yet again. All the mandatory and optional prayers became instinctive to me. Once I had sought to fulfil my desires, now I sought to repay debts. I wonder if this was recognizing Allah. I wonder if it was Him who occupied the vestiges of my heart.

FINDING ALLAH THROUGH FINDING THE SELF

Man is just another social animal, but a closer look turns him into a miracle of creation. The galaxies that surround him lie within him, as well. The proof lies in his very makeup, but only for those who contemplate and ponder over their existence. **When man understands**

his creation, he begins to recognize the majesty of the Creator. So to know the self, is to know Allah.

Like a car is a screaming proof of man's existence, man is a deafening proof of God's. The creation speaks of its master. It is tragic that some men, in their arrogance, deem themselves as the highest authority. They would mock all who deny the role of man in the creation of a car, but are too close-minded to accept the role of a bigger and brighter entity in their own creation.

Unlike a car, man is not a simple machine. He is complicated and functions on many different levels. He has two different command rooms, the brain and the heart. If there is conflict within the soul or a problem within the body, man has been programmed to help himself. Plus, like all who leave their signatures on their work, man also carries the insignia of his Master. His soul has been marked to help him recognize his Creator, but for that, man must understand his own self first. Only after achieving a certain degree of self-awareness or higher consciousness can man truly recognize Allah.

In Surah Qaf, Allah reveals His stance:

It was We who created man, and We know what dark suggestions his soul makes to him; for We are nearer to him than his jugular vein. (The Quran, 50:16)

Only the author is aware of the vulnerabilities in his work, or in man's case He, Himself. The above verse is a revelation for those who seek Allah. He is right there, and right here, with me and with you. If man fails to see and recognize Him, it is because his heart is shrouded in darkness.

FINDING ALLAH THROUGH UNVEILING THE HEART

Their similitude is that of a man who kindled a fire:
When it lighted all around him, God took away their
light
And left them in utter darkness, so they could not see.
Deaf, dumb, and blind, they will not return (to the
path).

(The Quran, 2:17-18)

Light bounces off a veiled heart. It simply does not enter and, therefore, does not allow the heart to see. Unfortunate men are those whose hearts are covered with veils. The shrouds not just hold in evil but also keep out the light of truth. **Without unveiling the heart, man cannot achieve higher consciousness which is necessary for recognizing Allah.**

Such men are lost, unless they turn back towards Allah. **They must recognize their faults, and fight off the darkness that resides in their hearts rendering them deaf to the truth of the Quran, dumb to its words and blind to the signs of Allah's existence.**

FINDING ALLAH THROUGH SELF-PURIFICATION

Purification of the self invites the Pure One into the heart. Allah is *Al Quddus*, the Uniquely and Unimaginably Pure and Perfect. He declares in the Quran that He has proportioned the souls of men, but that those who mar them with corrupt ways fail. He further reveals:

Indeed, he succeeds who purifies his own self. (The Quran, 91:9)

Purification of the self, i.e., of the heart, the body and the soul, leads man towards the path of enlightenment, and what is enlightenment,

if not recognizing the true Lord. A healthy heart works as a medium between man's soul and Allah. It causes man to unify with all His creation and seek and establish peace on Earth.

When Adam and Eve erred, they lost their intimacy with Allah. To return back and win the favor of Allah again, they had to repent and accept their wrongdoing. Later, when they descended to Earth, they knew that Allah expected them to discipline their souls and purify their hearts. They both understood that the heart was the only vessel through which they could return successful, and for that, they put it under strict checks and guarded its purity.

The hopeful seekers who wish to find Allah must realize the significance of purifying the heart and of bringing it out of the darkness by enjoining good and shunning evil.

FINDING ALLAH
THROUGH DEVELOPING SPIRITUALITY

Spirituality is another door that leads man straight to his Creator. It is the answer to inner peace and is developed through rites, rituals and different practices. **When men cleanse their hearts, they invite spirituality into their lives.** Although the techniques employed for acquiring it are different among different groups, the goals are the same.

From the earliest times, Islamic rituals were molded to polish man's spirituality. They were a fusion of Divine decree and human aptitude. All the prophets of Allah had the same goal: they relayed the message of *tawheed* and introduced practices that developed spirituality among the believers. Therefore, the acts of worship like *salah*, *saum*, *hajj* and *zakat* were not just measuring instruments for *iman* and obedience, but drills for developing and strengthening the spiritual self.

Ritualistic worship can also be viewed as an avenue for finding Allah. The better a person's *salah*, the stronger his spirituality, and the bigger his chances of finding Allah. It is the same with all other forms of worship. When man understands the significance of spirituality and recognizes it as means for gaining proximity with Allah, he increases his chances for success.

—ɯ—

In my little apartment, my life revolved around my Lord, not around me. I fed myself on His love and learned to live without grief and fear. I kept in touch with my family, and Yasmeen visited me from time to time, worried about my health and my mental state. When she insisted that we both go see Dr. Quarton, I agreed if only to appease her. The reality was, I hadn't felt this good in ages. I was working on forging a new relationship and maybe my willingness to go with the flow was unsettling her.

After a dozen sessions with Dr. Quarton, which were a test of my patience, we finally quit. Seemingly, we had achieved nothing, but I believe that no experience is worthless. Sometimes the lessons learned through such encounters are stored deep inside the brain and understood in their own time.

THE HOPEFUL SEEKER

The aspirants who wish to find Allah must first equip themselves with the right tools before they undertake such a journey. Intelligence and knowledge concerning the Quran, *hadith*, law and the *nafs* is mandatory. Intricate knowledge may not be necessary, but a person must understand and know his faith. He should tame the self by keeping his *nafs* under check and nurturing the qualities of sincerity, patience, justice and insight. Above all, he must remain conscious of Allah at all times.

Finding Allah might be easy for some people, but difficult for others, depending upon Allah's will, His mercy, and man's capability. However, a certain intimacy can be developed through His remembrance and worship.

Transformation of the self is possible, if man is willing to change. The more aware and conscious he becomes of his self, the more

distance he covers. The more he bows before his Lord in worship, the more he gains in character and regard.

The hopeful seeker must be willing to transform into Allah's slave. For that he must repulse his ego and false pride. Once the ego is restrained, the true self, the true spirit or the true essence of man will surface, transforming him, from a Muslim to a believer and a *muttaqi*, one with true awareness of God's presence.

Finding Allah in this world guarantees that man will find Allah's mercy on the Day of Judgement. However, the one who loses to his weaker self or ego in this world, must fear Allah's wrath in the next.

Allah declares in His book:

> *Allah is the Protecting Friend of those who believe. He takes them out of darkness into light. As for those who disbelieve, their patrons are false deities. They bring them out of light into darkness. Such are rightful owners of the fire. They will reside therein. (The Quran, 2:257)*

Finding Allah may seem like an arduous task, but with an unfaltering belief in *tawheed*, the will to succeed, and the strength to persevere, it becomes easy. Besides, Allah does not ignore those who strive in His path.

In Surah Ankabut, Allah promises guidance for the hopeful seekers:

> *And those that strive in Our (cause), We will certainly guide them to Our Paths. (The Quran, 29:69)*

WHEN WE RETURN TO HIM, HE RETURNS TO US

Through understanding, awareness and, ultimately, through deeds, when man shows Allah how much he cares for His approval, Allah shows him how much He cares for His slave. He blesses his understanding with truth, his awareness with love and his actions with purity, thus elevating his rank.

A successful seeker seeks forgiveness from Allah for his short-comings. He practices patience and perseverance, but he does not forget to praise the Lord or to supplicate before him. He gives from what Allah has given him, if only to earn His pleasure, and guards his heart, *salah* and chastity. **He loves Allah unconditionally, fears His wrath and prays for His mercy.**

While some of the above traits can be acquired through diligence and hard work, others are a blessing from Allah.

As I sit alone eating an early dinner, loneliness quietly pulls up a chair beside me, and before I know it, I am back in Patna. The little boy I recall is naive and ignorant, and surprisingly, knows more about his pretty neighbour's pooja than his own. The stark contrast between then and now amazes me.

I was a Muslim who was not, a soul that could have been so easily lost. A few remnants of a long lost tale float through my mind. I hear dadi telling me about a boy who wanted to make the tallest ladder so he could reach Allah, he did make the ladder and climbed higher and higher, carrying a dagger so he could kill Him. When he reached the sky he plunged the dagger into it, stabbing again and again. Allah told His angels to paint the dagger red and the boy climbed down thinking he had killed the Great One...

I wreck my brain for an ending, for the message that must have accompanied this tale, but there is nothing. I know there is no truth to the above story, but it still bothers me. Hate, like love is a very strong emotion, and like love, it propels people to do fantastic things, like finding Allah. While hatred is born out of pain, ingratitude, and the inability to see beyond the self, love is born out of kindness, gratitude and the ability to look beyond the self.

I found Allah and saved my faith, only when I learned to be grateful for all I had, the good and the bad. But the boy with the ladder, who did find Allah, only to lose Him again, turned into his own biggest enemy. My heart ached for him, for his loss, for his struggle with faith, but most of all, for his failure to recognize Allah and His greatness.

This story resurfaced after decades to deliver a message which must have eluded me years ago: Guidance and acceptance are not bestowed on just anyone who finds a way to reach Allah. Without the key of recognition and Allah's mercy, man, like the boy with the ladder, will fail to achieve both.

My alarm rings, jolting me out of my reverie. In a few more minutes, it will be time for the adhan. I reach for my coat and car keys. As I make my way towards the Novi mosque to give the call for the sunset prayer, maghrib, I see the sun disappearing from the horizon. Another day has gone.

A truth slowly sinks in.

Like the sun, I too have started my descent. My journey through this world is about to come to an end. Like the sun, I travelled far and wide, assisted life in some places and scorched it in others. Like the sun, I climbed higher and higher, and like the sun, I must go down. But someday, like the sun, I shall rise again in another place, at another time, for the final reckoning.

My thoughts are cast aside as I enter the masjid. I make my ablutions and prepare to call the adhan. As I raise my hands and turn towards the Kaaba, I pray that my call is heard far and wide, and that my message is delivered to as many people as possible...

اَللَّهُ اَكْبَرُ اَللَّهُ اَكْبَرُ

اَللَّهُ اَكْبَرُ اَللَّهُ اَكْبَرُ

اَشْهَدُ اَنْ لاَّ إِلَهَ إِلاَّ اللَّهُ

اَشْهَدُ اَنْ لاَّ إِلَهَ إِلاَّ اللَّهُ

اَشْهَدُ اَنَّ مُحَمَّدًا رَسُوْلُ اللهِ

اَشْهَدُ اَنَّ مُحَمَّدًا رَسُوْلُ اللهِ

حَىَّ عَلَى الصَّلوةِ

حَىَّ عَلَى الصَّلوةِ

حَىَّ عَلَى الْفَلاَحِ

حَىَّ عَلَى الْفَلَاحِ

اللهُ أَكْبَرُ

اَللَّهُ أَكْبَرُ

لَا إِلَهَ إِلَّا اللَّهُ

"Allah is the greatest! Allah is the greatest!"

"Allah is the greatest! Allah is the greatest!"

"I bear witness that there is none worthy of worship except Allah"

"I bear witness that there is none worthy of worship except Allah"

"I bear witness that Muhammad is the Messenger of Allah"

"I bear witness that Muhammad is the Messenger of Allah"

"Come towards prayer!"

"Come towards prayer!"

"Come towards success!"

"Come towards success!"

"Allah is the greatest! Allah is the greatest!"

"There is none worthy of worship except Allah"

QUESTIONS FOR REFLECTION

- **How do we find Allah?**

- **What leads man to Allah?**

- **What are the characteristics of hopeful and successful seekers?**

MUSLIM

In Transit

What's Next–Time to Act

Questions for Discussion

Love, Peace & Justice
What's Next?

THE MESSAGES PUT forth in this book are not intended to just make us think. We must act. My goal is to start a non-profit Islamic Scholarship foundation to support the continuing study of the themes presented in this book. My humble intention is to connect with others who are ready to join together for the positive advancement of Muslims and all humanity. Therefore, we ask you:

1. Do you believe Muslims' *Iman*, in general, has deteriorated?

   Yes   No

2. If yes, do you believe we need to cleanse our hearts?

   Yes   No

3. If yes, then would you support this project

   Yes   No

4. If yes, would you support financially?

   Yes   No

5. Voluntarily?

   Yes   No

Together, we can make a strong impact. We invite you to join us in this effort.

Connect with me on Facebook: Facebook.com/MusliminTransit

About the Author

MOHAMMED QAMRUZZAMAN, KNOWN to friends as Qamar, was born in India in 1940. In 1964 he traveled to America to pursue his education and received his BS Degree in Mechanical Engineering in 1969 from Howard University, and MS Degree in Management in 1976 from Frostburg State College. He worked for the US Army for 32 years in Defense Program Management and retired in Dec 2013. He has one daughter, a journalist, and two sons, a doctor, and an engineer and former US Marine who served in Fallujah. Qamar's dream is to have fellow Muslims realize that Islam is more than just acts of *Ibadah* (worship) but also a deep spiritual connection with God.

Visit him online at Facebook.com/MusliminTransit

muslimintransit@gmail.com

ORIGINAL BOOK CLUB
DISCUSSION QUESTIONS

1. Are Muslims truly following the teachings of Quran and of our prophet (pbuh)?

2. How does the author's personal life elucidate his views on Islam and the downfall of Muslims?

3. The author believes Muslims are raped, killed and humiliated all over the word. Do you agree?

4. Do you believe Muslims are united? Is unity ever truly attainable?

5. Would the Quraish have refused to accept Islam if they did not have to get rid of their vices, especially social injustice and economic inequality?

6. We are taught to do good deeds and stay away from bad, but more than 1400 years of teaching has not improved our character a bit, why?

7. Why is suffering allowed in the world? Why are not more hearts crying with sleepless nights at the condition of many around the globe?

8. Does God's "all-forgiving" nature mean we can sin freely?

9. If we believe God will forgive all our sins and reward us Heaven because He is loving, caring and compassionate, why doesn't He save the people from suffering all over the world?

10. How we can stay away from evil deeds and rid ourselves of our evil characteristics?

11. How we can fill our hearts with love?

12. What can each person do as an individual to correct their path?

Do you have a story to tell?
Join us at BookPowerPublishing.com *to learn more about how we can*
help you share your message with the world.

www.bookpowerpublishing.com
support@bookpowerpublishing.com

Made in the USA
Monee, IL
28 September 2020